D1495918

POST

The Theory and Technique of Digital Nonlinear Motion Picture Editing

C. Melinda Levin

University of North Texas

Fred P. Watkins

University of North Texas

Boston   New York   San Francisco
Mexico City   Montreal   Toronto   London   Madrid   Munich   Paris
Hong Kong   Singapore   Tokyo   Cape Town   Sydney

Series Editor: *Molly Taylor*
Editorial Assistant: *Michael Kish*
Marketing Manager: *Mandee Eckersley*
Production Editor: *Michelle Limoges*
Editorial-Production Service: *Omegatype Typography, Inc.*
Composition and Prepress Buyer: *Linda Cox*
Manufacturing Buyer: *JoAnne Sweeney*
Cover Designer: *Kristina Mose-Libon*
Electronic Composition: *Omegatype Typography, Inc.*

For related titles and support materials, visit our online catalog at www.ablongman.com.

Many of the designations used by manufacturers and sellers to distinguish their products are claimed as trademarks. Where those designations appear in this book, and Allyn and Bacon was aware of a trademark claim, the designations have been printed with an initial capital. Designations within quotation marks represent hypothetical products.

Library of Congress Cataloging-in-Publication Data

Levin, C. Melinda.
 Post : the theory and technique of digital nonlinear motion picture editing / C. Melinda Levin, Fred P. Watkins.
  p. cm.
  ISBN 0-205-33525-X (alk. paper)
  1. Motion pictures—Editing—Data processing. I. Watkins, Fred P. II. Title.

TR899 .L48 2003
778.5'35—dc21

2002023056

Printed in the United States of America
10   9   8   7   6   5   4   3   2   1   07   06   05   04   03   02

Credits appear on page iv, which constitutes an extension of the copyright page.

In loving memory of my father, William Brooks Matney, and in grateful honor of my mother, Carolyn Weaver Matney. Thanks for the support, love and laughs to my brothers Bill, James and Rob Matney. To my best friend across the Atlantic, Angie Boakes, in appreciation for the "rules of friendship." Most of all for my husband, Ben, who inspires me every day and reminds me of the privilege and responsibility of creativity.

—Melinda Levin

My efforts in this book are dedicated with thanks to my family, Shirlene, Jaret, Julie, Isabella, Ian, Conni and Kathryn; my parents, Edna and Paul; my brother, Bobby, and his family; and the many film crews and actors I have had the privilege to work with over the years.

—Fred Watkins

Credits

Chapter 2: pp. 14, 15, 16, 17, William Stacy IV.

Chapter 3: p. 27, William Stacy IV.

Chapter 4: pp. 41, 42, 44, 45, Art Today © 2001–2002, www.arttoday.com, layout by William Stacy IV; p. 43, © Adobe Systems Incorporated. Adobe and Premiere is/are either (a) registered trademark(s) of Adobe Systems Incorporated in the United States and/or other countries. Screenshot content by William Stacy IV.

Chapter 5: pp. 57, 58, 59, 60, 61, 63, William Stacy IV; pp. 66, 67, photos courtesy of Milestek Corporation.

Chapter 6: pp. 70, 71, 76, 79, William Stacy IV; pp. 73, 78, Art Today © 2001–2002, www.arttoday.com, layout by William Stacy IV; p. 80, © Adobe Systems Incorporated. Adobe and Premiere is/are either (a) registered trademark(s) of Adobe Systems Incorporated in the United States and/or other countries. Screenshot content by William Stacy IV.

Chapter 7: pp. 83, 84, 88, 89, 97, William Stacy IV.

Chapter 8: pp. 100, 101, 102, 104, 105, William Stacy IV; p. 106, Media 100, Inc., www.media100.com

Chapter 9: pp. 108, 110, 111, 112, 113, © Adobe Systems Incorporated. Adobe and Premiere is/are either (a) registered trademark(s) of Adobe Systems Incorporated in the United States and/or other countries. Screenshot content by William Stacy IV; pp. 109, 114, Media 100 Inc., www.media100.com; p. 115, William Stacy IV.

Chapter 10: pp. 119, 120, 122, 123, 125, William Stacy IV; p. 120 (Figure 10.3), photo courtesy of Video Post and Transfer, Dallas, Texas; p. 124, © Adobe Systems Incorporated. Adobe and Premiere is/are either (a) registered trademark(s) of Adobe Systems Incorporated in the United States and/or other countries. Screenshot content by William Stacy IV.

Chapter 11: pp. 129, 131, 133, 137, William Stacy IV.

Chapter 13: p. 174, William Stacy IV.

CONTENTS

11 Shooting Film and Editing on a Digital Nonlinear System   126

12 Interviews with Film and Television Editors   145

ACKNOWLEDGMENTS

We extend heartfelt thanks to our graduate and undergraduate student assistants at the University of North Texas, Przemek Budziszewski, Georgeanne Elder, Hank Fawcett, Trysh Foley, Julie Furnas, Beth Holder, Leslie LeMond, Marshal "Max" Hall, Kelli McKinney, Michael Mullins, Ashley Smith, Jill Snyder, Hongyi Yang, Mi Jung Youm and Emily Young, and to industry professionals Tony Bifano, Tony Buba and James A. Sullivan. Melinda Levin appreciates friend and colleague, anthropologist Alicia Re Cruz, who remained wonderfully patient while our own film edit was temporarily put on the back burner. Our immeasurable thanks go to several motion picture editors who were generous enough to sit for thoughtful and inspiring interviews. In particular, we would like to formally express our gratitude to Jonathan Mednick and his family; Jonathan passed away a few weeks after our conversations. Special gratitude and recognition go to our art director, William Stacy, for his patience and professionalism in designing and creating many of the graphics and photographs used to illustrate key concepts and to Walter Deed, Media Services Specialist, and Wayne Hassell, Television Engineer, at the University of North Texas for their technical support. Much appreciation goes to our series editor, Molly Taylor, for her timely and supportive efforts. We would also like to thank the following reviewers for their technical and artistic insights: Ann Alter, Humboldt State University; Ken Dancyger, New York University; Mary Jane Doherty, Boston University; Joe Flickinger, Radford University. In addition, we thank our colleagues in the Department of Radio, Television and Film at the University of North Texas for their help and encouragement in developing this book. Last, we offer our admiration to the many wonderful students along the way.

1 Introduction

Computer-Based Editing Systems as Tools

So you want to edit. As you are no doubt aware, motion picture editing has undergone an astounding technological revolution. Maybe *evolution* is a better word, for the tools are developing and changing in ways that oftentimes better support artistic freedom and fluidity. Computer-based editing systems now dominate the postproduction stage of motion pictures, and vast improvements in capability, storage and access occur literally on a monthly basis.

But these systems are merely tools that do what you tell them to do. They are like the paint, the plaster, the musical notes, the mathematician's calculator, the architect's ruler, the photographer's camera or the athlete's trained physique—instruments that allow you to create and accomplish your goals. And while any change in tools will always have an effect on the end result, many of the theories and techniques of visual editing are still firmly rooted in practices developed many years ago by some of the first motion picture artists.

The Term *Motion Picture*

Before going much further, let us agree on a term that will serve to encompass the various visual media we will be discussing in this book. For most discussions on postproduction editing, the theories and techniques can be applied not only to narrative fiction film, but also to various documentary genres, experimental explorations, television news, commercials, corporate productions, digital presentations on the Internet and home videos. When the theories and techniques can be broadly applied to each, we will simply refer to them as *motion pictures*. When specific approaches and/or technological applications are indicated, we will revert back to *film, television sitcom* or other such terms, as needed.

What Is an Editor? What Does Good Editing Mean?

In this book, we will discuss both some of the technologies and the techniques of motion picture editing. First and foremost, however, we should come to some agreement on what the goals of a motion picture editor are. What, exactly, does an editor *do?*

You will most likely agree that the editor works as part of a collaborative team to tell a story (unless the "team" is one person doing all the directing, producing, camera, lighting, sound, gripping and editing, in which case the "editor" still must understand and support all of the other efforts). The editor also shortens the film, selecting appropriate takes, eliminating some shots, cutting out slates and getting rid of unnecessary or unusable footage.

Of course, the editor's job is also to put the footage in the correct order, given that scenes are often shot out of order. If you are new to motion picture editing, taking your first class or using your home system to put together your own videos, these are usually your first concerns: Make it shorter, put things in the right order and tell a story.

For me, editing is the selection and arrangement of sounds and images. Like a musical composition, editing provides the basis for the language and structure of the art form.

Jonathan Mednick, Founder and President of Other Picture Production Company and Co-Producer and Editor of the "American High" Television Series, New York City

---

The Goals and Responsibilities of the Motion Picture Editor

But is that it? Of course not. The editor is an artist who helps endow the motion picture with a richness and resonance that did not previously exist. By using rhythm and pacing; holding back information; allowing pauses; utilizing music, dialogue and other sounds; emphasizing the emotional character of an actor or subject; crashing in close-up shots when least expected and crosscutting between scenes and actions, the editor prods the motion picture toward the psychological and intellectual domain that we have come to expect from great art and effective communication.

So what does this mean for you as a motion picture editor? Let's back up and examine how we might apply this to life. On a daily basis, all five of your senses are engaged, and your emotions are affected by what you experience. The sensory input may include music, dialogue, pacing, ambient sound, sensations of warmth, coolness and taste, and morning light bathing the world around you. You absorb and evaluate this input and make emotional and psychological decisions on the basis of it. In a sense, we are the editors of our own lives. We might not always directly control our experiences, but we do decide how to receive them, what to remember, what experiences to emphasize, what music to listen to, how to engage in dialogue, what and when to look at something. Our days and nights are made up of a tapestry of occurrences that are filtered through our past, our dreams, our fears and our goals. We "edit" on a minute-by-minute basis.

In some ways, then, the intellectual role of the editor should not be too hard to understand. And although the senses of taste, smell and touch are rarely part of motion pictures, nevertheless images, music, dialogue, ambient sound, the laying out of expectations, the indication of things unexpected, the heightening of emotion through pacing, and the holding back and releasing of information do make up the domain of the motion picture editor.

The primary role of the editor is to unfold a version of life before you, to use the aesthetics of film to create tension; to suggest contradictions; to hint at possibilities; to prompt excitement, dread, melancholy, passion and hope; and to allow you to "enter" the motion picture. The editor does this primarily by manipulating tools that you are already accustomed to dealing with in your daily experience: images and sound.

> Editing to me is the process of finding the right moments in the material and placing them in the right order. It is finding the best performances (whether they are actors or documentary subjects) and telling a story without losing your audience. You should always think about your audiences. Most television viewers (where a vast majority of film/video material is viewed) have a remote control in their hand. If you think about their thumb on the remote while you edit, you will edit differently. I would also define editing as "falling out of love with your footage." The famous Soviet filmmaker and film theorist Sergei Eisenstein said something like, "Editing is the ruthless suppression of the inessential." I would agree with that statement.
>
> Bart Weiss, Independent Video/Filmmaker Co-Director of the Association of Independent Video and Filmmakers and Director of the Dallas Video Festival

As you probably know, motion picture filmmaking is barely over 110 years old. Film and its offspring, video and digital motion picture technologies, are young art forms. Despite that, they have evolved quickly, both technologically and theoretically. We will talk about these changes in following chapters.

What *Nonlinear* Means

To begin our discussion of **nonlinear editing** (the cutting of picture and sound), we need to understand the term *nonlinear*. When new inventions come into a culture's public discussions, oftentimes the wrong label is given. For instance, Bandaid and Kleenex are brand names, not items, but how many people actually say, "Please help me put on this adhesive bandage" instead of "Could you help me put on this Bandaid?" or "Pass the paper tissues" in place of "Hand me a Kleenex"? The same kind of thing has happened with digital editing systems. If we were to all be semantically correct, we might refer to our Media 100 or Avid as our "disk-based computer editing system." But most of us, including the authors of this book, refer to them as nonlinear editing systems. Actually, it is the processes of accessing footage and editing that are nonlinear, not the equipment itself. This is an important distinction. So let's define the nonlinear editing process. In any nonlinear situation, whether it be film or digital video, the editor has the ability to assemble bits of source material in any order, place shots or audio or titles in between previously placed material without covering anything up and move elements of the edit around easily. This is what the hype is really all about. In both the film and digital nonlinear video domains, you can readily access images using internal search engines that will seek out your images and audio from your source material based on name, length, date, size or description, and you can manipulate these components while editing with ease.

Nonlinear Editing versus Analog Videotape Editing

Usually if something is considered good there is something it is compared to that is considered bad, or simply not as good. In the case of digital nonlinear, the *bad* is analog linear video editing using a source video deck and a record deck. The final product is assembled one image and sound at a time, from beginning to end. There is nothing nonlinear about that process. With linear analog video editing, there is a lot of shuttling back and forth on videotapes to access the needed footage, and once something has been edited, there is no moving it around on the edit master tape. If you have neglected to put shot number two in and are now already down to shot number twelve, you can't go back and place shot two in between shots one and three. Either you leave it out or you start the entire edit over and get it in there this time. Similarly, digital nonlinear editing is considered by some (certainly not all!) editors to be better than film editing. While film editing has always been an inherently nonlinear process, it can be cumbersome and slow.

Most of today's nonlinear editors are primarily disk-based systems. Simply put, this means that your footage can be randomly accessed, resulting in quicker edits. In addition, if you forgot shot number two, simply go back and place it in between shots one and three and go on with the edit! This clip is inserted, and the system can automatically bump the rest of the footage down the line to make room for it. On the flip side of the coin, in linear video editing, if you need to remove a shot in your edit, you are out of luck. You can either choose to cover the offending shot with another shot or begin the entire process over. In digital nonlinear editing, if you remove or shorten a shot, the system will back up the remaining footage in the edit, filling in the space left behind.

Terminology

Although each system is slightly different, there are fundamental similarities characteristic of all nonlinear editing equipment. Most incorporate certain basic features, and some are quite similar in concept and design (e.g., Adobe Premiere and Media 100).

Digital, computer, nonlinear, compression, layering, compositing—these are exciting terms for the motion picture editor. They suggest a whole new world of possibilities. As you begin to explore all that is occurring in this area of media production by reading trade journals, magazines and other books, you will learn more about hundreds of pieces of equipment, both software and hardware, computer applications, things like high-definition television (HDTV), CODECs and all kinds of other terms you might not be familiar with. Take the time to learn all you can about these new technologies. Learn the terms, and get a feel for what different pieces of equipment offer. Things change very rapidly, and every month you will have the opportunity to become more knowledgeable about the nonlinear world. Take hold of these opportunities and incorporate this new information into your chosen career.

How to Use This Book

This book is organized in chapters that can be read in the order that best serves your needs. Read them nonlinearly if you have specific questions that are addressed in later chapters. Some readers will have enough experience under their belt to skim chapters on early history and theory and go right on to some of the more technical chapters. However, as an editor, whether it be splicing and taping film, using a cuts-only video system or the highest-end Avid system, one should always consider the history of image making and communication and draw on the strengths of the past. The breath of fresh air that new technologies bring can prompt you to perhaps jump in too quickly without evaluating what was learned by many editors who preceded you. Making mistakes is fine, but learn from them and from mistakes of those who have worked out similar editing challenges many years before you.

Other readers will be very new to the field, perhaps taking their first course in editing, and will benefit from a more traditionally linear reading approach. This is fine as well, and you will find that several chapters do indeed build on one another. In addition to our suggestion that you become familiar with the history of motion picture editing, we would like to make two additional recommendations.

The first is to use this book as one of many support tools as you enter the world of motion picture editing. A book is great and often very helpful, but in this particular field, a book is never enough. You will also need to digest all of the equipment manuals for your specific system. Equipment manuals, email lists, experienced editors and company technical support will ease your entry into the digital editing domain. You should also delve into a wide range of motion picture genres to evaluate past and current editing practices. Although it is important to watch a wealth of mainstream films and television, we encourage you to actively seek out a wide range of alternative motion picture voices as well. These might be from community cable access television, low-budget streaming videos on the Internet, feminist and other activist documentaries, music videos from India, South African political advertisements, revisionist propaganda films using archival footage and the ever-improving video gaming industry. In addition, it will benefit your overall understanding of and appreciation for motion pictures if you are able to take part in critical studies courses that emphasize the art and theory of motion pictures. Perhaps just as important, you will get more out of this text if you are currently working in motion picture postproduction. This could mean cutting and splicing a silent 8mm film or editing a longer creative production on a high-end computer-based nonlinear system. In either case, you will better absorb the materials, will come up with your own understanding of why certain edits work and others don't seem to, and will better grasp the technologies if your hands are actually touching the equipment.

You should rent a DVD or videotape of your favorite film. Look at one scene. Count the number of shots. Make a graph about the length, the screen direction and all other elements of the scene. Then go out and shoot the scene. Then edit it exactly the same way. This will give you a feel for the intricacies of how a scene comes together.

Bart Weiss, Independent Video/Filmmaker Co-Director of the Association of Independent Video and Filmmakers and Director of the Dallas Video Festival

The Editor's Mindset

Our second suggestion is that you work on developing what we call the *Editor's mindset*. This is a frame of mind and a way of working that is open to the inherent creative possibilities of motion pictures and one that incorporates a concentrated effort toward proper time management, correct use of equipment and appropriate integration of critical feedback. It also means being very familiar with your footage and the goals for the project and pursuing the proper editing style for those goals. We will discuss each of these elements in the following chapters.

The fundamental core of filmmaking and therefore of editing is the expression of a thought, emotion or idea in a unique way. Your goal is always to communicate successfully and to initiate some sort of aesthetic or intellectual reaction in the viewer. It is also to create something new and powerful, something that will elicit emotion. You will learn how to do this successfully as you gain experience. Like all artists, you will find that creation of the profound takes effort, intense concentration and creative passion.

This book is one of many you will likely read in your life that in some way addresses the idea of such artistic creation. On a less philosophical level, this book will also address the artist's choice of tools to most effectively support an artistic endeavor, in this case motion pictures. A mere five hundred years ago, Michelangelo lay on tall scaffolding and used paint and wet plaster to create a masterpiece on the ceiling of the Sistine Chapel at the Vatican in Rome. Today, you can capture images and sound with celluloid, magnetic tape, digital tape or disks and can manipulate these images using powerful computer-based systems. As a media maker and editor, you have immense creative capabilities when using these tools.

What happens when you are in the editing room working with all of this footage? In this three- or four-day period that I was talking about, you've looked at assembly and it is dreadful, and you know that in three days you have to start showing this program to several people. At that point you don't know what will come into your mind. Will you see the way? There is a leap of faith that what does come into your mind is the right way. If you go down the wrong road, you won't have time to go back and fix it. I don't know where the ideas come from but sometimes you think, "let's try this or that," and trust that it will work. Time and time again, it is like writing a song. It just pops in your head. You don't know where it comes from. The great fear is that one day it won't pop in your head. I am thankful when it happens, but I don't know where it comes from or if it is going to work each time. I'm just thankful when it is there.

Wayne Derrick, Director and Camera Operator for "The Real Miami Cops" (Discovery Channel, USA and Channel 5, UK), London, England

We hope you use this book as one of many guides to help you travel the road toward becoming a better creator, communicator and artist, for the motion picture editor is all of these things. As we discuss various theoretical and technical aspects of editing, remember that we are, in a sense, sharing with you how to build the scaffolding, suggesting ways to spread the plaster on the ceiling and indicating the speed at which you must paint on it before it dries. Once you've got those basics down, it is time for you to make your own masterpiece. Let's plunge in.

2 A Brief History of Early Motion Picture Editing and the Introduction of Digital Nonlinear Systems

As we head toward our discussion about the current state of motion picture editing and what may be forthcoming, it is helpful to briefly examine what led up to current practices and technologies. As we mentioned in Chapter 1, motion pictures are barely over 110 years old. It is truly amazing to witness the power and domination of this form of artistic communication. At a time when many universities and smaller production companies have lower-end systems such as Adobe Premiere, Final Cut Pro and Avid Xpress DV and high-end postproduction facilities, broadcast news stations and film companies house multiple, connected Avids, Lightworks and Media 100s, it is good to take a quick look back at what led up to this digital revolution.

For films and television to become so pervasive in such a short time, pioneers in the form practiced, endured trial and error, tried new technologies, established theoretical premises and constantly evolved motion picture production. There are several very good books that analyze the history and theory of motion picture editing. With some exceptions, almost all motion pictures are *postproduced,* that is, they go through some stage during which the final product is honed and manipulated so that the message is as effective and powerful as possible. This applies to all kinds of motion picture productions, not only typical feature-length narratives or television programs. Experimental, documentary, travelogue, news, advertisement, personal essay and educational motion pictures are almost always edited. For that matter, so are animations, computer games and virtual reality experiences. We expect that you will spend time learning about your editing predecessors and rely on this and the following chapter to briefly introduce some of the early key editing theories, as well as a few of the stages in the technological development of the equipment used. Editing has come a long way in a short time. And as you watch the short films on BMWfilms (www.bmwfilms.com), filmmaker Alan Berliner's documentary "Intimate Stranger," Jonas Mekas's film "Reminiscence of a Journey to Lithuania" (each available from Canyon Cinema at www.canyoncinema.com), director Baz Luhrmann's groundbreaking film "Moulin Rouge" or HBO's acclaimed series "The Sopranos," you will note that they all either purposely follow well-established editing traditions designed many years ago or purposely and effectively break from them.

Early Motion Picture Editors

The editing of films was one of the first steps taken to manipulate and enhance the storytelling capabilities of motion pictures, but editing did not happen immediately. The earliest films were simply motion recordings of everyday events and included a sneeze, workers leaving a factory and a baby being fed. The sheer novelty of witnessing the recorded action of an event was so impressive that initially, there was no need to tell complex stories such as those the public would have expected from novels or dramatic theatre. Quickly, however, the inventors realized that by utilizing the already established technology of photography, combined with a phenomenon called "persistence of vision" (the eye working with the brain to fill in gaps of information), stories could be told in new and persuasive ways.

The very first "editing" was simply done in-camera. Short stories were filmed in the order in which they were to be viewed, with one take for each scene, usually a wide-angle shot. This required that the action and setups be very well thought out, since what you shot was what you saw in the final version. Many beginning filmmaking classes require that students edit in-camera for the first project or two. The emphasis here is on planning the film and learning how to load the camera, set up lights and tell a simple story without yet having to go through the formal process of postproduction.

Groundbreaking and Innovative Early Filmmakers and Film Theorists

Obviously, motion picture artists wanted new tools to expand their manipulation of the film and realized that by rearranging and shortening shots and by intercutting between different lines of action, they could begin to intuitively express emotions in ways that expanded what was shot by the camera. They could take the footage to a new level and tell stories in ways that neither still photography nor theatre could approach.

In any artistic form, there are certain groundbreaking artists who simply cannot be overlooked in any historical summary of the form. Some of the first filmmakers spent considerable time and effort applying their newly formed theories of the art form to the postproduction stage. There are many good books on the filmmakers who are discussed below; please consider this section to be simply an introduction or summary.

American filmmaker Edwin S. Porter was one of the first to begin to apply the idea of *construction* to motion pictures. Instead of simply using a series of wide-angle shots, one following the other, to tell the story in a chronological order, Porter was the first to allow for a certain fluidity in his storytelling style. In his film "Life of an American Fireman" (1903), he shows a fireman sleeping, dissolves to a hand setting off a fire alarm box and then dissolves again to a shot of various firemen jumping out of bed and toward the fire engines. The story itself prompts the various shots, not the other way around. Toward the end of the film, Porter goes even further in his technique by showing one event from two different points of view. The rescue of the fireman's wife and child is shown from the inside, where the trapped and scared family members await their rescue, and also from the outside, from the point of view of the fireman who in the end saves his own loved ones.

With the hindsight of over one hundred years, this might seem to be a very simple technique, but remember that these filmmakers were experimenting with ways to apply well-established storytelling techniques already accepted in novels and theatre to this new form of communication. To do so in a matter of about ten years was nothing less than amazing. Compared to ancient art forms such as painting and sculpture, this art form evolved at lightning speed.

Another American filmmaker, D. W. Griffith, built on Porter's techniques with several films, including two that are often included in the required canon of film history viewing: "Birth of a Nation" (1914) and "Intolerance" (1916). Griffith explored filmic storytelling capabilities by using quick edit pacing to heighten tension when needed, intercutting close-up shots of two people talking to each other, using different camera setups within a scene, introducing various character's points of view of the unfolding action and, in "Intolerance" in particular, the brilliant unfolding of four stories simultaneously. By crosscutting among these four stories set in different periods of history, Griffith allowed the theme of intolerance to become even more powerful and atrocious than it might have been otherwise. And in a truly unique addition to the evolution of the editing vocabulary, Griffith tied all four stories together with a repeating shot of a mythical woman, clothed in a shaft of light and rocking a cradle. As "Intolerance" unfolds, this woman comes to represent the ultimate goodness of humanity. The editorial addition of this image pushed the power of filmic manipulation to new heights. Other early filmmakers learned from and were influenced by Porter and Griffith and were even more dedicated to articulating their theoretical applications of editing.

Russian film theorist Lev Kuleshov was one of the first to survey the effects of combined, successive images somewhat scientifically. He and V. I. Pudovkin created an experiment with images and examined viewers' reactions to what they saw.

These two men first showed an image of an actor with no expression on his face, then a shot of a bowl of soup, and back again to the actor, still with no expression. Invariably, the viewer deduced that the character was hungry. They combined the same image of the actor with other shots, and viewers tended once again to read into the series of shots some emotion or need. To Kuleshov and Pudovkin, this experiment proved that a succession of images could tell a story in a way that the images alone could not. Once again, this might sound simple in hindsight, but it is important to appreciate the power these early film theorists, directors and editors had latched onto. Depending on which other image was inserted between shots of the actor's face, viewers came away with totally different stories.

Actor/soup/actor = hungry
Actor/coffin/actor = sad
Actor/young child/actor = happy

On the basis of these experiments, Kuleshov deduced that "Shooting and acting are merely the preparation of the material, like mixing the paint or tuning the instrument." You can certainly appreciate how important this idea is today in television commercial advertising.

V. I. Pudovkin and Sergei Eisenstein were colleagues and friends in Russia, each active in the Moscow Cinema Institute. Both were film directors and were committed to practicing their competing and passionately held theories about the appropriate utilization of image pacing and placement. In a nutshell, Pudovkin's theories promoted constructing ideas by building shot after shot to relate meaning. Eisenstein's theories held that to best manipulate the material and affect an audience, a collision of images was required. The collision of one shot with another created a new meaning beyond that held by either of the two original images.

Even with their apparently contrasting approaches, the two filmmakers had three main similarities:

1. Like Griffith, both Pudovkin and Eisenstein worked within and actively commented on the political climate of their society.
2. Both Pudovkin and Eisenstein sought to transcend the inherent "realism" of film and take the art form to new philosophic levels. They worked against the transparency that existed between reality and the cinema and, through cinematography and masterful editing, told mythic tales of human struggle.
3. Both filmmakers worked to show that the lives of individuals were mere elements in a greater scheme. In this attempt, Eisenstein and Pudovkin not only followed the dominant Marxist ideology of their culture, but also followed the lead of D. W. Griffith, an American who addressed similar human struggles on a grand scale.

Because current editing practices still draw so widely on Pudovkin's and Eisenstein's theories, let's take a moment to lay out each of their styles.

V. I. Pudovkin saw in film a vehicle that could *construct* meaning. Shots were linked together like pieces of a chain, the order of which expounded an idea. He then pushed that linkage idea further to construct philosophical ideas about culture and society.

Pudovkin believed that he could best do this by constructing, detail by detail, a mental linkage of shots that would provide the continuous flow of the narrative. He wrote that it was most effective to unroll an idea with single close-up shots. His opinion was that a scene could best be constructed from purely significant details instead of long shots, thus allowing each shot to make a new and specific point. In this practice, he diverged from D. W. Griffith, who used many long shots and inserted close-ups for dramatic detail.

There is at least one additional way in which Pudovkin branched off from his predecessor. Whereas Griffith was concerned with presenting broad human conflicts (such as the U.S. Civil War in "Birth of a Nation" and ongoing human failure in "Intolerance"), Pudovkin was concerned with implications and overtones, with emotions. He did this best by building up these implications through linked close-up shots throughout the film.

Perhaps Pudovkin's most famous film is "Mother," released in 1926. This is a fiction film about an individual's transformation from political naivete to Marxist awareness. Set during the 1905 Revolution in Russia, the film portrays the plight of a working-class woman who is oppressed, laboring only on behalf of the powerful. She becomes politically conscious through witnessing the activities, imprisonment and escape of her worker son, Pavel. The film's power results from Pudovkin's utilization of **montage,** piecing together shots like a work of music. The images are built up, combining action and reaction.

One of the key scenes in this film, and the one that perhaps best portrays Pudovkin's construction/linkage theory, is Pavel's escape from prison. Including not only close-up shots of his face, but also images of a babbling brook, sunlight hitting the snow, birds in flight and a laughing child, the film unfolds the powerful emotions felt by this formerly oppressed man. If you have never had the chance to view "Mother," it would be well worth your while to read more about Pudovkin's theories and then spend some time analyzing this truly powerful motion picture.

As was mentioned earlier, Pudovkin and Sergei Eisenstein were contemporaries and were very much aware of each other's philosophies and films. Their works of art were quite different in basic design and implementation. Eisenstein considered Pudovkin's linkage theories essential but simple and elementary.

Instead of linking shots in a smooth sequence as Pudovkin did, Eisenstein saw film editing as fertile opportunity for a mental clash of images and ideas. His goal was to shock, with each cut creating conflict and a fresh impression in the viewer's mind. You might think of each cut as combustion in the engine that drives the film forward.

Eisenstein worked to create a sense of meaning not held only by the images themselves, but also derived from this conflict or juxtaposition between shots.

In the 1920s and 1930s, there was an art movement called Cubism. This movement, directly influenced by photography and the new field of motion pictures, attempted to show an object from several points of view simultaneously. One of the most famous Cubist paintings is Marcel Duchamp's "Nude Descending a Staircase."

It is interesting to note that while such paintings and sculptures were in some way shaped by motion pictures (as well as various philosophies and ideologies), Cubism in turn affected the art of motion pictures. Where it influenced them most directly was in the editing of films. Eisenstein, a very intellectual artist, saw film editing as one way to promote the task of viewing an object from several points (almost) simultaneously. Through colliding images, the film compared each aspect of an object or action with others, setting differences against similarities. Eisenstein saw no value in directing only the emotions but preferred to direct the whole thought process through forcing image A into image B and forming C, a third thought or idea.

As Eisenstein worked to codify his various theories, he deduced five major chronological montage designs for editing. Briefly, these included the following:

1. *Metric montage:* In this first style of editing, pace is determined by the absolute lengths of the shots and follows a specific formula. For example, shots might be a series of three 12-second shots, followed by three 6-second shots, followed by three 3-second shots, followed by three 1/5-second shots and so on. Tension is produced by the mechanical acceleration or shortening of the pieces

while the original proportions are preserved. In this particular instance, a certain excitement and tension would be forced by the quickening pace.

2. *Rhythmic montage:* In this type, continuity arises from the visual pattern within the frame. Editing is forced by content. For example, matching action would force an edit to occur between a long shot of a woman beginning to wipe a tear away and a close-up of the same woman's hand just as it reaches her cheek.

3. *Tonal montage:* In this type, editing decisions are made specifically to establish the emotional quality of the scene. Tonal montage would include the insertion of specific shots such as close-ups to promote the emotional quality of the scene.

4. *Overtonal montage:* This type involves an interplay of the first three types, mixing pace, ideas and emotions to induce the desired effect from the audience.

5. *Intellectual montage:* This type includes all of the above plus the introduction of new and possibly shocking or unexpected ideas into a highly charged and emotional scene. In this type of montage, which Eisenstein considered the final goal of editing, the filmmaker might introduce new images that would clash with, comment on and add to what the viewer had already seen.

In "Battleship Potemkin," arguably Sergei Eisenstein's most famous film, he attempted to include each kind of montage in its editing style. The celebrated "Odessa steps" sequence in this film is considered Eisenstein's masterpiece and the arena in which he most successfully followed his own montage theories.

Of course, there have been many, many other filmmakers, both before and after those listed above. Although the ones we discussed are still considered some of the most important founders of various film editing styles, there were and are filmmakers of a different gender, from different cultures, with different goals and motion picture styles, audiences, stories and ways of visually articulating their messages. Some motion pictures are created to sell a product. Some are born out of a need to artfully challenge the governing ideology of a culture or to "subvert the dominant paradigm." Some films, television shows, CD-ROMs, DVD-ROMs or websites are created to tell simple narrative stories. Some ethnographic documentaries are made to record cultural activities before they are usurped by "progress." In almost every case, the editorial manipulation of the images and audio will make a more powerful, effective and enjoyable motion picture.

Other filmmakers that you might want to seek out as you continue your exploration of motion picture editing include Woody Allen, Robert Altman, Michelangelo Antonioni, Bruce Baillie, Ingmar Bergman, Bernardo Bertolucci, Stan Brakhage, Luis Buñuel, Charlie Chaplin, Michelle Citron, Jean Cocteau, Cecil B. DeMille, Maya Deren, Rainer Werner Fassbinder, Federico Fellini, Robert Flaherty, Su Friedrich, Jean-Luc Godard, Werner Herzog, Alfred Hitchcock, Stanley Kubrick, Akira Kurosawa, Fritz Lang, Spike Lee, Richard Lester, George Lucas, Chris Marker, Sam Peckinpah, Satyajit Ray, Jean Renoir, Leni Riefenstahl, Roberto Rosselini, Amalie Rothschild, Jean Rouch, Walter Ruttman, Martin Scorsese, Steven Spielberg, François Truffaut, Dziga Vertov, Orson Welles, Wim Wenders and Basil Wright. There are also several good websites and suggested readings listed at the end of this book, all of which will guide you to other established and emerging motion picture makers and editors, as well as alternative media voices.

As a motion picture editor yourself, it is truly important that you not be educated solely by the standard, common styles dictated by narrative feature "Hollywood-style" motion pictures or television. Actively seek out alternative styles, forms, experiments and voices. In doing so, you will not only learn more about life, but also more about potential ways of telling your own stories. Now, let's move on to some technology!

Early Editing Equipment

Film editing can be accomplished on a table, as long as there are reels to unwind and rewind the film and magnetic audiotape as the editor goes through the process. However, the introduction of a new piece of equipment in the 1920s included motor-powered rewinds. This first film editing machine is called an upright **Moviola,** and some editors still use the system today.

A few years later, other engineers and machinists invented a similar system but one that imitated the ease of access to material. These new systems are still referred to as *flatbeds* (in contrast to the upright systems), and possibly the most famous maker of these systems remains a German company called Steenbeck. Figure 2.1 shows a flatbed film editing system. The Moviola, Steenbeck and various other systems are simply ways to support and enhance the needs of the film editor. Many filmmakers, editors and even major motion picture directors such as Steven Spielberg and Tim Robbins still use such systems in certain stages of the film editing process. We will discuss the reasons for this in later chapters. For now, however, bear in mind that such systems work well and some editors prefer to keep the entire process on film. Many editors were trained using these original cut-and-splice systems, and the mindset of the motion picture editor is often based on these simple technologies.

It was not only film that was cut and spliced together—videotape was as well! However, you can imagine the hassles involved in physically cutting video-

**FIGURE 2.1   A Flatbed
Editing System for Film**

tape. If you have ever opened up the hinged door on a videocassette and looked at the tape itself, you know that a blank tape looks exactly the same as one that has been recorded on. The electronic signal representing the shot is invisible to the human eye, with no visual guide to alert the editor to where one frame ends and another starts. Literally cutting videotape with a razor required ingenious efforts, including looking at footage on a monitor, then removing the tape from the playback equipment and hoping you were making the splices in the right place. A system was devised by applying a chemical mixture of fine iron powder that made the 1/200th of an inch space between frames barely visible. These types of cuts more often than not lost picture signal. The development of an expensive video splicer, the Smith splicer, in 1957 allowed the editor to see the guard band (the space between frames) with a microscope. In 1958, Ampex developed a less complicated splicer, but editing problems persisted because of the difference between where the picture and sound were located. Sync-cuts were laborious and time consuming.

For those beginning their video editing in the twenty-first century, it's hard to believe that in the "old days" (the late 1950s lasting into the mid-1970s), the vast majority of video editing was done with open reel-to-reel videotape recorders (VTR) like the one shown in Figure 2.2.

These VTRs recorded in black and white only and had no editing-control unit, a piece of equipment that connects and controls both the source and record video editing decks. The person doing the editing was, in a sense, the editing-control unit. Editors had to push their buttons and use both hands to edit on the fly. They wound the reel manually to their preroll spot and guessed the exact location by watching the videotape as it went over the heads. This method required coordination and a developed skill to minimize the glitches and accompanying vertical rolls. Early video editing was difficult, prone to problems and very time consuming. However, the search for precise, filmlike video editing was underway.

In the late 1950s, edit sync for video finally arrived. NBC developed what it called *edit sync guide* (ESG). ESG was an electronic beep that was placed every second on one of the tracks and followed with a human voice announcing each minute and second. This type of coding of the videotape and the kinescope (film) copy allowed television editors to edit videotape using traditional film methods.

Perhaps one of the greatest advances in the movement of linear video editing toward nonlinear techniques, occurred in 1962 when a CBS technician, Dick Hill, working in Los Angeles, learned about the Defense Department's use of a time clock recorded on magnetic tape. The military used this magnetic tape clock to monitor close and distant locations around

FIGURE 2.2   A Reel-to-Reel VTR

missile test sites. Hill reported this to CBS headquarters and suggested the need for a similar reference system on videotape. The Society of Motion Picture and Television Engineers (SMPTE) soon developed a new referencing system, called SMPTE timecode, that allowed for truly accurate electronic edit points without physically cutting the videotape. Timecode is an electronic reference or address that is stated in hours, minutes, seconds and video frames that is assigned by a timecode generator to every video frame. We will discuss SMPTE timecode in much greater detail in Chapter 7, "Management of Your Material." Suffice it to say for now that playback decks can read these additional signals on the videotape and provide a numerical reference to coincide with the images and audio on the tape. Once the editor made a decision about which shots to use, she or he didn't physically cut the original tape but instead copied the images and sound in the appropriate order from one tape to another. Obviously, this was in many ways a positive change in the video postproduction process.

In moving to this stage, however, video editing became an interesting aberration in the creative process. Because this evolved form of analog videotape editing requires making copies of parts of one tape onto another tape, you lay one shot down, find another and then lay it down, locate a third and edit it, and on and on. You sequentially lay down copies of the desired shots and sounds onto a new tape, as shown in Figure 2.3. You are forced to work linearly.

Comparing this evolved type of video editing once again to film editing, you can see that you gave up some artistic freedom and flexibility with video. By physically cutting film, you could splice with tape, view the combined images, remove the tape, rearrange shots, resplice and view again until you were satisfied with the results. With analog video editing, making copies of shots from one tape onto another, you couldn't undo and redo splices, since there weren't any. You were simply copying information.

Any kind of motion picture editing is a time-intensive process. But in linear video editing, one is more or less stuck with the editing decisions that had been made and carried out. Linear analog video editors often try to redo edits a few times until satisfied and then move on to the next and start the process again. Sometimes, after lots of edits, a problem occurs. For example, imagine that the editor has spent two hours laboring over ten shots. After two hours, she decides to show these edited shots to the director. "Well," says the director, "it looks really good except for that second shot. I think it would be much more powerful if we include a close-up shot of the character's hand lingering on the doorknob just a bit longer before cutting to the wide-angle shot of him slowly opening the door."

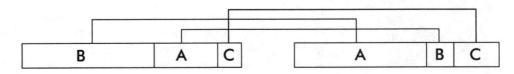

FIGURE 2.3   Laying Down Shots from One Tape to Another

If the poor editor has been editing on an analog video editing system, she cannot go back and insert a shot in between two other shots. Laboriously going back, covering up the second wide-angle shot of the character opening the door with a close-up of the hand on the doorknob, then including the wide-angle shot of opening the door, then once again laying down all of the other shots would be the answer. Of course, you can appreciate how frustrating and time-consuming this would be.

Digital Nonlinear Systems Enter the Market

With different degrees of success, many editing systems followed, each utilizing timecode and a linear process. But the quest for a nonlinear frame of working with video was still going on, and in 1968, CBS gave up tape and moved to magnetic disk platters for storing analog video. Owing to some mechanical problems, they went to the Memorex Corporation for help. Memorex was interested in developing a system with random access for recording video on disk. Together, they formed CMX (standing for "CBS, Memorex, experimental") and by 1970 had developed the CMX600, a computer that controlled removable disk platters that held 56 kilobytes (nearly 5 minutes) of video information. The information was stored in half-resolution black-and-white dailies and used timecode.

The CMX600 was attached to the CMX200. This was a linear tape assembler that took the 600's edit decision list and built a master 2-inch broadcast videotape. By 1972, perhaps because of cost, maintenance, image quality and limited storage space, the CMX600 had not reached sales expectations. What did sell, however, was the CMX300, a linear system that allowed direct interface through the keyboard terminal with the assembly editor.

In 1973, Sony introduced the 3/4-inch machine, and Sony's U-matic equipment, shown in Figure 2.4, became the standard for 3/4-inch tape. CMX developed the first commercial edit controller for 3/4-inch decks, called the CMX50. The CMX50 had a standardized edit decision list, previews and assemblies that created a standard for video editing that continues today.

The mid-1970s saw the development of some software programs to increase the usefulness of the CMX systems. CBS developed an advanced form of the CMX600 using the newly developed Sony Beta 3/4-inch videotape. Cash outlay

FIGURE 2.4   A 3/4-inch U-Matic System

for the new format's tape decks was costly, so the Beta systems mostly remained in-house at CBS.

LaserVision videodisc players also began to be sold to the educational market in the 1970s. MCA teamed up with Pioneer to form the Universal Pioneer Corporation to bring the videodisc players to the mass market. MagnoVision used a different technology to play videodiscs and was introduced by Magnavox in 1977.

By 1978, a variety of formats for video was flooding the mass market. Among the leaders were Sony's 3/4-inch Beta, Panasonic's VHS 1/2-inch, Magnavox's MagnoVision videodiscs and DiscoVision. A partnership formed in the mid-1970s by MCA and IBM also introduced their version of videodisc: LaserVision.

During this time, CMX was developing a plan to move videotape editors from dependence on number-type editing systems to a non-number-dependent editing system. This system was to have a database management system and a graphics user interface.

For most students and independent motion picture producers, projects were either shot and edited on film or, if originating on video, were taken to their final version using linear analog video systems. For producers with deeper pockets, early rough cuts of a video might be completed on similar linear systems, but the final version was often completed at very expensive postproduction facilities utilizing video systems controlled by computers. They still weren't the digital nonlinear systems we are surrounded by today, but they were yet another step in the integration of computers and motion picture postproduction.

Today, digital storage of the film/video image and audio, along with random quick access of footage, has moved video editing to a new dimension. Digital methods of postproduction are now complementing, and often replacing, traditional film and video editing. Computer-based random access picture and sound editing often overshadow both hands-on film splicing and linear videotape editing. Creative freedom and edit speed are by far the biggest lures of digital nonlinear editing systems. You have random access to any frame of footage (provided that you have enough storage space to digitize your footage), eliminating the need to shuttle back and forth or locate additional source tapes trying to find a shot. It is, of course, interesting to note that digital video editing is finally nonlinear—something film editing has always been.

Hollywood Helps the Move
to Nonlinear Editing

Hollywood filmmakers, ever aware of the cost of time, were looking for ways to use video in their postproduction of features. Director/producer Francis Ford Coppola was active in the mid-1970s using video to help in film production. He used a video camera side by side with the film camera to record the action and view the scenes. With his film "One From the Heart" (1982), Coppola is considered to be the first filmmaker to use *video assist* in film production. The video camera fed the signal to a production trailer, where it was recorded and provided instant viewing of the scenes.

Around 1979, George Lucas began looking into ways to improve filmmaking. His primary interest lay in using computers and video in postproduction. He set up a division at his production company Lucasfilm, Ltd. for research and development using these technologies. The company's first development in 1980 was a high-resolution graphics workstation along with sound and picture editing devices. The results were the EditDroid (picture editor), the SoundDroid and Pixar (graphics). The EditDroid was controlled by computer, was nonlinear and had disc storage. The EditDroid could also control tape decks for emergency linear editing.

> My first work as an assistant editor, the editor was not happy and the director turned to me and said, "Here, you edit." I had unprecedented opportunities. Shortly after completing that film, they asked me to run Droid Works. George Lucas seemed to have no interest in going digital with the Droid; he was more interested in selling this newly designed software to Avid.
>
> Bennett Goldberg, Vice President of Editing Services at Digital Symphony, Los Angeles, California

The main idea of the system was to be a user-friendly system that was easier to use than the current (1980–1983) crop of computers and video editing systems. There was no desktop computer industry at this time, but development activity was high, as some companies were trying to compete with IBM for the smaller high-powered workstations.

Talks were underway with DiscoVision Associates about developing LaserVision discs that could record. All this activity and publicity caused Lucasfilm to become the Mecca for companies, organizations and individuals that were interested in investigating or developing computer-based nonlinear editing systems.

By 1983, Bell & Howell, a fifty-year-old film equipment manufacturer and distributor, had bought Telemation, acquired the Mach-1 editing system and were developing Envision, a video-for-film editing system. Shortly after this development began, Bell & Howell was taken over in a buyout, and the new owners decided to sell off pieces of the company. Bell & Howell Professional, the research and development division, was bought by some of its employees. Bruce Rady bought the rights to the Envision system. He developed a low-cost VITC (vertical integral timecode) reader and changed the name of the editing system to TouchVision. (See Chapter 7, "Management of Your Material," for more information and a full definition of timecode, including VITC.) This system was demonstrated at the 1985 National Association of Broadcasters (NAB) Convention. TouchVision was based on a film editing flatbed and allowed editors to control the source decks independently. TouchVision was able to use various decks similar to a multiplate flatbed. Using 3/4-inch decks, the system had a price around $100,000.

The end of 1983 saw a great deal of advertising from Montage Computer Company and Lucasfilm about their new edit systems. Montage's system was initially called the Montage Picture Processor because of its resemblance to a word processor. Desktop PC makers had strong promotions going on at this time, and IBM PCs and their clones dominated the personal computer market. With a creative and visually oriented commercial, Apple introduced the Macintosh operating system during the 1984 Super Bowl. At the time, Macintosh was more graphics oriented than the IBM PC, and the nonlinear editing gurus began to move in that system's direction.

During this same period, the high cost of manufacturing laserdisks and some other software problems were slowing development of the EditDroid and the Picture Processor. Both Montage Computer Company and Lucasfilm revealed prototypes at the 1984 National Association of Broadcasters' (NAB) annual convention in Las Vegas but were not ready to deliver systems to the field. Laser Edit was experimenting with Optical Disc Corporation's two-headed laserdisk players and using it in a linear editing system with the dailies on laserdisk.

I would say that regardless of the toolset, an editor is an artist and an integral part of the creative team. The demands are great to stay on top of technological changes. However, it is important to remember equipment is a tool to accomplish something artistic. Editing is now attracting a different type of person. Before, people said, "I want to be an editor." But now, my children of seven and nine know how to edit.

Bennett Goldberg, Vice President of Editing Services at Digital Symphony, Los Angeles, California

Montage and EditDroid were shown again at the 1985 NAB convention, and they were making some headway in the marketplace despite their cost of about $200,000. At the same convention, Bruce Rady finally unveiled his TouchVision, a film-style editing system. That year saw the beginning of development by CMX on its film-specific nonlinear system, the CMX6000. The CMX6000 was very advanced for its time and had little in common with the old CMX600.

Feature Films Edited Electronically

Also in 1985, "Power," a feature directed by Sidney Lumet, used the Montage Picture Processor, becoming the first feature film to be edited electronically. Pacific Video was using the Montage, the Ediflex and the EditDroid to edit television shows that were originated on film. Pacific Video President Emory Cohen first started using the term *the electronic lab* to describe the new environment of film in a video post house using electronic editing processes.

The Montage Picture Processor won the 1987 Academy Award for Scientific and Technical Achievement in cutting several features, such as Stanley Kubrick's "Full Metal Jacket." William Warner's work led to the development in 1988 of the Avid/1. At the 1989 NAB show, Avid Technology began to take orders for its Avid/1. The disk-based system E-PIX by Adcom was also introduced at the 1989 NAB show.

The beginning of the 1990s saw steady improvement and growth in all digital systems. In London, O.L.E. Ltd. began to market a new system called "Lightworks." Adobe bought ReelTime from Rany Ubillos and named it Premiere. Apple released QuickTime. (See Chapter 6, "Getting Your Footage into the System: What the Steps Are and What You Need to Know," for a complete description of QuickTime.)

By the end of 1992, Hollywood had begun adopting digital nonlinear systems to replace the older analog systems. In 1993, J&R Film Company, the owner of Moviola, started to phase out its Moviola rental business and move into digital nonlinear rental for film postproduction. J&R also bought the EditDroid from LucasArts, Ltd. and ended Lucasfilm's connection with the product. ImMIX's VideoCube and Avid's 4000 and 8000 series, along with Lightworks' Heavyworks, were becoming the must-have on-line nonlinear systems. Many new systems such as the Media 100, TouchVision's D-Vision, FAST Electronic Video Machine and Matrox's Studio aimed at industrial, independent and corporate postproduction.

Early in the 1990s, Kodak introduced its high-end Cineon system, which changed the use of special effects in large-budget features. By using a high-quality film scanner, a shot could be scanned into the computer and manipulated and then brought back out to a high-quality film recorder with no loss of image. Built to work with 35mm and 65mm film, this system gave digital special effects a high-quality tool that worked with high-end Silicon Graphics computers.

In the mid-1990s, Avid continued its heavy market penetration. Desktop computers became more powerful with more memory. Software supported Macintosh, PC and Silicon Graphics computers. Avid began to add effects and compositing systems such as the Matador, a 2D paint and animation system. While all these developments were happening, new video formats such as Hi8 and digital Beta were being used extensively. Much speculation about HDTV (high-definition television) had been going on for most of the 1990s, and this technology is slowly being incorporated in broadcast and location recording.

Affordable Systems Catering to the Independent and Student Markets

Beginning in the early 1990s, independent and student motion picture makers and editors had access to digital nonlinear systems. Although they were still expensive, smaller production and postproduction houses as well as campuses could purchase any one of a wide variety of systems on the market. The penetration of these systems radically altered how smaller-budget films were postproduced and prompted quick and necessary changes in curricula. In the early years of the twenty-first century, it is not at all unusual for independent and student filmmakers to at least have access to, if not own, digital nonlinear editing systems including Adobe Premiere and Final Cut Pro.

At this writing, desktop computers continue to grow in power, memory and capability. Many companies have merged or been sold and operate under new names or have gone out of business. The major digital nonlinear systems continue to increase their market share. After much speculation about HDTV starting in the late 1980s, the standard for broadcast digital television was set in the spring of 1997, and the networks and the large-market stations began to prepare for the expensive change in broadcasting technology. However, in January 2001, the chairman of the FCC decided that the previously imposed deadlines for transition to HDTV placed on the U.S. market were too optimistic and reopened discussion on this changeover.

With all the bells and whistles and convenience that digital nonlinear editing and video have and will have, some media makers worship each new advance in technology. Continuing improvements and change in capture systems as well as digital nonlinear editing will be the norm as we move farther into the twenty-first century. Be reminded that these are but tools of the process. There will always be the need for creative and talented people who can tell the story through writing, performing, directing, image capturing, audio recording and the art of editing. All of these elements combine to create a strong, cohesive and moving story.

Despite the new technologies, content still reigns in terms of what makes a good film or video. As an editor, you must first and foremost be concerned with the storyline, the strength of the characters, the production skills and the needs of your audience. No amount of fancy wipes or flying text will overcome poor production or editing aesthetics.

The advent of computer-based editing has put the capability of film editing in the hands of anyone with access to enough **RAM** (random access memory), hard drive space or external storage device and some editing software. Although at the more inexpensive levels, this type of digital editing involves certain compromises (most obviously the quality of the video image), prices are dropping for devices that are capable of digitally capturing the video and copying the edited version back to video. Editing software, too, continues to drop in price. Using such lower-end equipment, however, can create what are called **artifacts.** These artifacts are simply by-products of low-resolution. Digital video noise is emotionally and aesthetically unappealing. Higher compression rates and more expensive equipment help to eliminate video artifacts.

Random access nonlinear editing allows possibilities to be explored quickly and easily. In a sense, the nonlinear approach to video postproduction equates to desktop publishing. You can manipulate the image and the order as often as you like without having to start the entire process over. If you are confident in your goals for the project, know your raw footage and are familiar with your equipment, the editing process can move quickly through the rough cut stage and on to the fine-tuning of your film. However, if you are unsure of exactly what your editorial goals are, then the process can easily get bogged down in an endless number of possibilities tried and rejected. The advantages of nonlinear are many, but in the wrong hands, the process can be ineffective and time-consuming. This is in fact no different from any other form of motion picture editing except for the fact that the new technology can tend to prompt multiple edit attempts without fully thinking through the ramifications. These and other concerns will be addressed in following chapters.

CHAPTER

3

What the Editor Must Know: Basic Motion Picture Stages and Crew Positions

The Basic Process of Production

If you are interested in motion picture editing, you are probably also interested in the other stages of motion picture preparation and production. There are some truly good books on what we call preproduction for motion pictures (including generating ideas, formulating stories, writing scripts, seeking funding, putting together a budget, hiring actors and crew, deciding on what equipment to use, location scouting, etc.), and if you are new to the field, it will be well worth your time to seek some of these books out. You might be taking a course that will cover various aspects of some or all of these areas. Preproduction and well-organized producing for any form of motion picture communication is crucial. The entire postproduction process rests on the existence of properly recorded material (both visual and audio), as well as capable and impassioned story-telling. Many students and new motion picture producers tend to gravitate, at least initially, toward a narrative filmmaking style. Certainly, narrative feature films tend to dominate the media market worldwide. However, both of us have successfully worked in documentaries, experimental/interpretive films, commercials, music videos and news broadcast productions. Many of the stages and crew positions exist in these other genres, though sometimes in slightly altered capacities.

It is extremely important to understand the basic process of production, for if you haven't recorded an image and sound, there is no way you are going to edit them! If you are familiar with the basic processes of video and film production, feel free to skip over this section. If not, or if you need a refresher, dive in here.

First, as was mentioned previously, it is rare that the shots or scenes of any motion picture story are recorded in the exact order in which they are to be presented. If you consider the recent film "Gladiator," directed by Ridley Scott, you might recall scenes that were supposedly set in Rome, Spain, old Germania and

Africa. Of course, motion pictures are often shot somewhere that simply resembles another place, but let us assume that this particular film was actually shot in these various locations. The film begins with a battle in Germania, cuts to a wheat field in Spain and goes back to the snowy battle. Eventually, the film's main character, played by Russell Crowe, finds himself a slave in northern Africa. From here, we cut to scenes in Rome with the new Caesar (Joacquin Phoenix) beginning to make changes to his deceased father's policies and dreams for Rome. The film intercuts between Phoenix and Crowe, from Rome to Africa, as the story unfolds.

Of course, it would make no sense at all to fly the crew from a snowy field somewhere in Europe off to a wheat field in Spain, back to the snowy battlefield, down to Rome, on to Africa and back to Rome. If at all possible, all scenes in one location are shot before moving on to another location. It doesn't matter that in the final version of the film, we will see inserted into the middle of a snowy battle scene a shot of Crowe's hand grazing the top of wheat slowly blowing in the Spanish wind. Things are shot out of order for convenience and because of financial and scheduling considerations.

But in addition to shooting out of order in different locations, you also need to consider the fact that within a particular scene, there might be several different camera setups—first a wide-angle shot of all of the action, then close-up shots of the same actions, cutaway shots of a hand on a sword, a slow-motion shot of a horse running swiftly toward the enemy, several takes of the action to get just the right movement and expressions, and so on. The director, the director of photography, the producer and probably the editor, key actors and others will watch this footage every day or so and begin to formulate ideas about what needs to be reshot, what should be included in the film and in what order to position shots.

Shooting on Film

So let's assume that instead of shooting on video, we correctly guess that this motion picture was recorded on celluloid film stock. Film is very expensive to shoot and process—much more costly than videotape. Since in many filmmaking scenarios there are several takes of the action, it would push the film budget through the ceiling if every single one of these were printed. What often occurs is that immediately after shooting a take, the director will quickly evaluate what happened and then indicate whether she or he want the film printed. All of the film will be processed, but often only the best shots will actually be printed to positive film stock for viewing. In narrative fiction and some other film genres, the director can be helped on the set by both a camera assistant and a script supervisor. The camera assistant writes down what scenes from the script were shot on that particular film roll (giving the roll a particular number designation), indicates the number of takes of each shot and writes down which shots the director wants to have printed at the lab for viewing. These camera reports go to the laboratory along with the footage so that the technicians know what to print and what negatives simply to process and store away. On the set, the script supervisor works very closely with the director, watching the action, making notes of exactly where props were placed, which hand held a cup of coffee, where the lights were set up, where the actor walked across the room and other important continuity information. These notes are particularly important if a shot needs to be redone for some reason. They help the directors and actors make sure that the audience will not be able to tell that shots from one scene were actually filmed on totally different days. The script supervisor's paperwork not only supports the director's plans for the next day's shoot, but also goes along with the camera report to the editor.

In order for these crew members and actors to even be able to watch this raw footage (called **dailies** or *rushes*—watched daily and rushed from the set to the lab and back), the exposed motion picture film must be carefully protected from light, packaged with directions and sent to a laboratory for processing and printing. For the sake of simplicity and following normal protocol, we will assume here that the motion picture was shot on negative film. You can easily and correctly compare negative motion picture film stock to the film you might put in your camera. You load the film, take your pictures, roll the film back into the canister to protect it from light, go to the photo laboratory at your local store, give them directions about what you need and wait for them to process and print the film. Once they do this, you can pick up not only a positive copy of the image (the print), but also the processed negative, which is actually the film that went through your camera.

Motion picture film stock can also be reversal film. This type is easily compared to slide film you might use in your still camera. You shoot your pictures, take the canister to the lab and give them instructions, and what you get back is positive still images that you can shine light through to view, usually mounted in white frames for ease of handling. Have you ever noticed that when you get slides back, you don't get negatives? This is because the actual image in the slide is the film that went through your camera. The chemicals simply "reversed" your negative into a positive image instead of processing the negative in a way that will allow a positive print to be made from them.

It is important to note that some films are shot with very small crews (sometimes only the camera operator, who also serves as director/producer and editor). Some documentaries, personal biographies, experimental examinations and short narratives truly do not have the need or budget for additional crew members. In these cases, notes about what was shot, decisions about what to print and specific directions for the lab are quickly jotted down without the benefit of an added pair of eyes. If decisions can't be made about what shots are worth printing, all of the film that was shot is printed by the lab, and decisions about what to use are based on all of the available film, not just the "best" shots chosen by the director in advance and printed by the lab.

If you have ever shot motion picture film or watched on a set or location, you will remember that the audio is not recorded on the film. There is always a separate audio recording device (often a 1/4-inch reel-to-reel recorder or digital audiotape deck. The visual image is recorded onto the film, and the audio (dialogue, ambient sound, etc.) is recorded onto some type of audiotape. We will briefly discuss how this affects film editing below.

Shooting on Video

Now you have the basics of shooting on film. What about video? In many ways, video is much simpler. You put a cassette in the camera, set up the lights, white balance the camera and shoot; you can then immediately rewind the tape and look at it in your viewfinder or on a monitor. There is no lab to which you must send it, no negative to be processed and no printing onto positive stock. Videotape is an electromagnetic recording medium, much like audiotape, and the image and sound are available immediately for playback. You may eventually manipulate this image in various stages of postproduction (make the image black and white, raise the luminance level, add strobing effects, etc.), but at this early stage, you can immediately view what you shot. Both the visuals and the audio are recorded directly onto the videotape, as shown in Figure 3.1.

In the early years, both motion picture film and videotape required a razor blade to cut shots apart, thus allowing the editor to rearrange them to tell the story. This process still makes sense for cutting film, because the editor can literally see the images on the celluloid, frame by frame. Running the film through a viewfinder at twenty-four frames per second, the film editor can make appropriate decisions about what to shorten, what to move and where to cut. Once shots are cut apart by the razor blade, the editor can either store them in a bin nearby or splice them together with other desired shots. So, despite the seemingly high-tech buzz word *nonlinear*, film editing has been a nonlinear editing process from day 1. Let's briefly examine the postproduction process for editing your visuals on film—that is, actually cutting and splicing the celluloid.

Early in the development of equipment for cutting film, technicians invented **splicers** that cleanly cut the film directly on a frame line, thus leaving the individual photographic frames untouched. The film editor could now easily cut out unwanted frames and/or move shots to other places in the film and splice them in, using tape or liquid cement. Once the editor removes shots, shortens takes and rearranges material, she or he can run the film through a viewer and easily evaluate the effectiveness of the edit. If the editor decides that a clip doesn't work—

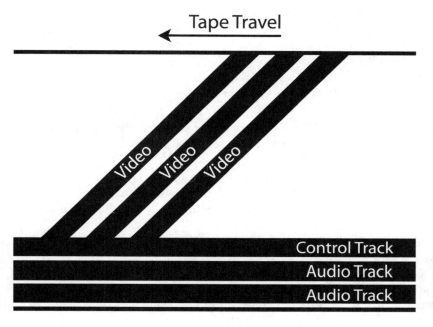

Tape Travel

Control Track

Audio Track

Audio Track

FIGURE 3.1   Where the Various Signals Are Recorded on Videotape

maybe it is still too long or simply in the wrong place—it is relatively easy to move the shot and splice it back in as needed.

Let's go back to audio for a second. Remember that the sound is not recorded on the film itself but instead on some type of audiotape. How does this affect film editing? Remember that we are cutting and splicing film, whether it is 8mm, 16mm, 35mm or 65mm. If we have audio to concern us, we must cut and splice it as well. In many films, the audio goes directly along with the accompanying visual. If we see someone speak on the screen, we expect that we will hear the person's voice in sync with his or her lip movements. So of course the editor needs some way of syncing sound up with the image. How is this done?

When film is shot (as opposed to video), you will see the use of a slate at the beginning of each shot (see Figure 3.2). Many people who are not involved in motion pictures assume that this slate is simply meant to indicate which scene and shot are about to be recorded. However, those are only two of the reasons for taking the time to slate a shot. One of the key goals of the person slating the shot is to make sure that the film camera records the action of the top, hinged clapboard hitting the slate body and

FIGURE 3.2   Movie Slate

that the sound recording device "hears" the sound of this hit. On a set, often the director will say the following:

"Quiet on the set"!

"Sound"!   The sound recordist will start the audiotape device and, once the machine is up to speed, will shout back, "Speed!"

"Camera"!   The camera operator will start the film camera and, once the film is rolling at full speed, will shout back, "Rolling!"

"Slate"!   At this time, the camera focuses on the slate, the microphone points toward the slate and the scene and take are announced before the clapboard is lowered with a sharp hit.

"Action"!

With a smaller crew or for a nonnarrative film, there might not be actors to direct or someone to hold up the slate, but there must be some way for the camera and the audio recording device to reference a common starting point. This can be done as simply (although less precisely) with a hand snapping. The goal is to designate an accurate starting point where the visuals and the audio can lock up.

Why is this necessary? You certainly don't need to do this with video, because the audio and the visuals are already synchronized: They both go onto the videotape. Remember that in film, the film records the visuals and the audio is recorded separately by an audio recording device. You must have some way for the editor to sync them up in postproduction. The first step in that process is to transfer the audio onto what is called magnetic film stock. This is a form of audiotape that is the same gauge (width) as the film you are editing (for example, 16mm). This magnetic film stock also has sprocket holes in it so that it can be pulled along at the same speed as the film.

The editor will find the first frame of visuals where the clapboard hits the slate and the first audio frame where that same hit can be heard and will simply lock down the visual with its accompanying audio. This way, if a few frames are taken out of a shot, the same number of frames can be deleted from the accompanying audio, and the shot will remain in sync.

Three Basic Stages of Constructing a Motion Picture

A production's life is usually divided into three major stages. A fair amount of what will be covered in this chapter is based on the narrative fiction film model, but these stages often apply as well to documentary, television series, news programs and experimental productions. The editor's familiarity with crew positions and their responsibilities will aid in understanding the production's purpose and theme and can assist in the editor's overall success. Though the editor is usually not fully immersed in the project until the last few days or weeks of the preproduction phase, the editor's work ordinarily begins with reading the script and discussing the film with the director toward the end of the preproduction stage.

Preproduction

For narrative fiction productions, the preproduction stage is sometimes divided into two parts: script development and shooting preproduction. In the development stage, the producer has commissioned a script or has purchased a script and usually required rewrites to hone the story. A director is hired, and more rewrites to the script usually occur. The lead actors are usually also hired at this time. The producer prepares a detailed budget. With the director and lead actors on board, financing, which is also sometimes tied to distribution, is sought. Once the financing is in place, script development proceeds to the preproduction stage. During the preproduction stage, the rest of cast and crew are hired, and locations are scouted and selected.

For all motion picture genres, the preproduction stage may also involve fundraising, historical and cultural research, acquiring archival materials and commissioning music. Off-camera preinterviews with documentary subjects or auditions of actors take place during this phase, as do researching and testing appropriate production equipment. For many motion picture makers, the preproduction stage is as collaborative as all other phases of the process. For some independent, autobiographical or exploratory motion pictures, this stage may lean more toward personal brainstorming and writing.

Production

The production stage, sometimes called principal photography, follows the preproduction stage. It is during this time that all the major shots in the production are captured. Be aware, however, that often production begins on one part of the film (scene, act, location) while preproduction is still in full swing for other sections of the film. During production, the script supervisor makes note of all shots taken, along with comments from the director. As the postproduction stage begins, the editor or editor's assistant logs all the shots (see Chapter 5, "The Digital Nonlinear Workflow and Environment"), using the production notes as a reference. As shooting continues, the editor prepares dailies (film shot each day and shown to the key production members for review) by syncing sound to each take shot on film, making dubs of the video master and/or inputting the material into the digital nonlinear system. The editor takes notes on the director's and script supervisor's comments as to where to cut various shots and then begins to cut the project. This process continues until the end of principal shooting. A good editor is always reliant on proper coverage and good footage. As they say, "If it wasn't shot, you can't edit it. And if it wasn't thought out, you can't edit it well." This is true of any editing process, whether it is for a news package, a narrative film, a documentary, a music video, animation or a sitcom.

Postproduction

Just before the end of shooting, the editor meets with the producer and director and sets the schedule for postproduction (see the section entitled "Some Postproduction Positions" for some of the elements that have to be scheduled). Obviously, in a scripted narrative motion picture, the editor is dealing with acted lines, scripted sets and locations. The editor may also work actively with graphics and compositing artists if there are special effects to be added during the postproduction phase. In a documentary or interpretive motion picture, the theme and key characters are often developed in the editing room. The editor truly has the ability to manipulate and form the footage into a cohesive story. The project begins to look more like a whole than just individual shots. Location sound is cleaned, and where it is unusable, it is replaced through the process of automatic dialogue replacement if actors need to rerecord dialogue. The process of adding sound effects begins. Music from the composer and/or music supervisor is added. In any genre of motion picture making, there may be several versions of the edit as the story is fine-tuned. Finally, after the producer, director and editor agree that the picture and the sound are working, the fine cut is locked, and a final sound mix that brings all the sound elements together is executed and then brought back to the visuals and merged with them for the final print in the various formats that might be required for distribution.

Motion picture making, whether it is 35mm film, digital video or bare-bones VHS, is usually a collaborative process. It is important that you work well with the entire production team.

Production Positions and Usual Responsibilities

The motion picture editor should be familiar with the various crew positions and their responsibilities. This will allow you to understand the overall production process and which crew member positions will likely be required to interact with you as you enter the postproduction phase. This communication will ensure a smooth postproduction process. The following list includes the usual major crew positions, but bear in mind that this list might not entirely represent what is used in student, news, documentary, interpretive, music video or various other motion picture forms.

In large-scale motion picture productions, crews are primarily assembled from pools of skilled freelance production technicians. In the past, each major studio had its own pool of technicians on the payroll and assigned them to the various productions. With the demise of the studio system, even well-known and skilled technicians and motion picture artists became freelance workers, and this practice continues today. Obviously, the size of the crew will vary. Typical Hollywood features may have hundreds of people working on location; a small-scale experimental autobiographical video might have one person fulfilling all tasks. We will list here some of the production positions and their usual responsibilities. If they are included as part of the motion picture process, they will likely have some interaction with the editor.

Producer

The producer has the responsibility to supervise the production from the beginning to the initial distribution of the completed production and beyond. The responsibility varies with the size of the budget and, depending on the situation, ranges from a great degree of hands-on interaction to being a mere figurehead with the money. Under the larger title of producer, there may be a line producer and associate producers who perform some of the various day-to-day functions listed herein. In documentaries, studio films and some smaller independent works, there is often an executive producer, who may indeed oversee production but more often is the commissioning agent or one of the major financiers of the motion picture. This may be the person who developed and financed the project but wants the help of an on-set or on-location producer to supervise the day-to-day operations of the production.

Producers may purchase the script or story concept and work with one or more writers to develop it into a master scene script, and they may hire the director and major characters. They usually consult with the director in hiring the editor, the other actors, the director of photography and the production manager. Producers are the main influence in organizing the production during preproduction. During production, they often work through the director and production manager, and in postproduction, they may work with the editor and oversee the completion of the project.

For television documentaries, the producer may also serve as the director. For television commercials, the producer is occasionally someone from the ad agency who is overseeing the production for a client. For television sitcoms, dramas, game shows, reality television series and the like, the producer is usually attached directly to a network or cable station.

Production Manager

In the preproduction phase, the production manager (PM) has the responsibility for working with the producer to develop a budget. As the script is completed, the PM usually develops a more complete detailed budget. Working with the producer and the director, the PM develops the shooting schedule by breaking down the script into its individual scenes and the individual elements of each of those scenes. Some of the elements the PM looks for include what actors, extras and cars are in the scene, whether it is an interior or exterior scene, how many pages the scene covers, which helps to estimate how long it will take to shoot, and many other details. Weather, backup scenes to shoot in case bad weather occurs and how long an actor has been working (which is important because of overtime requirements for Screen Actors' Guild members) are among other details the PM has to consider.

In the shooting phase, the PM has to cope with a variety of details, from ordering and making sure specialized equipment is in place when needed to film stock to ensuring that food, water and restroom facilities are available. In smaller productions, the PM's responsibilities might be handled by the producer. In post-production, an associate producer, line producer, or postproduction coordinator usually replaces the PM.

In smaller productions, the PM may also serve as the editor. The PM oversees so many details of the production and is so in tune with the various elements of the story and what was shot that occasionally this position flows very naturally into the editor's responsibilities.

Director

The director, along with the producer, is the main energy driving almost every part of the production. Working with the writer(s), the director and producer help to hone the script into a shooting script. In documentary productions, the director may have developed the idea for the project and may also operate the camera and location sound recording.

The director drives the daily shooting schedule by determining when shots are complete and when to move to the next shots. In the case of narrative, the director works closely with the actors to ensure mutual interpretation and appropriate performance. Working with the director of photography, the director plans the shots, the camera moves and the look of the film. The editor and the director should meet before production starts to discuss the director's thoughts on how the editing should be approached.

The editor should attend daily screening of the rushes, take notes and communicate at this early stage with the director on shots, pacing and additional coverage needed. Directors vary in how they prefer to interact with their editors. Some are very hands-on, some like to provide regular input after looking at rough cuts and some want to see only the fine cut before giving feedback.

If the editor is working in a postproduction facility and working on commercials, public service announcements and/or training videos, the time schedule for completion can be very rushed. For instance, an editor might have only one or two days to complete the editing, music mix, graphics and animation for a commercial. In these cases, the director and producer are often on hand at every stage to provide guidance.

Because of their nature, smaller-budget productions often combine crew positions. In many cases, the director of such a project will work with other crew members, such as the camera operator and director of photography, but will choose to serve as editor as well.

Script Supervisor

The script supervisor, if part of a crew, is someone the editor should go out of his or her way to get to know on the crew. The script supervisor notes every shot, every take, what's happening in the shot and whether the director indicated that it was a good shot. In narrative films and commercials, a good script supervisor's work will save the editor hours of work. When the director says, "Print it," that means the director thought the shot was a successful one, barring any technical problems with the camera. A "print it" shot is usually circled in the script supervisor's script book and also on the camera and sound logs. When the editor is ready to lay out the usable shots in chronological order, she or he usually only digitizes those circled shots to save time and storage space.

At the end of shooting, the script supervisor hands over the script book to the editor. The editor is also usually given all camera and sound logs and any other production notes that may be helpful in the postproduction phase. In other media forms, such as documentary, there might be no script, but the script supervisor can note the takes, indicating what was included in the take, making the editing to go more smoothly. Often in such nonfiction forms, there is no official script supervisor on location. In such cases, it is often the director or even the camera operator who makes notes about what was shot, what worked and what still needs to be covered. Good documentary camera operators tend to be very organized and have exceptionally good visual memories. They can usually write their notes at the end of the day, in collaboration with the director.

Assistant Director

In many productions, the assistant director (AD) reports to both the producer, keeping him or her up to date on how things are proceeding on the set or on location, and the director. The AD can serve as the director's right hand, communicating with the crew about technical considerations. The AD often then makes judgment calls and decides what is important enough to share with the director. This discretion allows the director to concentrate on the actors' performances, the story and the camera. The AD is sometimes involved in the preproduction process, working with the director, producer, and production manager in preparing the daily shooting schedule. On large productions and/or ones with large casts, there are sometimes second and third assistant directors working with cast and crew to ensure that they are on the set when needed and to help with background extras.

Director of Photography

The director of photography (DP) collaborates with the director to determine the look of the production. This look is achieved through lighting, camera angles, makeup and costumes, camera and actor movement, and editing. In narrative productions, the DP usually tries to work with the director to ensure that shots will cut together and, if the director plans special transitions in a film print, that there are enough frames to accomplish the desired transitions.

Location Sound Mixer

The location sound mixer is responsible for recording all the sound during the production phase. The sound mixer tries to record all the spoken words as clearly as conditions allow. The sound mixer also keeps a log and makes comments on it after each take—for example, "Airplane was heard toward end of shot." A copy of the sound log is usually given to the script supervisor and placed in the script supervisor's script book. This gives the editor a reference when trying to look up sound takes to determine which one was the best or whether a portion of one could be used.

On many sets, there are several additional production departments, each with its own set of collaborating crew members. These may include set design, wardrobe, makeup, craft services (food/catering), gaffers, grips and production assistants. Usually, the editor's interaction with these is minimal.

Some Postproduction Positions

Editor

The editor works with the producer, the postproduction supervisor and the director during the shoot but especially during the first days of the postproduction phase to plan and schedule the postproduction phase. This schedule may be governed by completion to make a festival date, release date, broadcast commitment date or director's cut date (in the case of Director's Guild productions) and by budget considerations.

The editor works to assemble the production and helps to inform the rest of the postproduction crew what services may be needed from them. Such services could include automatic dialogue replacement, titles, computer-generated effects and music composition/recording. The editor usually has one or more assistant editors to help with some of the details in logging, digitizing and keeping up with the various elements of postproduction. We will discuss the editor's possible artistic goals in later chapters, but bear in mind that for many nontheatrical motion pictures, the editing stage is one of discovery and rediscovery as the footage unfolds.

My entry into the postproduction world was as a foot messenger. Usually it is still like this. Or you might start out as a receptionist in the building. Nobody gets out of film school and gets a job here as an editing assistant. We've had some stupid people turn down jobs as a receptionists. They say that they didn't go to school to work in that kind of position, but that is simply oftentimes the way you get in. In terms of moving up, it is just being lucky. But in my experience, if you are good, it takes about six months. Usually you are then a second assistant or a floating helper. The greatest skill you can have is organization.

Mark Block, Editor at Crew Cuts Postproduction House, New York City

Re-Recording Engineer/Sound Mixer

The re-recording engineer/sound mixer is responsible for bring all the sound elements such as dialogue, automatic dialogue replacement, music, special sound effects and any other sound elements into a final mix that will sync up with the visuals. Separate sound editors such as music editor, special effects editor and dialogue editor also work under the sound mixer and editor to aid in the completion of the sound for the final release print of the production.

Composer and Music Supervisor

The composer and/or music supervisor is responsible for composing the music and recommending additional music for the production. The composer works with the producer and director, noting the type of music needed to enhance the emotional content of a scene or ambient music, as in the case of a bar scene, and writing or finding the music to fit the scene. Many times, the composer/music supervisor will work with the editor to assemble several songs and pieces of music to copies of the visual to help choose which best suit the story or emotional content of the scene. The music supervisor also works with the producer to secure the synchronization (sync) rights for the final music selection. In commercial work, the editor often lays in a scratch track of music during the rough-cut edit. The editor will then indicate that the composer is to write similar music. This new song should not directly imitate the scratch track but should flow along the same emotional lines.

Visual Effects Supervisor

The visual effects supervisor works with the director, the DP, and the editor to plan for and execute any computer-generated effects or other methods for the production. This planning sometimes takes place months before the shooting of the project, since such graphics-intensive production takes time. Once completed, the individual effects are placed in the project. The visual effects supervisor sometimes oversees titles and opticals, digital compositing and animation effects.

ADR (Automatic Dialogue Replacement) Editor

The ADR (automatic dialogue replacement) editor works with the editor and post-production supervisor to replace any dialogue from the location recording that was unusable. Usually all the actors whose dialogue is affected are scheduled on the same day to try to save time and money.

On-Line Editor

Productions that are finishing on video that have been edited on an off-line system will also deal with an on-line editor. See Chapter 10, "The Edit Decision List," for an explanation of the duties of the on-line editor.

Foley Artists

The foley artists are a team of professionals who re-record all needed sound effects for a motion picture. These sounds may range from footsteps to rushing water and are recorded in sync with the projected film.

Understanding the various positions and functions on the production and postproduction crews, especially those most involved with the postproduction phase, will help the editor in the execution of his or her duties. For the editor, the way to successful postproduction is to be planned, resourceful and systematic without compromising the motion picture.

Remember that different kinds of productions require different kinds of crews. Fairly small-budget student productions may have several crew members, or they may have one person completing all of the necessary tasks. Television game shows obviously require a different crew makeup than a television show such as "Survivor III." Personal video diaries, such as Michelle Citron's groundbreaking autobiographical film "Daughter Rite," have different postproduction requirements than the big-budget narrative feature film "Traffic." But each and every one of these will have some type of editor. There will always be someone there to sift through the footage and execute manipulation of this footage in order to unfold the story. Whether it is live television switching during "The Today Show" to lay in commercials or the delicate intercutting of interviews with footage of the Holocaust, there is someone there who serves as the artist in this final stage of the motion picture process.

4 Editing Conventions and Styles

The Lure of High-Tech Equipment

Before we discuss the specifics of organizing your media before and during editing, this chapter reviews some basic editing conventions and styles. If you are going to be a good nonlinear editor, it is not enough that you take the time to sit down with the equipment manual and feel competent pushing buttons in the digital environment. Although equipment manuals are absolutely necessary and should always be close by, they do not generate the art of postproduction. Frankly, although any new piece of equipment takes a dedicated amount of time and effort for an editor to truly understand, most of us will move into the digital environment with relative technical ease. This is not to say that there won't be head-scratching problems at times—but when working with equipment, when is that not the case?

There is a lot of excitement surrounding nonlinear editing both in the industry and on campuses nationwide. An unfortunate occasional side effect of this excitement is that students and other editors want to skip right over the well-established theories and techniques of editing in the visual storytelling process to get their hands on the digital equipment. The result of this is a lot of quickly but poorly edited material. The equipment should never be the end-all of any phase of video or filmmaking. Ever. Period.

Manipulation of Time and Space

So as a way of beginning our discussion on editing conventions and styles, let's spend a bit of time examining some of the basic tools of visual storytelling. Any film, video, CD-ROM game or Internet movie exists on two planes: time and space. Think about it.

Time

Unlike the arts of painting and sculpture, the art of the motion picture depends on an element of time. Over a specific time period, you feed your audience a message or story. For the message to be successfully communicated, the attention of the audience is generally required throughout the process. The members of the audience are therefore investing a period of their own lives to take part in the motion picture.

Space

Unlike music, the motion picture also deals with space. You are communicating your story within a particular area. In the visual realm, you might compare it to a painting, since you have a fixed screen and you are optically manipulating and representing physical spaces on this screen. In the audio realm, it is almost like listening to music; you can surround your audience with sounds in their own physical space. The editor's attention to time and space allows him or her to effectively communicate a story. You manipulate (compress or lengthen) actual time into perceived time. Of course, there are exceptions to this and every rule. Artist/filmmaker Andy Warhol, among others, was known for a refusal to compress time in some of his films, including "Sleep."

Classical Hollywood-Style Editing

There are some basic rules or tenets that were established very early in the history of motion pictures. Remember that films are just over one hundred years old, and video and other motion picture media take many cues from film. These basic rules weren't established arbitrarily. They evolved as techniques of manipulating space and time in order to make logical sense to audiences. We now refer to these rules as classical Hollywood-style (CHS) editing, although of course the films don't have to be made in Hollywood, nor do they have to be narrative fiction motion pictures.

So what are the main points of CHS editing? Before going over them, let's recognize that although you should always understand rules before taking it upon yourself to break them, there are instances when breaking the rules is certainly appropriate to the story. The international television conglomerate known as MTV (Music Television) made its mark not only by showcasing musicians and music videos, but also by breaking editing rules.

In the past twenty years, new and aesthetically evolved editing techniques have been incorporated into everything from narrative features and documentary films to commercials and television series, newscasts and web presentations. Such editing methods include quick cuts, the eliminating of action, music as the major driving factor in the unfolding of visuals, complex graphics and animation, stop-motion action and sophisticated sound design in postproduction. These and other editing techniques play into a new visual aesthetic and have in a sense created a new filmic vocabulary. Media studies professionals have indicated that such approaches work in direct correlation the psychoanalytic approaches of Sigmund Freud, Carl G. Jung and others to evoke an emotional or intellectual response.

We believe that it cannot be stated strongly enough however, that even though new editors may be fluent in the *reception* of these new editorial visual aesthetics, it is often not appropriate to skip right over the firmly established editing storytelling techniques. Challenge them when appropriate to your editing experience, but try them out first. Having said that, let's go over some of these typical rules. These lay down the basis for some of the most commonly used motion picture editing practices.

The Four Main Points of Classical Hollywood-Style Editing

The four main points of classical Hollywood-style editing are these (note that when we refer to cuts or edits, we are referring not only to visuals but also to the addition and manipulation of audio):

1. Do not call attention to the editing—make it invisible. The visual transitions and manipulation of audio is hidden from our perception.
2. Edits are there to move the story forward—to give more relevant information. Don't spend time on unnecessary information.
3. Cuts are psychologically motivated from the audience's point of view. A transition occurs when the audience wants or needs to see or hear something else.
4. Editing gives the illusion of continuous space and time.

Shooting for the Edit: What You Need to Consider during Production

What do these rules and goals have to do with preparing for your edit? Simply this: You must begin to organize your edit while still in the production stage. This is called *shooting for the edit*. Shooting for the edit means taking steps, while on location or in the studio, to plan for the editing process to make it go more smoothly. It means following the basic goals of classical Hollywood-style editing by ensuring that you have gotten sufficient coverage of both visuals and audio. This takes organization and planning! Your editing mindset begins way before you sit down to edit. Following are some areas you will most likely need to consider while in production.

Establishing Shot/Master Scene Shot/Individual Shots

This is a well-established series of shots and is used in film, television sitcoms and dramas, as well as documentaries. An **establishing shot** is often an exterior shot of the location in which the action will be occurring. The establishing shot(s) is incorporated to help the audience get their bearings and to understand "where" they are. This establishment can also be set up with a rapid series of shots that show various locations, people and objects. An example of such a series occurs at the beginning of the television show "ER." Here we see various images of doctors and patients in the emergency room dealing with a variety of situations. This series of establishing shots sets the location and subject matter for the viewer.

The **master scene shot** is a wide-angle shot of the action, allowing the viewer to see each of the characters and their proximity to each other.

The **individual shots** are close-ups of each character as they go through the action or dialogue.

Obviously, in a narrative motion picture, to get these shots, you must plan in advance and have your actors repeat actions. You must also have done sufficient location scouting to find an appropriate exterior image. Once you have this coverage, editing this scene will be relatively easy to do. In a documentary or news story, it is also good to shoot establishing shots of the various locations you are shooting in and around. Most documentary shooters also begin by shooting actions and interviews with wide-angle shots and then get in closer as things move along. Editing documentary footage can be a bit more challenging in terms of incorporating master shots and individual shots, but is made easier either with the insertion of cutaways (discussed below). Potential editing problems can also be virtually eliminated by covering the action or conversation with two cameras, one staying wide and one going in tighter for the close-up shots.

Cutaways

This type of shot is used for different reasons. Basically, the cutaway shot is a shot of something within or around the environment where the action or conversation is occurring. Usually, it is a fairly close shot. If you were shooting a documentary about long-distance track runners in training, you might get cutaway shots of the coach looking at a stopwatch, a friend in the stands cheering a runner on, a competitor tying his shoes, a dog running across the field and the sunset. Figure 4.1 shows an example of a cutaway shot. Each of these shots can be used to help give more information about the event. They are visually interesting and help move the story along.

Cutaways can also be used to get rid of jump cuts. For instance, if you have inadvertently crossed the 180-degree line (discussed later in the chapter) and need to edit those two shots together, the insertion of a cutaway in between them will help cover the visual jump that otherwise would occur. In addition, cutaways are often employed to eliminate part of the action or dialogue, therefore compressing time. If we have a scene in which someone needs to walk across a room and sit down in a chair, it might not be necessary to see that entire action. As long as we see enough of the action to understand that the character is walking across the room and then the main part of the action where he actually sit downs, we can insert a short cutaway of coffee brewing or some other item relevant to the shot and eliminate the several seconds it would take in real life to cross the room.

Parallel Editing

Many narrative fiction motion pictures incorporate the idea that two or more things are going on at once. This makes perfect logical sense to viewers because we are always aware that in reality, millions upon millions of things are happening in the world while we are doing whatever we are doing at the moment. In the motion picture world, you will occasionally see a split screen to incorporate this idea, but more often, editors incorporate parallel editing. This simply means cutting back and forth between different locations to imply that the events are occurring simultaneously.

When on location, you must shoot each of these scenes in their entirety. Often they will be shot on different days. With this editing technique, you are manipu-

FIGURE 4.1   Cutaway Shot

lating the concept of time. The classic example is a film scene in which we see the damsel in distress tied to railroad tracks as a train approaches. We then cut to a shot with the hero racing on a white horse to rescue her. We cut back to the woman and the train getting closer and closer, back to the hero, and so on (see Figure 4.2). This is parallel editing and implies that the actions are occurring simultaneously.

Match Cutting

Unlike many of these other ways of manipulating time and space, **match cuts** don't have some kind of basis in our day-to-day lives. Match cutting puts the audience in a privileged position of seeing part of an action from one angle and then seeing it complete from a different angle. We might see someone pick up a phone in a long

FIGURE 4.2   Parallel Editing

shot from the right side. Just as the phone reaches the person's ear, we might cut to a much closer shot taken straight on from the front. The action would match so that none of the movement is repeated in the second shot but it matches perfectly with where the first shot left off.

Of course, this immediate jump in space is not something we do in reality, but audiences have accepted it as part of the vocabulary of filmmaking. In fiction filmmaking, you have your actors repeat actions and move the camera to a different angle for the various takes. In documentary filmmaking or newsgathering, if an action is repeated (a dance is run through a second time, for instance), you might move the camera to a different angle for the next performance, thus allowing for potential match cutting in the editing room. This editing technique is sometimes also called *cutting on the action* and allows you to manipulate space.

L-Cuts or Split Edits

The **L-cut** or *split edit* manipulates aural space. All you are doing here is letting the audio of one shot continue under the visuals of another shot (see Figure 4.3). This idea makes perfect sense in our day-to-day lives. Unless we have a hearing disability, we are not capable of turning off our ears the way we can close our eyes. We

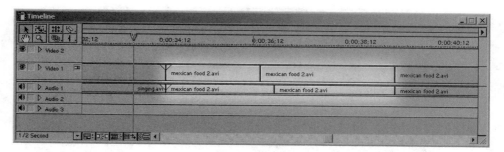

FIGURE 4.3   L-Cut or Split Edit

are constantly barraged with audio information. I might be looking at a cat but hearing an airplane or listening to music but watching a bike race. These are "real-life L-cuts." Here is another example, one that corresponds with a common use of L-cuts in motion pictures: Suppose you are watching and listening to two people having a heated discussion. You are not taking part in it but witnessing it. As Richard talks, you look at him. When Hannah responds, you look at her. But then things begin to get really interesting, and as Richard's voice rises and he makes his point, you are curious to note Hannah's reaction to all of this. Your head turns to look at her even as Richard continues his speech. This is an L-cut! Of course, it is easy to transfer this idea to motion picture editing and manipulate the audio space of the story.

Reaction Shot.   A **reaction shot,** sometimes also called a *noddie shot* (as in head nodding) in news and a cutaway shot in a documentary, is simply the visual portion of the example we just explored. You force your viewers to look at what you want them to look at through close-up shots, therefore manipulating screen space. Figure 4.4 shows examples of reaction shots. Once again, to incorporate this or any editing technique into your motion picture, you must be organized and ready to shoot for the edit while in production. These shots do not just appear out of nowhere.

180-Degree Rule.   Also called the *axis of action,* this is a very basic rule of visual storytelling and one that the novice media producer often neglects. The **180-degree rule** states that when on location or in the studio, you mentally place an imaginary line between two people talking or based on the direction of the action. The camera is placed on one side of this imaginary line, and it can move anywhere within 180 degrees of the line. If it stays on that one side, screen direction of movement and the direction in which your actors or subjects are facing on the screen will not change. However, if you move the camera across the line, the direction of the action or position of the actors or subjects will appear to suddenly flip. This is considered a **jump cut** and is disturbing and disorienting to the viewer.

Think about it this way: You are watching a football game on television, and it is the beginning of the first half. The Northern University Cardinals and the Southern University Eagles are battling it out, with the Cardinals moving from left

FIGURE 4.4   Reaction Shots

to right and the Eagles moving right to left. All of a sudden, you see a shot of the Eagles' wide receiver moving from left to right. Wait! Has the player gotten so turned around that he is about to score for the wrong team? Probably not; more likely, the television producer just decided to cut to a camera placed on the other side of the stadium (see Figure 4.5). This is an editing faux pas unless a little graphic has been put on the screen letting the viewer know that this is a reverse-angle shot. Otherwise, you end up with a huge and unexplained jump cut. There are ways to save your edit if you crossed the line for some reason on location. You could, in the above scenario, incorporate in between the two disorienting shots a neutral shot of the action moving directly toward or away from the camera. In this case, the camera is considered neutral because it is actually on the 180-degree line. Another option would be to cut to a cutaway shot in between the two shots, such

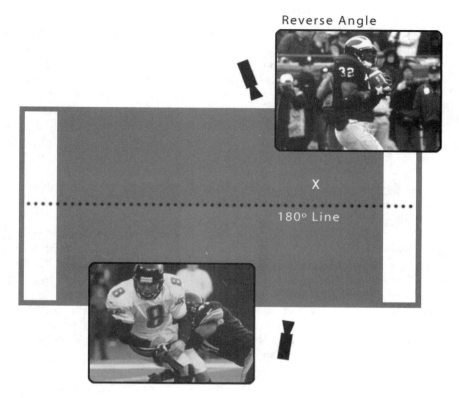

FIGURE 4.5 180-Degree Rule

as a shot of fans going wild in the stands. This would smooth the jump out a bit but would not totally eliminate the problem. If you find yourself in the postproduction editing stage and have footage taken from all over the place, crossing over the line, and have no neutral shots or cutaways to help the situation, you've got a problem. Remember that editing begins on location!

30-Degree Rule. Another production and editing rule that has a number attached to it. The **30-degree rule** states that if you are planning to edit together two shots of the same person or thing, the camera should be placed 30 degrees away in the second shot from its placement in the first shot. If you have a medium shot of someone sitting in a chair and want to cut to another shot of the same person sitting in the same chair as she picks up a cup of tea and the camera is in virtually the same position in these two shots, a visual jump will occur. This creates a type of flash: The person might be in almost, but not quite, the identical position, and when the cut occurs, she "jumps." By simply moving the camera 30 or more degrees away (think of an arc), you eliminate this visual jump. You have, in this instance, manipulated the visual space of the screen.

Wide Variety of Angles and Distances.   It is important to have sufficient coverage of your action and dialogue. It is extremely frustrating to sit down to edit only to realize that you really don't have enough footage or that all of your shots are taken at a distance. Include a variety of long shots, medium shots, close-up, point-of-view shots, cutaways, over-the-shoulder shots and so on. The availability of a wide range of appropriate footage is what allows you to be creative at the editing stage.

Continuity.   **Continuity** is the successful and unnoticeable continuation of a scene in terms of placement of objects, weather conditions, clothing, camera placement, and so on. You have no doubt seen a television show or film in which the main actor had a book in one hand and in the next shot it was in the other or had shoulder-length hair in one scene and short hair in another, only to go back to shoulder-length hair in the following scene. Or what about shots within the same scene in which it is cloudy and then sunny, cloudy and then sunny. These are obvious examples of breaks in continuity and yet another thorn in the editor's side. It is agonizing to attempt to edit this kind of footage together, and the potential problems must be thought out and corrected while in production. Of course, with advanced computer imaging, you could "lengthen" someone's hair or clear up the sky, but that's another (expensive) story. On location, there should be a crew member who keeps a close eye on continuity issues. Sometimes this is the script supervisor or editing assistant whose whose job it is to keep his or her eyes open and take Polaroid or digital still photographs of sets and actors or subjects.

Sound.   Problems with audio can wreak havoc in the editing stage. If there is an airplane flying over during your interview with the Dalai Lama and no one on location heard it, you've got a postproduction problem. Or if you need to edit out a minor audio blooper but this would cause a hole in your audio track, you need to have a bit of something we call room tone to fill in the hole. Room tone is a simple recording of the sound of any interior space. It can be used in editing to smooth out audio jumps. Ambient sound is an all-inclusive term describing any location sound, either inside or outside.

Extra Time before and after Shooting a Shot.   There is nothing more frustrating for an editor than to have a great shot in which the action or dialogue occurs at the very beginning of the shot or a shot that ends just as the action or dialogue ends. Simply put, this is the sign of an inexperienced director or camera operator with little understanding of the creative process of editing and poor production values. Always remember that editors are not just technicians, they are artists. Editors need extra footage to work with before and after the dialogue or action to establish proper edit pacing. If every line of dialogue has no breathing space before or after it and it must all be slammed together—well, you can imagine how irritating that would get!

Any editing style also had to consider shot length. A good rule of thumb is this: Leave a shot on only long enough to get the necessary information across to your audience. There are a lot of things that come into play here. Is it a wide-angle shot with lots of information? If so, you might need to leave it on longer than a close-up shot. But if it is a close-up shot and we see a character going slowly from sadness to a small smile, you wouldn't want to cut it too short. If there is a lot of dialogue or if music or sound effects are important, you make take this into consideration when deciding on shot length. Such pacing is an integral part of the art of editing, and most editors spend a fair amount of time making decisions on the timing of shots. Pacing is the rhythm of a motion picture. It is the flow that, along with the content creates the feeling of your program. If your goal is to create tension, a short rhythmic cutting might be appropriate. If romance is the theme, longer flowing takes might be a better decision. Consider the full range of human emotions and incorporate pacing and length of shots into your artistic palate.

Effective Storytelling

The editor's job is to collapse footage and manipulate time and space in a unique, effective way that communicates the goals and story of the film effectively. We've heard editors compare the creative and artistic side of their job to that of the great painter and sculptor Michelangelo. Michelangelo is said to have answered the question "How did you know how to create your masterpiece, the sculpture 'David'?" with the comment "I didn't create it. It was already there. I simply released David from his stone prison." The job of the editor can be thought of in this way as well. The footage is there (hopefully). You are just deleting unnecessary elements and releasing it. Alternatively, you are building up a creative masterpiece from the raw elements.

There are several things you might want to consider as you begin to look at the raw footage that will make up a motion picture. These questions include audience, purpose and content. Let us take a look at each of these considerations separately.

Audience

The editor should always consider the potential viewer of a film and use knowledge of the viewers' tastes, expectations, viewing patterns, knowledge of the subject, age, cultural background and the like to create the most effective story possible. Of course, we are not suggesting that a film editor's job is to pander only to the audience in making decisions, but the good editor utilizes his or her talents, intuitions, discipline, analysis of the material and emotional expression to speak to a presumed common understanding. If the audience is made up of young children, the editor might choose to stay on shots a bit longer and to incorporate soothing yet upbeat music and to add a narrator track to help explain actions on the screen. If the film is aimed at an audience of 15-year-old males, the editor might speed up the pacing, include more aggressive music or sound effects and break typical continuity rules. And if the motion picture is meant to confuse, challenge or alienate the viewer, the editor will use knowledge of audience expectations to his or her editorial advantage.

Purpose

Imagine that the purpose of your television commercial is to sell a particular brand of computers. The editor will likely repeat information that the director chose to incorporate, such as price, design, ease of use, availability and personal power. The pacing will emphasize clean visuals and the clear articulation of why this is the best computer available. If the goal of your television documentary is to show the bad effects of global warming on drought-stricken farms, your editing might include repetitive intercutting between archival footage of green fields with flowing streams and withered plants, parched land and dry riverbeds. Your music might be dispirited, and the pacing slow and emphatic.

Content

An editor who is working on a typical narrative feature might utilize common and standardized techniques such as crosscutting action, using 2-shots (usually a medium shot with two people in the frame) intercut with close-ups of romantic conversations and paying attention to screen direction with movement. If, instead, the content of the film is much more experimental in content and potential form, the editor might let go of all standard editing techniques and adopt a much more free-flowing structure. The presentation of content through pacing is an area in which you will especially want to consider your viewers' assumptions, knowledge and preferences. For example, if your use of a popular culture reference is integral to the story or documentary representation, do you assume the audience will immediately recognize this reference or do you linger a bit longer on the image to draw their attention to it?

There are many good books on the theories and techniques of motion picture and television editing that add greatly to what has been discussed in this chapter, some of which are listed in the Appendices. Your grounding in the history and current practices of the art of postproduction will make you a more skilled, sought-after and successful visual editor. Think of it like this: If you are a musician, you start at the beginning, learning scales and basic techniques. You learn how to read a sheet of easy music before playing at Carnegie Hall. If you are a painter, you learn how to draw in two dimensions and how to represent the human body before you go on to exhibit your masterpiece at the Museum of Contemporary Art in New York. Likewise, if you are a motion picture producer and editor, take some time to practice, practice, practice the basic and established rules of postproduction story-telling. Your future masterpiece will be all the better for it.

Theory and Technique of the Editor— The Editor's Mindset

Every system differs in terms of precisely how it allows you to edit your footage and insert additional materials such as animation and graphics, but as we've stated before, the technology does not make the editor. Editing is a creative process. Many editors refer to an "editor's mindset" when asked about their career. They may differ in terms of their preferred system, their love of fast or slow cutting and their dislike or affinity for complex transitions, but almost across the board, editors describe a state of truly delving into the material and then allowing the visuals, audio and other elements guide them through the process. This process has been likened to many things, from a runner's second wind to Zen Buddhist meditation. You might not take the analogy to these extremes, but it is appropriate to recognize that editing is an art and a craft above and beyond any equipment available. The nonlinear system you have chosen should allow you to sculpt your footage, utilizing all of the elements available (sync visuals, music, transitions, graphics, titles, imported files, silent images, sound effects and ambient audio). You shape it and reshape it and then polish it up. Using a nonlinear system, you can quickly see what your intuition tells you is a good edit.

As an editor, there are some tried and true rules to consider following whether cutting film or video or in the digital domain. Many of these were covered in the section on shooting for the edit earlier in this chapter. A couple of additional concerns for the editor are the edit pacing and the edit structure. The edit pacing is simply the length of each visual or sound. You might weigh the following areas when making your pacing choices:

- Amount of information in a shot: If there are lots of people or there is heavy action in the scene, you might slow the pacing down a bit so that the viewer has time to absorb the information.
- A long shot or wide-screen shot: These give more visual information and so might need to stay on the screen longer.
- New information: The first time the viewer sees important characters or information, leave them on the screen a bit longer than usual.
- Important cutaways: The same rationale as above applies. If it is critically important information to the story, leave it on a bit longer.
- Pauses in dialogue and action: The sign of an inexperienced editor is one who is too anxious to cut and doesn't let important pauses stay. Silence says a lot and is a powerful tool for the editor.
- Speed: To create tension and/or excitement, speed up the pacing of your edits.

Edit Pacing

You always want to pay attention to the content of the visuals and audio when contemplating pacing. You should understand the effect of the transition relative to the content. Editing is a finessing job, and the two stylistic extremes—from rapid fire edits, to minimal edits—orchestrate how the information is fed to the audience. Edit pacing can be quite a challenge, a responsibility and a pleasure.

Let's briefly examine the edit pacing in some films you have likely seen and a couple you might not have. "Peter Murray" is an ethnographic film from the "Vermont People" series by Herb DiGioia and David Hancock. This film, like many anthropological films you might have seen, speaks volumes about the power of hesitant editing. The goal of the film is to share the working process of

Peter Murray, a craftsman chair builder. We see every movement he makes with the camera following his expressions and hands. When he sits simply absorbing his most recent creation for quite a long time, the filmmakers didn't cut away to something more "exciting." The editing respected the integrity of his character enough to pause along with him. This is particularly important in such ethnographic films but can easily be utilized to great effect in fiction narrative films as well. Louis Malle's film "My Dinner With Andre" is a prime example. In this particular film, the content of the conversation at dinner and the friendship of the two men are of the utmost importance. The edit pacing respects this and holds back without interfering (in fact, most of the edits occurred when the film roll ran out).

"The Player" follows the lead of its famous predecessor "A Touch of Evil" by Orson Welles in integrating a long tracking opening shot that brings in several scenes without an edit. The camera movement takes the place of cuts between the shots. The opening is paced by using the action and powerful tracking and dollying of the camera. Edits would have interfered with the content.

The opening of Oliver Stone's "JFK" is an example of an opposite approach to edit pacing. These first few minutes are a barrage of multilayered images, rapid cutting, audio overlaps, combinations of documentary and fiction footage, and contrasting and complementary visuals and audio. The editing lays out the premise of the rest of the film by drawing on nostalgic images and audio and compression history into a digestible capsule.

In the digital world, you can see how quickly you are cutting by looking at the timeline. You have a visual representation of the footage laid out, and every cut or transition is represented. You can immediately assess whether there is equality or disparity in your tempo. This similarity or difference is what creates tension.

Bart Weiss, Independent Video/Filmmaker Co-Director of the Association of Independent Video and Filmmakers and Director of the Dallas Video Festival

Edit Structure

In addition to basic edit pacing, you should consider edit structure. Structure is simply the form in which the story unfolds in or how you as an editor maneuver the content of the film. Think of it as the packaging of the message. Many films are told in a straightforward manner. We have a simple story, and it is told from beginning to end with little structural creativity. As an editor, you need to ask yourself, "If the possibilities for structuring this piece are endless, why use common techniques if there is a more effective way of constructing the film?" Use your craft to create a powerful work of art.

You might decide that unpredictability is appropriate—staying one step ahead of your audience keeps them interested. Incorporating flashbacks, intercutting, use of dialogue or no dialogue, radically altering time and offering opposing views of events are all possible through editing.

Quentin Tarrantino's film "Pulp Fiction" starts out in the present, and then most of the film is actually a flashback to previous events leading up to the scene. Director Christopher Nolan's 2000 film "Memento" also uses an unusual structure to tell a story. The film is literally told backwards, with the ending of the film told first, and progressing toward the present. "Extreme Measures" disorients the viewer early on by opening with two naked men escaping from somewhere underground into the streets of a large city. The audience does not find out until well into the film who these men are and from what they were escaping. "Casino" with Robert DiNiro and Sharon Stone alters the sense of time by occasionally incorporating the use of edit strobes to draw attention to an action. A wonderful film by Canadian director Richard Girard called "32 Short Films About Glenn Gould," concerning the life and death of the brilliant Canadian pianist, allows the editorial creation of a rich tapestry of information about the musician.

There are specific (and sometimes changing) rules that you can follow or break regarding most any type of film or scene you will ever deal with, including action, dialogue, music videos, how-to programs, typical broadcast documentaries, news features and many others. Film, video, digital—it doesn't matter what equipment you are lucky enough to be using; your job is to help the story unfold.

The Editor's Concerns and Goals

Film or video is a conglomeration of many, many elements, some tangible, some philosophical or psychological. In most media productions, you will be involved in most (though not all) of the following areas of concern for you as an editor:

- Narrative clarity, drawing the viewer into the plot and lay out the story
- Identification with the character
- Give sense of the environment
- Development of conflict
- Intensification of emotions/excitement
- Struggle to resolve conflict/intensity

You achieve each of these by manipulating your visuals and other elements such as music, sound effects, dialogue, transitions and voice-over narration. As an editor, you know the elements of editing technique such as the 180-degree rule and matching action, and you are concerned with edit pacing and structure. In the non-linear environment, you have the elements readily at hand and easy to manipulate. Your challenge and pleasure is employing the techniques into a powerful and engaging film, video, CD-ROM or other motion picture media form.

5 The Digital Nonlinear Workflow and Work Environment

Workflow

Digital nonlinear editing systems are almost always complicated combinations of hardware and software, and you must make the effort to learn them properly. You need to budget time in your schedule to go through any available tutorials, read and understand the user's manual and do trial edits. Some folks jump in feet first and attempt to edit on a system without ever going through the appropriate supporting materials. Most of us have enough basic computer savvy to somehow find our way into the editing software, but if you don't fully understand the limitations and capabilities of the system, you risk never using it to its full capabilities or, worse, harming the system software or hardware. Do take the time to really learn a system before you charge into a full edit. Appendix A has a list of potentially useful websites related to editing, and it would be in your best interest to browse through some of those as you begin to learn the system. Others who have come before you have made mistakes, learned about problems with various software versions and tried things that work or don't work, and many people are happy to freely share their experiences, horror stories and successes.

Editors work with directors and other people to tell stories. This is an aspect that a lot of editors don't seem to grasp. I learned with old-school editors and they taught me that we are visually telling something, whether it is a 30-second commercial or an hour-long show. There is now a tendency for people to skip a lot of steps in their knowledge as an editor. They are learning how to push buttons. They are getting caught up in the technical aspects of it. They are hung up in various programs, systems, knowing how to rewire machines. That is wonderful and increasingly a larger part of our job, but if you don't know the fundamentals of visually telling a story, then you aren't an editor.

Lisa Riznikove, Editor and Co-Owner of Absinthe Pictures, Los Angeles, California

At its most basic level, the workflow of digital nonlinear editing consists of input, editing and output. But each of these stages has various components and requirements for successful technical and artistic completion. Although it is easy to look at the whole process and get a bit overwhelmed, if you break the components down into manageable sections and stay organized, your workflow will, well—flow!

Possibly the most important step in this process happens, at least to some extent, before you even input your footage into the digital nonlinear system. This two-part stage begins with becoming familiar with your footage and creating written logs of the visuals and audio. A well-kept logbook can save an editing session. (Note that there are good logging software packages to sort and describe footage that has already been put into the computer system.) The second part of this step is deciding on some basic editing structure. This does not mean making all of your editing decisions before you even sit down at the system, but it will give you some guidance as you begin to build up the story or whittle down the footage (whichever your approach may be). The logging and planning stage becomes even more important when you are working on a digital nonlinear system than it might be if you were working on an analog video editing system. You are probably well aware that these computer-based nonlinear systems allow you to make changes, additions and deletions within a matter of seconds. The number of versions you attempt is limitless. The now-old adage that editing on a digital nonlinear system speeds up the editing process can be quickly proved false when an editor cuts, recuts, revises, adds transitions, deletes graphics, cuts again, and so on and so on. The process could (and sometimes seems to) go on forever if you don't have some kind of plan already in place. Once you have an idea of the direction in which you want to go, the benefit of a digital nonlinear system is that it speeds up the time it takes to incorporate these changes. Don't let the fact that changes can be made quickly and at the last minute deter you from good preparation and familiarity with your footage and goals. We will talk more about management of your material in later chapters.

After all of the material has been input into the system, the actual editing of the footage, audio, graphics and other materials begins. Editing in the nonlinear environment offers the utmost in creative flexibility and freedom. However, with this freedom come new expectations about speed, fancy graphics and continued alterations. You are the artist, and you call the shots. Make the best decisions you can in editing, take time to do them well and finally, once you are satisfied, call the project finished and go to the final step, which is outputting the material to a viewable format (e.g., video, film, or CD-ROM, DVD).

Potential Problems

Trust us, you are going to love digital nonlinear editing. It is fun, satisfying, creative and technically hip. For most people, any downsides the digital nonlinear process has are far outweighed by its good points. However, it is worth mentioning a few of the potential problems you might come across as you work in the digital domain:

1. The first and second of these have already been mentioned. It is new equipment, and you have to learn it. This takes time and effort.

2. People (including you) might expect a final version more quickly. But remember that just because you can make changes more quickly doesn't mean that you complete the final editing version more quickly. In some cases, the ability to make changes delays the final edit.

3. You are expected to do it all. Because digital nonlinear systems incorporate so many things, the nonlinear editor not only practices the art and craft of story-telling, but also is responsible for checking waveform monitors and vectorscopes, designing graphics and animation, sweetening audio and so on. These stages always used to be completed by trained specialists whose job was to concentrate on these particular needs. You might be responsible for some or all of them now. In addition, in the past, these stages could be completed on various pieces of periph-eral equipment while the editor continued to work on the story. Now most of this work can be completed on the same piece of equipment that the editing is done on, thus slowing things down.

4. Probably the best thing about editing on an analog video system was the fact that the editor was forced to shuttle back and forth on tapes to find needed shots. This forced him or her to continuously evaluate and consider footage for possible inclusion. With digital nonlinear systems, random access means that you can choose a specific shot from your bin and never look at the original shots before or after it on the tape. This is not necessarily a good thing for creative flow.

5. Working on an analog video or motion picture film edit forced a certain orga-nization and forethought. Changes were not as easy to make, and a certain mind-ful creativity was required. In contrast, digital nonlinear editors can find that trial and error without organization is possible, thus depriving themselves of disci-plined creativity in the visual unfolding of a story.

The Learning Process and Developing a Strategy

It is important to know what is in front of you as you learn the technicalities of any editing system. As you begin to learn your equipment, you will go through three learning stages (which apply to most experiences): You will first work at under-standing a concept. With a digital nonlinear system, this includes things like "A clip is really just a pointer to the actual media that is stored elsewhere" or "If I hit the space bar, it makes the footage play on the screen." Once you understand a basic concept, you will slowly begin to memorize things about the system. The steps, terminology and processes will begin to seep farther into your memory. The last learning stage (and the one in which the fun really begins) is in remembering what you have learned without having to go back and look it up. Once you remem-ber things about the process or techniques, you can actively apply them quickly and under pressure.

Organization and strategy are very important as you work on an editing sys-tem, and your efforts will be rewarded down the line if you can begin to enforce a certain discipline on yourself as you learn the system. There are thousands of non-linear editors in the world and thousands of preferred approaches to dealing with the equipment and software. The most important things for you to do are to learn the system fully and then to be methodical in your approach. Being disciplined and methodical in no way takes the fun out of editing but instead supports your creative juices. If you know that you always make a backup copy of your day's edit onto tape at the end of the day, you will be able to automatically let your creative mind be concerned with starting a new version at the beginning of the day. If you always digitize several extra seconds at the beginning and end of a clip to give you more room to edit, you will know that you have the footage available to make the very best edit point possible.

Learning the system includes such basic things as knowing how to properly turn on your digital nonlinear system. The "brain" of any digital system is the main hard drive. The hard drive monitors all aspects of the computer's hardware and executes commands. This brain has an interesting way of thinking. You know that when a computer is turned on, it takes a few moments for it to fully get up to speed. What is happening during these moments is the computer's reminding itself that it is a computer, remembering what it has inside of it (hardware, software, applications, documents, etc.) and finding out what it is hooked up to and can therefore interact with. Once it has done all of these things, your computer is ready to go. So part of the workflow mentality involves starting up your computer in the proper way. If part of what a computer does is analyze what other systems or pieces of equipment it can talk to, it makes sense that if one or more of these peripheral devices (such as external hard drives, video decks or vectorscopes) are not already turned on, the computer might not recognize their existence and may therefore assume that they are not there. Therefore, you should turn on all peripheral external devices and let them get fully up to speed before you turn on your computer.

Basic Stages of Editing in the Digital Nonlinear Environment

There are several specific stages of editing in the digital nonlinear environment:

1. Becoming familiar with your original material (logging and transcribing) and organizing it
2. Inputting your material into the digital system (if it originates as an analog signal, this step will also involve compressing the signal/digitizing it)
3. Frequently saving work to the appropriate drive and folder
4. Naming your clips and sequences for easy retrieval
5. Editing and assembling your material
6. Fine-tuning your edit and enhancing your audio
7. Outputting your final project to tape, CD-ROM, DVD, a website, or some other format

Workflow also may include specific approaches to editing. Are you planning on having multiple versions of a project? If so, how will you name and organize them? Will there be more than one editor working on the same project? If so, how will you and the other editor(s) compromise in your own organizational styles and editing preferences to work together successfully? Will one person be responsible for these scenes and someone else for other scenes? Will you collaborate and make all editing decisions together? Will you start out with a low-resolution rough cut and move toward a high-resolution final edit, or do you have enough storage space to work at high resolution throughout the process? How will you manage and organize project data? Will each version of an edit go into its own bin? Will you break up long programs into various folders? These and many other important considerations will be discussed in later chapters. At this point, the most important things for you to remember are these: Make a real effort to truly learn the system, and begin to formulate organizational strategies that allow you to be a disciplined and outstanding editor.

Work Environment: Studio Setup and Ergonomic Considerations

As you sit down to edit on a digital nonlinear system, it is important that you consider several key areas that will make you not only a happier and more effective editor, but also a healthier one. The physical layout of your system is something you must be concerned with. If you find yourself in a situation in which you are editing in a student postproduction lab or using someone else's system, make every attempt to follow the suggested layout below. If you are lucky enough to have control over the design and setup of a digital nonlinear editing system, these points will help guide you. Let's look at specific points of concern.

The Fundamentals

1. The computer monitor(s): You are certainly aware that having a monitor positioned too high or too low can cause neck and back strain. Place your computer monitor at eye level. If your working space will not allow you to place the monitor at eye level, change the horizontal angle of the monitor so that the screen plane is parallel with your eyes. If you are using only one computer monitor, place it directly in front of your keyboard, not off to one side. Incorporate as large a monitor as your space and budget allow. We suggest at least a 17-inch color monitor to lessen eyestrain. In most cases, professional editors prefer to have two computer monitors side by side, as in Figure 5.1. Dual monitors (or one widescreen monitor) give you additional screen "real estate." In other words, you now have the ability to keep more windows open by moving them around on the two monitors. You might choose to keep your bin window and timeline open on the left-hand monitor and the window where your editing choices are made open on the right-hand monitor. If you are using an audio-mixing window or software-generated vectorscope and waveform monitor, you will have more room to keep them open in a dual-monitor setup. Your mouse will move the cursor easily back and forth from one computer monitor to the other. If you are able to incorporate two computer monitors, place them fairly close together and rotated so that they are facing slightly inward. Your chair and keyboard should be between the two of them. You should set up your monitor in a way that

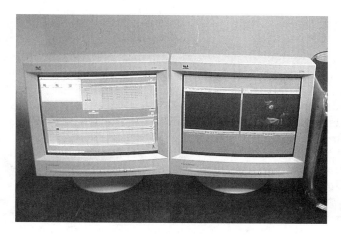

FIGURE 5.1 Multiple Monitors

eliminates glare. Don't have a light pointed toward it and, if necessary, add a glare-reducing glass attachment to the monitor (available at computer stores.)

2. Keyboard: We have all become familiar in the past few years with what is commonly referred to as carpal tunnel syndrome or repetitive motion disorders. Repetitive movements and awkward angles required by computer work can damage nerves and muscular function. Anything you can do to eliminate these will be to your benefit. So your first consideration is the placement of the keyboard. It should sit where your arms can hang comfortably from your shoulders, allowing your elbows to bend at a 90-degree angle. One of the main causes of wrist strain is a keyboard that forces the wrists to rest on a table and then bend up toward the keys (see Figure 5.2). Many newer keyboards have an extension that allows your hand to remain more or less flat as your fingers type. If yours does not, consider getting a foam pad or other wrist rest that can be placed along the bottom of your

FIGURE 5.2 Improper Placement of Hands

keyboard for your wrists to rest on. These are commonly available at computer stores and office supply stores.

3. Another problem with typical keyboards is that they force the arms and hands into a slightly awkward and unnatural angle. For most of us, the hands most commonly come to rest turned slightly inward. A common keyboard forces the arms to extend straight out away from the body instead of each angling slightly in toward the center of the keyboard. Ergonomically correct "split" keyboards work quite well to eliminate this particular form of strain. As shown in Figure 5.3, all of the keys that the left hand uses are tilted slightly so that the far left keys are farther away from the body and the far right keys are closer. Similarly, keys that the right hand uses are tilted so that the far left keys are closer to the body and the far right keys are slightly farther away. There is a space between the left-hand keys and the right-hand keys—hence the name *split keyboard*. This type of keyboard may take a day or two to get used to, but it makes for healthier computer use. Some digital nonlinear editing systems come with color-coded keyboards. Specific keys are given different colors that relate to specific commands required by that particular system. Some editors swear by these keyboards; others find them an unnecessary expense. In terms of the health of your hands and wrists, it is wiser to make keystroke editing commands than to use a mouse. Often you can also work much faster in this mode. If split keyboards and/or color keys prompt you to become a keyboard editor, look into them.

4. Mouse and mousepad: The right hand is often the one that first develops nerve and/or muscle damage due to mouse use. We will readily admit that many people prefer to use the mouse for their editing commands (the "drag and drop" folks) and will hesitate to make a keystroke when their hand is already resting on the mouse. However, human anatomy was not designed for the awkward position in which a mouse requires your hand to sit. A typical mouse forces your arm to rest on the table and your wrist to bend up as it grabs the mouse. This is similar to the

FIGURE 5.3 Split Keyboard

keyboard problem listed above. We strongly suggest one of two remedies to this. The first is to use a mousepad with a raised, soft pad that supports your wrist, thus allowing your hand to reach straight out to rest on the mouse (see Figure 5.4). The second is to choose a trackball (see Figure 5.5). Your fingers move the trackball around instead of having to use your whole arm to move the mouse around the table. Additionally, it is very important that you incorporate some basic hand, arm and neck stretches into your routine as you edit on a computer. You may want to get a soft rubber ball to grip onto a few times every hour, stretch your fingers out, rotate your wrists to make circles, stretch your arms out away from your body, slowly and gently roll your head from front to side to back to side. Many editors become so involved in their editing that after several hours, when they finally stand up, they find themselves stiff and sore. There is certainly no need for this. Just a few minutes each hour for some basic stretches and a good walk around every couple of hours will help immensely. Also, don't get so wrapped up in a project that you eat lunch or dinner in front of the computer. Not only is this bad for your keyboard, but you simply need to get out for a fresh breath of air, get the circulation going in your legs and take a mental break from your masterpiece to continue with a fresh eye. Some editors set their computer alarm to go off every hour as a reminder.

5. Chair: You can certainly tell by this point that you may easily spend hours, if not days and weeks, in front of your digital editing system. Because of this, your choice of a chair is important. There are many ergonomically designed chairs on the market, and it would behoove you to look into them. These chairs can be raised or lowered so that you are sitting at eye level with your computer monitor. Many have arm rests and can swivel, thus allowing you to turn your whole body instead of just your head. Often, they are designed with some amount of additional support for the curve of the lower back (see Figure 5.6). If your chair does not have lower back support, you may improvise by rolling up a towel or sweater and placing it behind

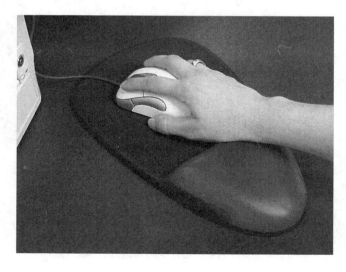

FIGURE 5.4   Mousepad with Wristpad

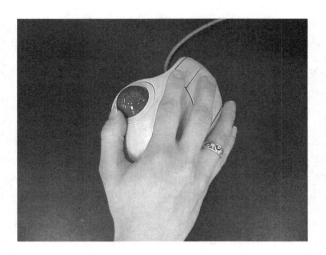

FIGURE 5.5   **Trackball**

FIGURE 5.6   **Ergonomic Chair**

you. In addition, be sure the height of your chair allows your feet to rest comfortably and flat on the floor.

6. Speakers and sound: Computer stores sell some very nice speakers for computers, and most are relatively inexpensive. We would suggest that you not spend lots of money on mega-bass speakers or the like unless you are certain that your viewers will also have such speakers available for screening your project. Professionally, it is better to listen to your film with speakers similar to those that the final project will be heard on. If your final version will be streamed on the web or otherwise viewed on a computer, computer speakers will allow you to make appropriate audio editing decisions. However, if your project will be screened in a theatre with rich and loud audio, make every attempt to duplicate such speakers in your editing suite. Many nonlinear systems also incorporate external mixing boards and CD players for inputting music and sound effects. Audio is a critically important element of any motion picture but is usually overlooked to some extent in setting up an editing system. External mixing boards are still often preferable to mixing your sound using the editing software.

7. Uninteruptable power supply: One of the many horror stories you may hear is of an editor, up all night to make a deadline, who just completes an edit when there is a power surge or power outage, and some or all of the project is lost. Even minor surges (which are fairly common) and brownouts (when the normal flow of electricity is lowered) can cause problems with your editing system. This is why you should consider adding an uninteruptable power supply (UPS) to your digital nonlinear editing system. A UPS is exactly what the name suggests. It keeps a steady flow of power running to your computer for five to ten minutes until your normal power source is stable. It can be a lifesaver. An example of a UPS is shown in Figure 5.7.

8. Operating system: The basic decision you need to make about operating systems is whether you will work on a Macintosh or Windows system. Each has pros and cons. Many editors believe firmly that one system is better than the other, and some editors transition easily between these two basic computer platforms. It is outside the scope of this book to delve into the differences, advantages and problems with each system, but we do recommend that whatever platform you are using, you should be familiar with its nuances.

FIGURE 5.7   UPS

Editing Environment

1. Lighting and room color: If you have ever had the opportunity to visit or work at a high-end editing facility, one of the first things you will notice is the lack of overhead lighting. An editing environment is designed with the needs of the editor in mind, and often controlled pools of light strategically placed around an otherwise dimmed room eliminate a certain amount of eyestrain. Often there is a lamp placed somewhere near the actual editing system that illuminates the keyboard and notes, but care is taken not to overwhelm the light emanating from the computer monitors or to cause glares on the screen. Also, tests have shown that a flat, light gray paint on the walls eliminates glare, reduces eyestrain and lets you see the colors on the screen better. A light gray background on the computer monitor has a similar effect.

2. Noise level control: There are two things that can happen if you don't consider noise level as it relates to your editing system. The first is that you will have a hard time making appropriate audio edits if you are distracted by outside noises; the second is that you will irritate everyone around you as you play the same sound over and over and over trying to get just the right edit. If at all possible, set the system up in an acoustically quiet space. This doesn't necessarily mean that you need expensive sound-dampening panels on the walls, but do make every effort to remove your system from distracting external sounds. Make sure the doors and windows can be closed, let those around you know that you prefer not to be interrupted and certainly turn off any televisions or stereos around. If you are working in a lab environment where several editors are working on digital systems, respect each other's needs by not talking loudly or holding conversations in the editing room. One way to eliminate repetitive and irritating noises for those around you is to use headphones as you edit. And if you are working in a lab space, that may be the best way to go. However, if possible, try to set up your editing environment so that you don't have to use headphones. Remember, part of film and video editing includes the manipulation and placement of audio, and you should listen to it through speakers.

External Equipment

1. A viewing monitor: In almost all cases, it is important for you to have a regular television viewing monitor attached to your system, besides the computer monitor(s) (see Figure 5.8). This monitor will show you how your program will actually look to a viewer (and is therefore often thought of as the *program monitor*). You can attach your video deck to your computer with Firewire or SCSI cables and also to a viewing monitor using component analog video cables. Looking at your footage on a computer screen is fine, but unless your goal is Internet streaming or CD-ROM or DVD distribution, most viewers will see your film on a television monitor. This viewing monitor will also let you look at footage from your original video or digital videotapes before importing them into the computer. Your viewing monitor should also have an underscan option, thus allowing you to see the whole video frame (most television/viewing monitors overscan, slightly cutting off the edges of the frame). You might also want to consider a viewing monitor that can display the 16:9 aspect ratio, as this is the aspect ratio of HDTV (high-definition television) and Super-16 film. **Aspect ratio** pertains to the height and width of the image on the screen. Viewing monitors are often placed slightly off to the side, to the right of your computer monitor(s). It is very important that you make the effort to look away from the computer screen every few minutes. Focus your eyes on some distant object for a bit and then simply close them for several seconds. We know that when you are on a roll, looking away from the screen can be frustrating, but eyestrain and headaches are even more problematic.

2. Racks or shelves: Your work environment should allow you to easily get to all of the needed equipment without reaching too far. Many editing suites incor-

FIGURE 5.8   Viewing Monitor

FIGURE 5.9   Racks

porate racks that house various components, including any external hard drives, servers, external audio mixers, decks, monitors and CPUs (see Figure 5.9). These racks protect the equipment and allow you to properly mount cables for easy access. Cables are like the veins of the system, and when they are kinked or become slightly disconnected, your system won't work properly. Racks allow the cables to be properly wrapped and help to eliminate gravity stress and odd angles. You might also want to add shelves to hold your original tapes, notes and user manuals. Even if you normally consider yourself a sloppy person, work hard on designing and maintaining a neat editing environment.

3. Multiple decks: Some editors work with footage that originated on a variety of formats, from standard VHS to Beta, Hi-8 and Mini-DV. If you expect that this will be your situation, it might be worth the money and effort to include various format decks in your editing system. Of course, you can always use a camera as a playback device and connect it directly to the computer and viewing monitor. However, cameras are designed primarily to record images, not play them back, and you don't want to wear out an expensive camera because you used it too much as a playback device. Decks are always going to be less expensive than cameras. You might also want to consider incorporating timecode-generating decks. If your camera did not lay down timecode, you can play the tape back with a timecode-generating deck. This timecode will then be input (or digitized) along with the footage in the digital nonlinear editing system. The importance of having timecode references for your footage cannot be over-stated. This permanent, unchangeable address system for each frame of video will greatly improve your editing speed, enhance your creative ability and help to elim-inate frustration in the editing process.

4. External vectorscopes and waveform monitors: Many nonlinear editing soft-ware packages incorporate vectorscope and waveform monitor windows that allow you to more professionally analyze your footage. However, if you are truly going for a broadcast-quality signal, it would be better to add proper and standard measurement equipment externally to your system. Software is software, and it can develop glitches. An external vectorscope and/or waveform monitor through which you run your signal will be much more reliable.

5. Breakout box or patch panel: You may also have a special breakout box or patch panel for the various connections you are concerned with on a system. The Media 100 system is a good example, as this nonlinear equipment comes with a specially designed breakout box. Most cables go in to and out of this box, making setup easier.

6. External storage devices: You might also have external hard drives, servers or other pieces of equipment used to store footage. These are connected to the computer and interact with it. We will talk more about storage devices in a later chapter. For the moment, suffice it to say that your initial concerns include amount of space and for-mat. It is always best to store your footage on a different drive than that which holds your editing software. System software will almost always work better if footage is stored externally (on a RAID array, additional internal drives or other storage options discussed in later chapters) than if the footage is stored on the main hard drive.

Extras

In the film and television industry, there is a somewhat generic term used to identify a bag with items you will need on location. The term *gaffer's bag* or *gaffer's box* originally referred to all of the additional tools and equipment needed by the gaffer (the crew member who serves as the head electrician) on a motion picture set. In time, this term became a bit more generic and now refers to any bag of equipment, tools or supplies that need to be close at hand to accomplish a task successfully and efficiently. As an editor, you might not need to keep extra items nearby in a bag, but there are certainly supplies that you should have available to support your needs. Most of these are inexpensive, and you may already have them on hand. Keeping a neatly organized editing area where such supplies are easily accessible will make for a smoother, more enjoyable editing experience. These include the following:

1. System user manuals for the hardware, software, any peripheral hardware, including monitors, decks, and drives.
2. Office supplies, including notepads, sticky notes, pens and pencils, paper clips, stapler, business cards, dictionary and thesaurus, and plenty of labels for videotapes, audiotapes and Zip, Jaz or other storage disks.
3. A side table to place log sheets, notes and that cup of coffee or soda that you aren't supposed to have in the editing bay but can't do without.
4. Cleaning wipes to keep the computer screen and keyboard free of lint, dust and fingerprints.
5. Extra floppy or other disks to back up the edit decision list at the end of each day. This way, if the system crashes, you will have lost only one day's work (or less if you back up at lunchtime as well).
6. Remote controls for various decks.
7. A graph that shows how the cables are or should be connected back behind of all of the equipment. If you or someone else needs to make changes, this can be a lifesaver in quickly getting things back up to speed. Labeling each of your cables also helps.

The points we have just gone through include some of the things you might want to consider as you either set up your own digital nonlinear editing system or work on other people's systems. Make your editing experience as healthy and productive as possible, and you will have a more pleasant time and will most likely be a more effective editor.

The last point made indicated that cables are something you will need to be concerned with. The art of editing requires that to some extent you understand the basic science or technology of the equipment you are working on. If you have a 24-hour standby technician to answer your every question or need, consider yourself in digital nonlinear editing heaven. Most editors have some technical support (either via an on-site engineer or technician or by calling company tech support or looking up information on the web), but often it is best if you simply understand the basics of how a nonlinear system works in order to quickly troubleshoot on your own. This basic knowledge includes understanding a bit about cables, how things are hooked up and what to change if things aren't quite working right.

Cables

There are several basic cables that you will come across with many digital nonlinear editing systems. Remember that a cable is, at its simplest level, a bundle of wires that carry information from one piece of equipment to another. If you don't have your video and audio successfully connected from the deck to the computer to the monitor and vice versa, you will have problems. Before we list some of the basic cables and connectors, it is important to note that cables are actually technologically complex pieces of equipment that have certain engineering and placement requirements. It is not in the scope of this book to cover most of these specifics, but there are many good video production and television engineering books that explain specifics of cable technicalities and essentials. What we would like to emphasize here is that cables are the "veins" that carry the "lifeblood" of your project. They are important! They must be connected correctly, must be properly grounded and protected and must be stored and wrapped properly. Far too many system problems are caused by simple user setup errors such as crossing cables over one another (causing video or audio interference) or cables becoming disconnected because they aren't wrapped properly and pull on the connection. If you can, make sure there is room behind your system to easily view and access cables. Use Velcro or other ties to bind them carefully. Label the end of each cable, indicating what it is and where it would normally be connected. These simple steps, and knowing what each cable is for, will make your editing session go that much more smoothly.

First, let's go over some of the basic cables you will likely come across. Some of these are illustrated in Figure 5.10.

FIGURE 5.10   Cables

1. Coaxial cables are what you often see hooked up to your home television set. These are sturdy, relatively inexpensive and adaptable cables that can carry both video and audio signals. They are shielded (covered with relatively thick material that keeps out interference) and are used professionally.
2. SCSI, pronounced "scuzzy," stands for small computer system interface. SCSI cables are thick and have a greater bandwidth than many other types of computer cables.
3. AC cables are standard power cables that in the United States alternate at 60 Hz cycles per second. It is particularly important not to cross AC cables over other cables, because 60 Hz can cause an interfering audio hum. Be sure to use well-shielded cables.
4. Data cables carry computer data from computers to other devices. They can also carry Internet information into the computer.
5. Composite cables are analog video cables that integrate both the luminance and the chrominance portions of a video signal and can carry this signal along one wire.

6. Component cables divide the video signal into three parts, and therefore the cable is a bundle of three wires, separately carrying luminance, the red signal minus the luminance and the blue signal minus the luminance. Since composite cables don't require that the chrominance be imbedded with the luminance, component video is visually superior to composite video.
7. Ethernet cables carry fairly large loads of digital information.
8. IEEE 1394 cables are commonly called Firewire cables. This type of cable, designed by Apple Computer (other companies produce similar cables now), carries digital information. The Firewire cables have become very popular and are supported by many nonlinear editing systems, video decks and video cameras. This type of cable is small, flexible and hot-swappable (meaning that you can connect and disconnect the cable while the computer and other equipment are running) and carries information very quickly.

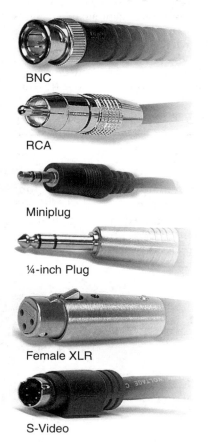

BNC

RCA

Miniplug

¼-inch Plug

Female XLR

S-Video

FIGURE 5.11   Cable Connectors

Cable Connectors

Next, let's look at some of the most common cable connectors. It is important that you take the time to learn the names and be able to visually identify cable connectors, which are shown in Figure 5.11. Often, when someone asks you to "get a BNC cable," what they are referring to is actually the connector attached to the ends of the cable. As a professional, it is your job to know what they are talking about.

1. A BNC connector is usually attached to coaxial cables and has a twist-and-lock mechanism, which is preferred by professionals. Such BNC cables are usually used to carry video (not audio) and time-code information.
2. An RCA connector has a single wide pin and is pushed into the female receptacle on the receiving equipment. These are often found on consumer-grade products, and sometimes such cables and connectors pick up interference.
3. RCA miniplugs are what you often will find on headphones for a portable cassette deck. These audio connectors are considered consumer grade.
4. 1/4-inch connectors are what you might find on the end of higher-end headphones. They are also audio plugs and are a bit more stable than the smaller 1/8-inch (3.5-mm) miniplugs.

5. An XLR connector is used to connect audio equipment and has three pins. This connector is considered professional.

6. S-Video connectors allow for the separation of luminance and chrominance of the video signal and are often called *component*. They are preferred to the *composite* carrying capabilities of the RCA and BNC connectors, which carry luminance and chrominance together.

7. Ethernet or DSL connectors carry high-bandwidth networking information and look similar to a telephone connector.

8. USB (universal serial bus) connectors connect computers to external devices.

9. Firewire connectors are either four-pin or six-pin and carry digital video and audio.

The second piece of advice is to always hold onto the artistic concept of what you want to do. Walter Murch is one of my favorites editors. He is a soft-spoken gentleman. He lights up when he talks about editing. The artist just jumps out. Bear in mind that the technology is a tool. Like any other tool, it is what you do with what you have. Many successful editors don't fully understand the technical side, but they do understand the art form. Regardless of money and politics, it is an art form. I'm fond of saying it is about emotional survival, not about anything else. If you believe in what you are doing, you will do okay.

Bennett Goldberg, Vice President of Editing Services at Digital Symphony, Los Angeles, California

---

As you can see, there are many things to keep in mind as you consider your own editing workflow and environment. If you are preparing to set up your own system, address as many of these as your time, budget and experience will allow. Good habits in workflow and environment are healthier, less stressful and more conducive to creative editing—and being creative is what it is really all about.

6 Getting Your Footage into the System: What the Steps Are and What You Need to Know

Definition of Terms

Sometimes terminology gets a bit confusing, especially when editors toss around terms such as "digitizing" inappropriately. Let's start this chapter by clarifying the difference between **inputting** and **digitizing.** If your footage is already digital (you shot it with a digital camera, you have transferred your analog footage to a digital tape or you are dealing with digital audio from a CD or DAT), you obviously don't need to digitize your footage—it is already in that format. You simply go through a series of steps to input this material into the nonlinear editing system (often storing it in a peripheral storage device accessed by the computer). Your footage, music, dialogue and/or effects are already written in the language that the computer speaks, so there is no need to "translate" it in advance.

The Digital Language and Why Compression Is Required If Your Material Is Analog

However, if your footage is still in the analog language (you shot it with an analog camera such as VHS, Super-VHS, Hi-8 or Beta SP), the nonlinear editing system's hardware and software can't accept it. It is not written in the 0s and 1s that a computer requires. The word *digital* refers to a numerical representation of information—in our case video and audio information—and the ability of this information to be processed electronically by a computer. So if you have analog material and want to edit on a system such as Avid, Media 100, DFast or Final Cut Pro, you must go through the process of digitizing your signals as they go into the system (see Figure 6.1). Digitizing video, audio and graphics almost always requires some type of **compression.** There is so much information in 1 second of moving video that you would quickly fill up your hard drive space if you didn't compress this material. So compression goes hand in hand with digitization. We will say more on what compression is and why there are different types of compression in a moment.

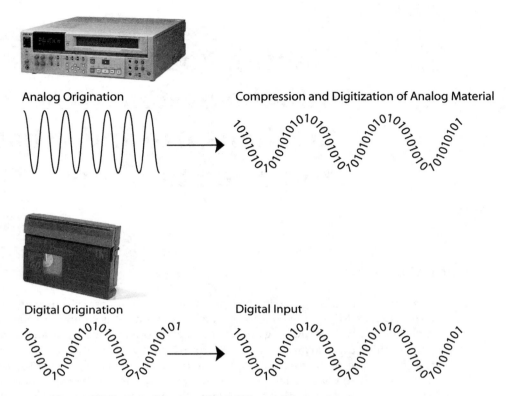

Analog Origination

Compression and Digitization of Analog Material

Digital Origination

Digital Input

FIGURE 6.1   Difference between Digitizing and Inputting

Some systems, such as Apple's Final Cut Pro, are set up to input only digital material. If your original source footage was shot with an analog camera, you must add a SCSI card or hook up some additional conversion box to change the analog signal into digital for you.

If you are shooting on film and planning to edit with a digital nonlinear system, there are several additional requirements as you consider technical specifics and prepare your film order for the laboratory. These issues are discussed in detail in Chapter 11, "Shooting Film and Editing on a Digital Nonlinear System." We recommend you read this chapter first and then familiarize yourself with the additional basics of preparing to edit your film digitally.

See Chapter 11 for additional important information on shooting film and editing on a digital nonlinear system.

So what is it about this word *compression* that makes everyone go crazy and generates so much discussion? As we mentioned, compression of the video data takes place during the digitization process. Raw video frames take up a huge amount of space. Computers can easily handle things like desktop publishing, data management and spreadsheets. But challenge them with full-motion visuals and audio and—well, things get interesting. So enters video compression.

Video editors are fond of saying, "Compression is like life. You can never be too thin or too rich!" The video signal is compressed so that the data stream is reduced to a manageable level and it simply doesn't take up as much space, making nonlinear editing possible. The compression rate requirements have dropped over the past few years (and will no doubt continue to drop) because of advances in the throughput speed of hard drives.

System Bottlenecks

However, if you've got a high-end camera and deck and a new, powerful capture card for the data but your computer drive is not an A/V (audiovisual) drive, the system will be incapable of letting enough information pass through quickly enough. This problem will cause a bottleneck in the system (see Figure 6.2), causing your video quality to suffer.

```
1010101010101010101011010101010101010101011010101010
1010101010110101010101010101010101011010101010101010101010
1101010101010101010101011010101010101010101011010101010
```
Fast-Moving Data →

```
1010101010101010
0101010101      00101
10101010101 10101010 11 1010101010101010101011010101010101010101
101010101010 10101 01 0101101010101010101010101011010101010101
0101010101 0101 01 010101011010101010101010101011010101010
010101010101010101
```
Slow-Moving Data →

FIGURE 6.2   Data Bottleneck

Throughput and Compression Rates

The quality of video coming out of a computer depends on the system's **throughput performance,** the rate at which data travels between the video source deck, disk drives and video-capture cards. When discussing the throughput of drives, we refer to interface protocols such as SCSI, Firewire, USB and fiber channel options. These will be discussed below.

One second's worth of uncompressed video and its audio at full color resolution and motion takes up about 30 MB of space. That's 1 second! Given other drains on the system, at 30 frames per second of video, the requirement would be that the drive sustain about 36 MB per second of consistent video.

This data transfer between the pieces of equipment that make up your nonlinear editing system must be uninterrupted and steady. If there is any flux or deviation, the data stream is impaired. Regular drives, such as those we use for simple word processing, continually adjust the speed of their revolution to compensate for internal temperature fluctuations (this is called the **thermal calibration** or *T-CAL function*). Because these processes don't incorporate visual motion, T-CAL doesn't cause a problem. However, with motion video, this fluctuation will result in image flickers, bounces, pauses, jumps and audio distortion during playback. Audio/visual drives spin faster and are also are geared specifically to eliminate these problems in the digital nonlinear editing domain.

Software and Hardware CODECs
and Compression Rates

During the basic digitization process, we must also compress or "crunch" the video data so that it is a small enough stream to travel within your nonlinear system. There are a few major types of compression in the world of video. We will specifically discuss a few here: JPEG, MPEG-1, MPEG-2 and MPEG-4, although there are many other less-known and some company-specific compression types. They all simply use different algorithms.

It is important to note that each of the various compression schemes falls into one of two camps. Some make use of a combination of hardware and software, and others are simply software **CODECs** (compression/decompression device). The hardware-assisted CODECs such as MPEG are faster and therefore cost more. On the flip side, software-only CODECs are cheaper or even come bundled with other software packages or may be downloaded from the web.

JPEG (which stands for Joint Photographic Experts Group) and **MPEG** (which stands for Motion Picture Experts Group) are very common compression schemes. JPEG is referred to as *spatial* or *intraframe* compression. JPEG is considered a fairly mild compression factor that promotes few artifacts (visual sparkles, video "noise," color streaks or blocky edges around the edge of an image; compression artifacts are the result of the system's inability to correctly reconstruct the original image) and allows for maximum editing freedom. It is the compression scheme utilized by many graphics-based systems. If your end goal is CD-ROM, broadcast quality or Internet movies, JPEG probably should not be your choice, as it is not the cleanest compression available (see Figure 6.3).

In JPEG compression, every individual frame is compressed. Basically, you are taking something large (the video frame) and making it smaller. Think of it this way: If you have a big empty cardboard box, it takes up a lot of space. But if you walk all over it and smash it down, it is still a big empty cardboard box, just smaller and taking up less space. Now you can move it around more easily. JPEG compression is something like that. If you can fit more video information into less space, more power to you.

Storage space on nonlinear editing systems (or any computer-based setup, for that matter) is probably the most cost-intensive consideration. If you can deal with that problem in creative ways, you will. By compressing the information, you also allow it to transfer at a quicker rate into the digital domain and back out to analog (and by the way, JPEG compresses symmetrically—that is, it compresses and decompresses information at the same rate of time).

FIGURE 6.3 Possible Artifacts Caused by JPEG Compression

So what is MPEG? Of course, in the computer world, you never have just one of anything; there are always competing pieces of software, hardware, platforms and, in this case, CODECs. MPEG is a CODEC just as JPEG is. The difference is that MPEG is a form of interframe compression (as opposed to JPEG's intraframe compression). What this means is that some frames of the image contain all of the information, an entire image, and others record only what differs from the previous frame or succeeding frame. MPEG is really just an extension of the JPEG idea; it compresses like JPEG but saves only the difference between frames and tosses out frames that are identical to previous frames. So why would we have these two different CODECs? Obviously, each has advantages and disadvantages. JPEG's interframe compression is easier to edit and compress. MPEG's intraframe compression allows for higher compression ratios without becoming unwatchable. That means that you could compress at 200 to 1 (greatly compressing the information) and get more footage onto your hard drive.

Because MPEG is so compressed, it is quite difficult to edit with frame accuracy. The picture information is dependent on the information that the frames are getting from each other. An edit might leave a frame without its preceding reference frame, causing problems. If you have an image in which there is very little movement or change, such as a golfer correcting his stance and looking down at the ball about to be hit, each frame is fairly similar, with a bit of movement in the hands and feet. MPEG would record only those frames in which there was discernible difference between them. However, once the player begins to swing the club back and then forcefully hit the ball, each frame differs from its preceding frame pretty radically. MPEG would be incorporating normal JPEG compression, since each frame is a change from the previous frame and therefore needs to be recorded.

But remember that one of the pitfalls of the otherwise admirable MPEG CODEC is that it is not editable on a frame-by-frame basis owing to the interframe compression. Editors loved the high compression ratio that MPEG allowed but were often forced to capture and edit video in another format and then compress the completed video using MPEG. This is labor-intensive and costly.

There are now new and improved versions of MPEG. MPEG2III is used for DVDs. Its compression can go as high as 30 to 1. The quality of the end result is rich and clean.

What about MP3? MPEG3 (more commonly known as MP3) is a compression system for *audio*. The MP3 format reduces the number of bytes in a song or other audio recording without noticeably affecting the audio quality. MP3 compression allows you to play audio with high quality using little storage space. A .WAV audio file is great in quality but can take up an immense amount of space—approximately 10 MB per minute of audio. Making your audio an MP3 file instead of a .WAV file makes the file dense so that it takes up less space. MP3 also retains the superior quality of the audio. Note that when you are digitizing and compressing your video footage, the audio is compressed along with the video image, so you will instead be using JPEG or one of the other MPEG CODECs.

Finally, MPEG-4 does for video what MPEG-3 does for audio. The goal is to take a DVD and compress it enough that it can fit onto a CD.

Partly because of the price war relative to the MPEG CODEC, a new hybrid form has arrived. This form is called editable MPEG or I-frame MPEG, and it is a semicompressed file that allows clean edits yet is still compressed enough to be practical.

Compression

Really high-quality nonlinear capture cards and hardware can capture and play back video that is compressed as low as 2 to 1. This is very high-quality video, because there is so little compression. However, video with little compression takes up a lot of space on your hard drive. There is always a tradeoff in the compression game. The more you compress the footage, the more footage you can get into the system but the worse it looks. JPEG compressed at 6 to 1 shows a good bit of artifacting. But JPEG at 2 to 1 is very clean; the eye can't tell the difference between this and raw uncompressed footage.

Probably the biggest area of concern when it comes to compression is the whole issue of a broadcast-quality signal. So let's attempt to define what that is. To most people, *broadcast quality* simply means video that looks good on a television set, with no dropouts, no color smears and a sharp image. Officially, broadcast quality signals must provide a certain degree of resolution. Television sets are capable of reading 350 scanned television lines, and therefore broadcast standards dictate that an acceptable signal include 350 lines of information. Because most delivery methods at this point are still analog (which degrades in transmission), the resolution rate must start out even higher. Digital signals, when uncompressed, do not degrade in transmission, and if they are delivered digitally to the television set, you lose no information. However, even current digital signals still go through an analog delivery channel and therefore lose some signal quality.

For more information on broadcast quality and broadcast engineering specifics, go to the Society of Motion Picture and Television Engineers website at www.smpte.org.

When using a nonlinear editing system, you will be rightly concerned with broadcast quality. In most cases, you will be shooting on analog video, compressing this into a digital signal, editing and then laying back out to analog tape. Because equipment is evolving so rapidly, you will need to do some research and talk with experienced nonlinear editors to make the best choices of equipment and CODECs. Still, there are bottleneck areas that can inhibit your final broadcast signals, including the quality of the original footage, the compression scheme you incorporate and the bandwidth of the computer bus.

The easiest of these potential problem areas to deal with is the quality of the source material. The now well-worn dictum "garbage in, garbage out" is certainly applicable to digital nonlinear editing. How clean your source footage is in many ways determines the quality of the finished product. The ravages of age, physical damage, generation loss and analog transport problems affect analog video footage. Add to this list all-too-common production problems such as low lighting, improper white balancing and poor audio, conditions that will affect any video recording and therefore the quality of the final version.

Audio Compression

As you probably know, audio is measured in frequencies. Quick and frequent waves represent a high-pitched audio signal. Slower and more widely spaced waves represent a low-pitched audio signal. Exactly how quickly these audio waves go up and down is defined as the wave's frequency. Figure 6.4 illustrates this concept

When an audio wave is being digitized, the system must check the volume of the wave very often and at a constant rate. How often the computer checks the wave is called the *sampling rate*. CD-quality audio is sampled at 44.1 kHz (about 44,000 times a second). Of course, this takes up a good bit of space because the computer must remember every point sampled. There are many good books, articles and websites on audio and compression, so we won't get overly technical here, but we do want to make sure you consider audio sampling rates as you digitize and edit. Most nonlinear editing systems let you set preferences, and one area you can manipulate is the audio sampling rate. Be sure to set this sample rate so that it is the same as your newly digitized footage or the same sample rate that your digital camera used in recording. If your editing system and editing timeline are set for one audio sample rate and you attempt to drag an audio clip with a different sampling rate into the timeline, some editing systems will force you to abort the edit. They simply will not allow you to place shots with different sample rates into the same program. Other systems, such as Adobe Premiere 6.0, have no problem incorporating different audio sample rates into one timeline.

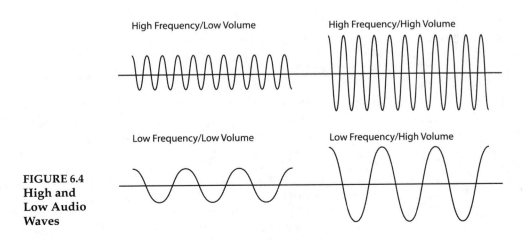

High Frequency/Low Volume   High Frequency/High Volume

Low Frequency/Low Volume   Low Frequency/High Volume

**FIGURE 6.4
High and
Low Audio
Waves**

Lossless and Lossy Compression: Different Ways of Compressing and Saving Storage Space

There are a couple of other terms you will hear thrown about when people discuss compression. They are *lossless* and *lossy*. **Lossless** refers to a compressed data file that is reconstructed exactly from the original data; all of the original information is there, just compressed. Obviously, if you choose this scheme, you are compressing the information but are still using a good amount of space.

Lossy means a compression scheme in which specific parts of the data (meaning video image content) are permanently removed. Lossy compression is acceptable when dealing with video, because the images will be viewed subjectively and our eyes easily fill in the small amount of missing information. The trick to compression is getting rid of data that we don't immediately perceive or that is redundant. Here is a visual example of the two: Imagine you've got a large double scoop of chocolate ice cream in a huge waffle cone. It's big. It takes up a lot of space. If you were going to do lossless compression on it, you might let the ice cream melt into a bowl and then break up the cone into smaller pieces and throw them in. All of the original information is still there, it is just taking up less space now. In a lossy compression scheme of this same scenario, you might put a few spoonfuls of the ice cream in the bowl and two or three pieces of the cone, then get rid of the rest of it because it is redundant. We still get the idea of ice cream and cone and can fill in the rest of the necessary information.

These are not the only ways to reduce the space needed on your hard drive. In the compression process, you can also reduce the video files by reducing the basic amount of information your video contains. There are a couple of ways to do this. The first is to reduce the **frame rate.** Video runs at 30 frames per second for full motion. If you reduce the frame rate to 15 frames per second, you have halved the information and therefore, in effect, doubled your potential space on the hard drive. Of course, when you go this route, you introduce jerky motion. A second way to reduce the space needed for your video files is to reduce the size of each frame of video (making the image smaller on the screen and reducing the pixels per square inch), as shown in Figure 6.5. Normal broadcast video is set at a rate of 640 by 480 pixels. You can reduce this to half, making it 320 by 240; this quarters the image size and therefore once again reduces the space needed on the hard drive.

Something should be pointed out about what we call *video noise.* In analog shooting and editing, we have all been taught to be paranoid about excess signal information in the visual portion of the video, known as **noise.** Video noise is usually perceived as speckles or muted edges of surfaces. However, when you are dealing with a combination of analog to digital to analog media in the nonlinear process, some such noise can be considered helpful in masking the inherent artifacts of compression. This is done during the decoding process (changing the signal back to analog) by visually covering up the ragged artifacts created by the loss of the high-frequency portion of the video signal due to bandwidth limitations.

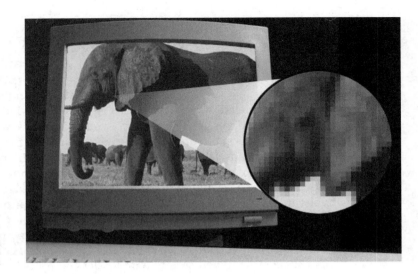

FIGURE 6.5   Reduced Pixels and Smaller Image Size on Computer Screen

Batch Digitizing

Digitizing and inputting are time-consuming and ultimately extremely important processes with all nonlinear editing systems. The various nonlinear editing systems handle this process in different ways. Some systems will allow for the creation of **clips** (comparable to a take or shot in film or analog video editing) based on control track or timecode breaks. Most systems incorporate a feature called **batch digitizing.** This allows you to log tapes in the field or after scanning through the source videotapes on a VCR, selecting the best takes—the ones you want to digitize for your nonlinear edit. The system is then capable of automatically digitizing these best shots directly from the logs based on your suggested timecode in and out points. This obviously saves time and hard drive space. Another way in which you can use batch digitizing is by following this process: Go ahead and digitize all of your source material but at a very low resolution. You perform a rough edit and make all of your creative editing decisions. Once you have decided which footage will be utilized in the final edit, go back and batch digitize at high resolution only the material you need.

Remember that batch digitizing requires timecode reference numbers.

The Digital Bin

Bin windows are visible on the monitor screen interface as a place to store your various clips. The terms *bin* and *trim bin* come from motion picture film editors. In a film editing room, the film is cut into strips or shots. There is a large bin with metal hooks around the edges where the editor stores footage before it is placed into the edit (see Figure 6.6). This concept has now made the leap to the digital domain. You are able to take the best of both the film and video postproduction worlds and see or access your raw footage clips with ease.

The topic of storage is covered in Chapter 8, "Storage of Media in the Digital Nonlinear Environment."

In the digital bin window, you are able to quickly retrieve various clips because they are catalogued on the screen by name, thumbnail image of the first frame of the shot, timecode in and out numbers, and so on. As Figure 6.7 shows, most systems also allow you to add comments to your clips and search for key-words when you are needing to access footage. For example, you could search for all shots of a snow-covered mountain or all shots taken inside a British pub. The best systems are flexible and allow you to organize your bin in the way that is most convenient to your editing needs. However, to best utilize these tools within the system, you must have first been very diligent in naming your "reels" (tape num-bers), scenes and shots. If you simply give each shot a number, you can imagine how difficult it will be to locate exactly what you are looking for. Most systems allow only a few words to name a shot, so you can use the notes or comments sec-tion of the bin to add additional information about each image or audio clip. The more organized your screen interface and your bin, the more you can concentrate your efforts on creative editing with appropriate speed.

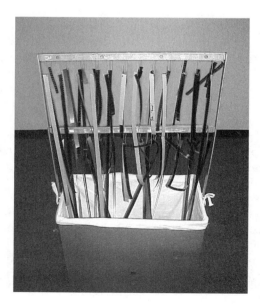

FIGURE 6.6   Film Room Trim Bin with Film

FIGURE 6.7   Computer Monitor Interface with Bin Window and Clips

QuickTime

Let's add one last term in here, since you have no doubt heard about it and might wonder what it has to do with nonlinear editing. QuickTime is a process that you will often hear people discuss relative to video movies, and it warrants at least a description in this chapter on compression, digitization and storage. QuickTime is Apple Computer's industry standard architecture for editing, creating and publishing digital media. In other words, it is a file format that can move and process digital video and audio. It is not a process or a product. It is a file format something like TIFF or EPS. Many software platforms, including Adobe Premiere, Apple's iMovie, Avid Cinema, Macromedia's Final Cut, Adobe After Effects and Radius Edit, incorporate QuickTime. Desktop editing products such as Adobe Premiere are fairly inexpensive. Therefore they are often being used in colleges and universities nationwide in entry-level classes to provide a first glimpse at the power and relative ease of most aspects of nonlinear editing. QuickTime is a rich file format that is an environment for media authoring. It is also a complete suite of applications that allows users to play back professional audio and video on their computers. One of the most impressive things about QuickTime is its continuing compatibility. This compatibility enables QuickTime developers to serve multiple distribution methods with one file. For instance, a single file can be used for streaming over the web, for downloading from a web server or for local playback from a CD to both Mac and Windows users. One of the newest innovations from QuickTime is QuickTime VR (virtual reality). This gives the option for 360-degree graphic representations.

Compression, digitization and inputting will be areas of critical concern for you as a digital nonlinear editor. This nonlinear form of film and video editing owes its very existence to these processes. Things change rapidly in this field, and you should always attempt to keep up with evolving applications, equipment and terminology. Magazines such as *Videomaker, Videographer* and *PC* often include well-researched and well-written articles on nonlinear editing and reviews of system equipment components. Keep on top of it!

7 Management of Your Material

Various Production and Postproduction Modes

It is in the area of postproduction editing that film and video have really come together. The strict boundary between the "film" world and the "video" world is blurring.

Of course, there are still many ways to go about the production process. Maybe you shot a silent fiction story on 8mm film. Perhaps you shot 29 hours of video footage for a documentary on an Alaskan wildlife refuge. Possibly it was a two-camera studio "how-to" show or an autobiographical video about your struggle with an eating disorder that you are going to make into an interactive CD-ROM. Maybe it was a 16mm film production about street musicians in Paris. There are an unlimited number of production possibilities. What they all have in common is postproduction, and there are many, many choices to be made in the postproduction process. These choices hinge on budget, creative preferences, past experience, deadlines and the medium in which your motion picture will be finished and distributed.

In the past, many motion pictures were shot on film and then transferred to analog video for a **rough cut** (a first loose attempt at putting together the image and dialogue). With new digital technologies, the original film image and accompanying audio are instead dubbed onto digital videotape and put into the digital system. The rough edit of these materials and any other audio or visual elements is then completed using this nonlinear system. Quite often, the production company then goes back to the original film negative and conforms it in the traditional manner for distribution.

Off-Line and On-Line: Different Definitions

If you shot analog video, you could, of course, edit completely on a linear analog system. If your intent were a television broadcast, you might go through a couple of stages in postproduction. First, you would make dubs of all of your original footage and put the originals away in storage for safe keeping. You then could use a fairly inexpensive cuts-only VHS analog linear editing setup to make basic editing decisions, using the dubs of your originals as source material. This is referred to as an **off-line edit.** Once you decided how the edit should be, you could then go back to

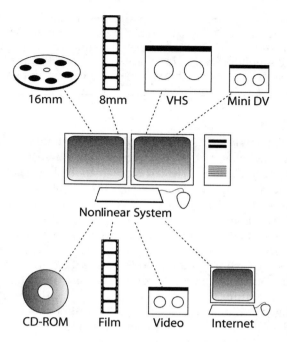

FIGURE 7.1   Origination and Output Sources

your original master tapes (these are first generation and therefore are of the highest quality) and perform what is called an **on-line edit.** In most cases, you would rent high-end analog linear editing facilities along with an on-line editor who was familiar with this equipment and perform a final edit with any necessary transitions, audio mixing, titles and so on. However, the days of final postproduction using analog systems are numbered. When shooting on video, many editors perform their off-line edit on a nonlinear editing system such as Lightworks or Avid. They digitize the footage and make these same basic editing decisions in the more accommodating digital domain. With a high-end nonlinear system, you can also actually perform your final on-line edit digitally complete with layered graphics, sound mixing, transitions and so on and output the signal back to videotape, CD-ROM, the Internet or whatever your chosen medium is, as illustrated in Figure 7.1.

As you enter the industry, read books and articles, and talk with others about motion picture editing, you will hear the terms *off-line* and *on-line* used in two entirely different ways. The alternative meanings of these terms have been prompted by digital terminology, and it is important that you understand both these and the earlier meanings. The ways in which the words have been defined in this text relate to different stages of the creative process of editing. Off-line can be often thought of as a working, early edit. On-line is the final, distributable version of a motion picture, complete with mixed sound, graphics and titles. However, in the digital world, these terms mean very different things. If a shot (footage or other element) is off-line, its corresponding media file is not stored in the computer. You might see a thumbnail image of the shot in the bin, but the actual footage (media file) is either corrupted or missing. If a shot is on-line, the thumbnail clip and the actual media file to which it is pointing can communicate successfully because the media file (the actual digitized footage) is stored within the nonlinear editing system.

In a studio production (unless it is live and therefore you are editing during broadcast with a television switcher, as shown in Figure 7.2), you've got some of the same basic postproduction possibilities. You can edit via an analog system, cutting between the two cameras in a way that best tells the how-to story, or you might employ a digital nonlinear system. (There are systems that are better suited for multi-camera work; this will be discussed in Chapter 13, "Choosing the Right System.")

There are many stages of editing film and video. All of the steps can be broken down broadly into two major steps: off-line editing and on-line editing. There are some very basic differences between the two. To define the difference between off-line and on-line for the nonlinear editor, let's discuss these terms as they relate to analog videotape or film editing.

There are many stages in film or video editing. An off-line edit is considered an early version or rough cut. In this stage, one uses dubs of the original footage as sources in order to keep the original footage (either the original videotapes or the film negative) in pristine shape. During the off-line edit, basic structural editing

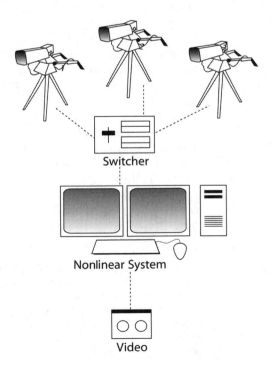

Switcher

Nonlinear System

Video

FIGURE 7.2   Flowchart of Nonlinear Editing for Basic Studio Production

decisions are made. What is important here is that you begin putting the major sections of information together. Often, editors will do a second, third or even fourth off-line edit, each one becoming more fine-tuned, with specific decisions being made as to pacing. Extensive notes are taken during this process, culminating in an edit decision list (see Chapter 10, "The Edit Decision List," for more information). This edit decision list is then used in what is called the on-line edit. During this stage, the editor uses the original material as source footage and creates a final edit master tape or film.

In the off-line stage of either video or film editing, usually one or two editors working together serve as the creative postproduction decision makers. Often, the off-line edit is technically a bit rough. At this stage, you are not concerned with video generation loss, unequalized audio, small scratches in the film workprint or matters of that kind. These problems are corrected in the on-line edit by professional film negative cutters, sound mixers, color-correction technicians (timers), and others. In the on-line edit, your job as an editor is to help finesse your footage into the best possible creative edit. You rely on hired technicians to ensure technical excellency.

So let's talk about the terms *off-line* and *on-line* as they relate to the nonlinear digital editor. In the digital domain, most editors prefer to go through these same processes for various reasons. The first reason is simple: Rarely is your first attempt at an edit the best. One of the joys of nonlinear editing is that it allows you to easily perform multiple off-line edits. The "nonlinear" portion of nonlinear editing implies that it is easy to randomly access footage and to move the material around with ease.

As you will read more about in Chapter 10, the terms *off-line* and *on-line* can get a bit confusing in discussing digital editing; these two terms not only refer to specific stages in the editing process, but, in computer language, also refer to information that is within the digital domain. Footage you have digitized is therefore *on-line,* and information or processes that occur outside the digital domain are *off-line.* In digital editing, it is possible to perform several off-lines in one sitting. If you were using film workprints or an analog video system, this would be much more difficult. So the nonlinear editor makes all of the basic creative choices with footage that is digitized at a fairly low (poor) resolution. At this point, the editor has several different choices, including the following. The editor might use the edit decision list created in this digital nonlinear off-line edit and go back to edit the original camera negative and audio (if the original footage was motion picture film and analog or digital audio recording). The on-line edit would then be out of the digital domain but would utilize decisions made within it. Following are the required basic steps:

1. Digitize your footage at a low but readable resolution rate.
2. Go through and edit the footage in the order you want, with transitions. Using this version and your log sheets as references, make an edit decision list (EDL). This is a written history of the editorial decisions that were made.
3. Use this EDL (it will have to include film edge code numbers using special EDL software) to go back and cut the original camera negative and audio.
4. Have a laboratory strike a release print with an optical sound track.

See Chapter 11 for a thorough discussion of the traditional film process of matchback and conforming the original negative.

If the original footage was videotape, the editor might once again use the EDL created during the off-line nonlinear edit and then edit the analog video source tapes onto a professional analog video master tape at a postproduction house with all of the fancy transitions, titles and audio mixing. Once again, the editor exits the digital domain for the on-line edit:

1. Digitize your footage at a low but readable resolution rate.
2. Go through and edit the footage in the order you want, with transitions.
3. Using this version and your log sheets as references, make an edit decision list (EDL). This is a written history of the editorial decisions that were made.
4. Transfer this EDL to a computer-assisted linear analog video editing system.
5. Load the videotapes into decks connected to this linear analog editing system.
6. Execute the edit on the basis of these decisions, add titles and graphics, and manipulate audio as needed, ending up with a master videotape.

Alternatively, the on-line edit might be accomplished within the nonlinear editing system, provided that it is a system with high-resolution or digital output. In this option, with an upper-end nonlinear system, the digitized footage is edited in its final form, with the addition of all the necessary graphics, compositing, still stores, image manipulation, audio mixing and so on. You must have a good bit of storage space available within the system to accomplish a truly digital on-line edit. Once this digital edit is complete, the program can be output to videotape, CD-ROM or the Internet or through a direct digital broadcast.

1. Digitize your footage at a low resolution.
2. Edit your clips with transitions.
3. Create an EDL of your decisions.
4. Go back and redigitize the footage you have chosen to include in the edit at a high resolution rate.
5. Edit clips, include transitions, manipulate audio as needed, and add graphics, animation, titles and digital video effects.
6. Decompress this edit and layback to final master videotape.

We bring up these postproduction differences here to indicate that you will need to organize the process according to how you will complete the final edit. It is not within the confines of this book to go into much more detail about production variances, but you should note that every decision you make in production (Is it shot on video? Is it intended for Internet distribution? Is it a multiple-camera shoot with an immediate broadcast deadline? Will it be shown on film in festivals, museums and galleries?) will affect decisions you must make in the postproduction realm.

Expanded Responsibilities of Editors

In the professional postproduction world, editors (whether they be film, video or digital) often have an apprentice or assistant editor whose main duties are to help keep material organized and logged. If editing in this industry is your high calling, you may spend a good bit of time at this level learning the tricks of the trade while providing valuable services to the productions currently underway. Digital nonlinear editing systems have radically altered the duties, responsibilities and expectations of people working in postproduction. There has been a blending of responsibilities. There are many examples of these changes due to digital nonlinear editing systems. Often, the editor is now expected to oversee graphics, titles and even animation. In the past, these duties were completed by other trained professionals. Editing assistants used to be integral to the postproduction suite. They would handle duties such as organization, preparation, logging footage, labeling tapes and naming shots. This not only benefited the editor, but also served as a mentoring opportunity for the assistant. Because digital nonlinear editing systems are often considered all-in-one, accessible suites, the responsibilities of the editor have greatly expanded in many cases. The editor not only has to take care of the above-mentioned duties in many cases, but also must now be more familiar with the technicalities of system interface and layout, broadcast-quality analysis of the image, audio mixing and other duties. We mention these kinds of changes here to further emphasize the need for organization and management at all levels of pre-production, production and postproduction for film and video. There are many things for you to be concerned with, and sloppy oversight will not allow for spectacularly artistic editing (which we assume is your goal).

In terms of storage, we have a high-speed server, so all of our media files are moved back and forth. All of the rooms are linked, so you can control anything from any other room. The editors no longer really have to focus on final mix of audio or graphics. They focus on telling the story, working with the client. Audio issues are handled by our sound designer in a separate studio mix. He cleans up the audio, equalizes it and sends it back to editor. It is the same for visual effects. Depending on editor's skills, if they can do effects during edit, that is fine. But if they are not graphically skilled but still a great storyteller, they send it out to graphics department and the editor drops into the show. In the old days, a lot of this was done in the on-line room. In the nonlinear world, it can be spread out.

Dan Sparks, Director of Post Production at Four Square Productions, San Diego, California

Control Track and Timecode

When discussing the organization of media, we need to define some more terms that editors use. The first one is the **control track.** The control track is a signal that exists on any videotape that has an image or audio on it. If you have picture or audio, you must by default also have a control track. It serves a few purposes, and one of those is a kind of cement that all of the other signals (such as visuals and audio) sit on top of (see Figure 7.3). The control track can also be thought of as the equivalent of sprocket holes in film; it is a way that the video "talks" to the VCR and allows it to move through at the appropriate speed. There is a control track pulse on each frame of video, and therefore it can be used to gauge approximately where you are on the videotape if you reset the counter to zero at the beginning of the tape. However, the control track is not frame accurate (not an exact unchanging address for each frame). If you are 1 hour and 3 minutes into your tape and the counter says this, but then you accidentally hit the reset button on the counter, it will go to zero. Now the equipment is telling you that you are at the beginning of the tape, but you know you are really 1 hour and 3 minutes in. To continue to use the control track as a reference, you need to rewind the tape and reset to zero again and then fast-forward back to the approximate spot where the shot exists on the tape. Tape shuttling eventually wears out your decks and stretches your tape. On the flip side, this is the time when most editors take a break to grab a cup of coffee or make other necessary trips. The loss of this time is one of the few unfortunate side effects of the digital domain. Because there is no waiting for tapes to shuttle back and forth, digital editors don't get up and around as much during their day. They therefore make fewer efforts to stretch, clear their mind and reflect on what has been accomplished and what remains to be done.

One of the most important technical elements of editing is the **timecode.** Sometimes, students find the whole issue of timecode confusing when they are first introduced to it, but it is really a very simple concept and important to understand. Timecode is a numerical reference for each frame of video. It takes the place

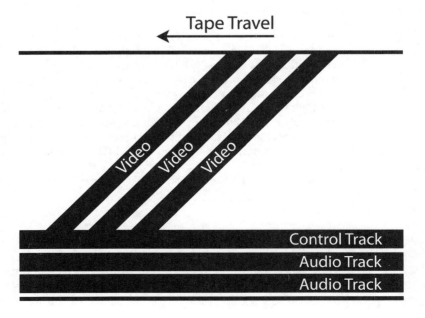

FIGURE 7.3   Control Track Diagram

of relying on the control track as an approximate location of your footage. Each frame is given an unchanging and specific "address." In many ways, it is like the edge numbers on film, but instead of measuring the physical length of the video-tape, timecode tells you the duration of the running time. The timecode measures hours, minutes, seconds and frames. You can quickly and easily locate any shot if you know its timecode address. The primary reason for timecode is therefore to function as a time reference to facilitate easily locating footage and setting precise edit points. Timecode allows for frame-accurate edits that would be impossible to achieve by simply using the control track as a reference device.

The timecode is a signal on the tape that is not seen along with the image. However, when you make dubs of your original footage for your off-line edit (see Chapter 7), you can create what is referred to as a timecode burn-in. This is a visual representation on the screen of your timecode numbers for making this off-line edit easier. The editor can then look at and log the footage anywhere there is a VCR. You would never burn in the timecode on your original source tapes or copy it onto your edit master.

The **Society of Motion Picture and Television Engineers (SMPTE)** is the association that governs timecode regulations in the United States. There are some variations in timecode—some choices that you make in production or postproduction that affect where the timecode is placed on videotape and how many actual pulse signals there are. Timecode is used in digital nonlinear editing just as it is used in on-line analog video editing, and you need to understand these different terms.

In terms of where the timecode is placed on the tape, you've got two choices, as illustrated in Figure 7.4. The first is **vertical interval timecode (VITC).** This kind of timecode is placed on the part of the videotape where the visual signals exist, in between the frames. VITC is laid down only with a camera that is capable of generating it, since it is going down right with the picture signals. If you don't have a professional camera that lays down VITC, there are add-on camera adapters that

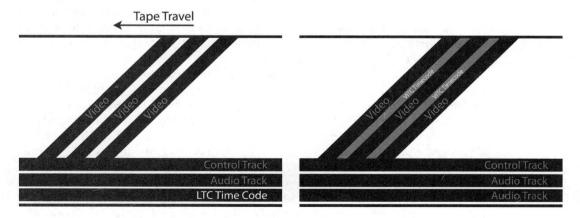

FIGURE 7.4   Longitudinal Timecode and Vertical Interval Timecode Placement on a Videotape

can lay it down. These are referred to as timecode generators. There is also **rewritable consumer timecode (RCTC),** which is laid down by Sony and some other Hi-8 cameras, but these are considered consumer-oriented versions and not industry standard. The second option is **longitudinal timecode (LTC).** This type can be laid down in place of VITC if your camera doesn't incorporate VITC timecode. LTC is striped onto your videotapes after production and takes the place of one of the two audio tracks (thus getting the name "longitudinal"). This is called **post-striping** using an external timecode generator. When you shoot on location, the same audio is going onto both available audio tracks, so although you are losing an audio track, you are not losing audio signal. Although this is not the ideal situation, it is not a huge loss to cover one of your audio tracks up to gain LTC timecode. If you lay down LTC, you need to watch the level. If it is applied at a high level, the signal can bleed over to the adjacent audio track and create noise. Whether you incorporate VITC or LTC, timecode serves the purpose of providing an unchangeable address for each frame in hours, minutes, seconds and frames.

The second choice you have to make, whether you are using VITC or LTC, is how many pulse signals are being laid down onto the tape. You've got two choices in this area: drop frame timecode and non–drop frame timecode; both are SMPTE versions with a slight but important variation between them. Remember that timecode is a set of four numbers indicating hours, minutes, seconds and frames. Each frame of video has a specific timecode number allowing you to quickly and easily locate an image or section of audio. Some form of punctuation, usually colons but occasionally commas or periods, separates the four sets of numbers when they are written out on a log sheet or EDL. The most common timecode notation form would be written as 01:14:07:28, meaning 1 hour, 14 minutes, 7 seconds and twenty-eight frames. At the standard rate of thirty frames per second in video, there are 1,800 frames every minute and 108,000 frames per hour.

So let's explain the somewhat technical reason for these two different versions. Videotape is displayed at thirty frames per second of timecode. A video frame is made up of two alternating fields of interlaced video. NTSC (the North American standard format, also used elsewhere in the world) video is simply and easily measured using a standard 1 volt peak-to-peak measurement. Television in the United States is operated at a fixed frequency of 60 hertz (Hz), with one frame of video cleanly created during two cycles.

Given this fact, 108,000 frames should be generated in 1 hour of video. However, there is a glitch: What we refer to as the "sixty-cycle" NTSC color video signals actually require a vertical scanning frequency of 59.94 Hz. Because it takes a full 60 Hz to produce thirty frames of video, we have a problem. To get around this inherent dilemma, **drop frame timecode** was created. If we went with the timecode generated by the fixed 59.94-Hz frequency, only 107,820 frames would be produced in an hour's time. Remember that 1 hour of timecode requires that 108,000 frames be displayed, so we've now got a difference of 180 frames. Therefore, when measured by the timecode clock, what appears to be 1 hour of video running at thirty frames per second would actually take 1 hour and about 3 1/2 seconds. Using normal **non-drop frame timecode** that read 01:00:00:00, the actual clock time would be 01:00:03:18. If you are editing a film for television, where the timing is absolutely critical, this difference is unacceptable. To get around the problem, drop frame timecode was invented.

Whenever the timecode on videotape must indicate actual running time, the timecode must be adjusted by using drop frame timecode. It is called this because the process "drops" (actually simply ignores) the extra 108 frames in every hour of video. Of course, for shorter programs, a smaller number of frames are ignored or not counted: 54 frames in every 30 minutes, 9 frames in every 5 minutes and so on. The way it works is this: At the end of every minute of videotape except for each "tenth" minute, two frames are simply not counted. Using this method, at the end of the second minute, the timecode would change from 00:02:59:27 to 00:03:00:00. Remember that there are thirty video frames in 1 second of video; therefore, normally, the last frame you would have on timecode would be 29. When it turned to "00," you would be on the next second. In the drop frame method, therefore, 00:02:59:27 shows that two frames have been eliminated in the count before moving on to the next second.

Most editors prefer always to use drop frame timecode simply because the video project can be edited precisely to actual clock time. However, when actual running time is not critical, non–drop frame timecode is sufficient. What you must always remember, however, is that your digital nonlinear editing system will have problems if you attempt to work with some drop frame timecode tapes and some non–drop frame timecode tapes.

If you have shot film and are ordering video dailies of your footage from the lab to help in the logging stage, there is one critical request to remember to make. As you fill out the lab ordering paperwork, be sure to indicate timecode start numbers on the tapes. Each roll of film can have a new timecode start number. Therefore, film roll 1 would be video-tape with timecode starting with 01, film roll 2 would be videotape with timecode starting at 02, and so on. If you forget to request this from the lab, you may end up with several tapes beginning with timecode 01, for instance, and you can see how this would complicate logging, batch digitizing and finding shots quickly.

The Paperwork of Editing

Logging and Log Sheets

Logging is the process of creating some type of written version of your raw footage so that you can easily locate the shots you need as you proceed through the edit session. If you have planned your production well, logging isn't as time consuming as it can be if you haven't planned well in production and have scattered source clips among dozens of videocassettes. The unfortunate editors of such footage are often pulling their hair out minutes into an edit session. In this case in particular, clear and concise log sheets are a necessity. You can log your footage in a variety of ways. Some professional editors still use a simple log sheet and a pencil. A blank log sheet usually contains columns for tape number, shot numbers, shot descriptions, and either control track or time code begin and end numbers. Sometimes in narrative filmmaking, there are several takes of the same shot or different angles of the same action. This information would be noted on the log sheets as well as comments such as "slightly out of focus," "shaky camera," or "great shot!" There are desktop software packages for editors who prefer to type in their log sheets.

Concise and complete log sheets can save hours of time in an edit session. If you are in school and have limited access to editing equipment or are fortunate enough to be able to rent on-line editing equipment, a situation in which every minute costs money (lots of money!), log sheets can help to ensure timely and cost-effective edit sessions. Thorough logging of all material to be used in the editing process is possibly the most important stage in the editing process. Thorough log sheets help to make the editing process more efficient, which means you can save time and money. More important, it means that you can let your creative ability as an editor come to the forefront instead of spending energy trying to locate shots or, worse, to remember whether you even have a specific shot or sound. New motion picture makers and editors are often so anxious to jump onto the equipment that they skip over detailed logs. Editors usually don't make this mistake twice!

Also, if you've logged and labeled your footage well, you are halfway there. You can use the comment windows attached to each shot to discuss thematic value, characters, describe the shot and so forth. On that note, logging must include all of the potential themes that the shot might incorporate into the final project. You need to list how many ways the shot *might* be used. Label the shot mentioning these. This requires forethought, and that takes experience.

Bart Weiss, Independent Video/Filmmaker Co-Director of the Association of Independent Video and Filmmakers and Director of the Dallas Video Festival

Logging in the nonlinear realm usually comprises two separate components. These include information entered into the system with the footage that identifies clips and bins and also some sort of handwritten or typed logbook, which is used to record this information in a written, detailed form.

A logbook can be customized to include necessary information for your particular editing needs but usually includes the following information:

- Picture roll number (if original footage is on film)
- Videotape number (if original footage is on video)
- Head/tail slate number for film shoots
- Sound roll number (if original audio was recorded on a separate recording device, as in film production and some video productions)
- Scene or shot number
- Description of the scene

- Comments and remarks (which may include the take number and comments such as "out of focus" or "great shot")
- Important dialogue or other audio
- Script page numbers (if you are editing a narrative fiction production)
- Timecode numbers of the original footage (if the original footage is on video) or key edge numbers (if the original footage is on film). These numbers would reference both the beginning and the end of the shot.

Log sheets force you to become very familiar with your material, thus allowing you to go beyond basic editing decisions such as "this shot goes before that shot" and on to a situation in which you can fine-tune and finesse your footage into a powerful and effective film. One sign of a good editor (and of a great film) is effective management of your material. In film editing, the editor must keep track of hundreds of strips of film, some as short as a few frames, as well as various tracks of magnetic audio stock. In analog videotape editing, tapes must be kept labeled, stored and logged. In the digital domain, editing is still all about organization.

See Appendix B for an example of a log sheet.

Logging your footage is where you link postproduction with all that you did in production. We have mentioned actually hand logging your footage using some type of form. There are also computer-based logging software packages, and several of these interact with editing software to make the whole process smoother and quicker.

Here is one example of how you might use this type of logging software: If your original footage has timecode on it, you can log your footage and type in these corresponding timecode numbers. You now have a digital log of all of your footage with timecode references. This software can then interact with the computer hooked up to a timecode playback deck to help you input specific, desirable sections of your footage based on the timecode numbers you choose.

Naming Your Clips or Shots: The Importance of Description

As important as timecode numbers are to the technical side of the editing process, they aren't very revealing to the artistic side of the process. Shot descriptions are certainly a step in the right direction, but at times, even these can be a bit cryptic, especially if it has been a while since you have looked at all of the footage. Desktop hardware and software can be utilized in the logging process instead of simply using a pencil and log sheet. If your VCR comes equipped with a connector port that will communicate timecode numbers to your computer, these two pieces of equipment will do a lot of the work for you. Of course, you still have to type in shot descriptions (the equipment hasn't reached that stage yet!), but entering each and every timecode number is taken care of. Big companies such as Sony and Panasonic include such connector ports (they are different for different companies) on some of their consumer equipment. Here is how they work: If you have one of these connector ports on your deck (or if you are using Firewire), the deck can communicate timecode numbers directly to your computer via a cable plugged into the computer's serial port. Given the proper computer connection and software plug-in, which is easily installed on your computer's local hard drive, allowing it to work in conjunction with other software applications you've got running, you can use the mouse to grab and copy timecode off your videotape and insert it into your list. With this kind of software, the only typing you need to do is a shot description. Utilizing the built-in log sheets the software offers, you can simply shuttle forward to a shot, see the timecode number displayed and type a description of the shot onto the sheet. Once you're done, shuttle forward to the next shot and continue this process until all of your tapes are logged. By using these specifically designed software packages within the nonlinear editing system you can incorporate thumbnails, or small graphic images, into your log sheet. These images, which are captured from the videotape, are copies of one frame from each of the shots in the list and serve to easily identify clips. Since you need these images on your log sheets or edit decision list only to remind you of the content or look of a shot, you don't need high-resolution color images taking up lots of your hard drive space. And since you will probably be printing your log sheets out on a black-and-white printer, even a simple low-resolution black-and-white image will serve your purposes. There are even software programs that not only grab and copy timecode, but automatically find the beginning of each new shot. They then note the timecode number and capture a picture from the start of each clip. In addition, the images are intentionally low resolution and compact so that you can copy your log sheet with these images onto a floppy disk (usually about eighty frames per floppy, minus text). This is an amazing help and obviously superior to the "shuttle and write it down method" you might use for analog linear log sheets. One feature that some of these software programs offer is a type of valuable search; if your shot descriptions are well thought out, you can use the search command to group your shots into various categories that are helpful to your particular edit. For instance, you might want to group and pull up all of the shots of saxophone players, or all of the shots taken indoors or all of the close-up shots. This search capability can help you quickly and easily compile your first rough edit.

Hardware and Software Support

Many companies have entered the market to support your logging needs. Each hardware or software element differs in its level of support and its goals. Once again, because equipment and packages evolve so rapidly, research will need to be done on your end once you have established your needs and expectations.

The issue with organizing multimedia is that they can be very complex in their makeup. Film, video and digital programs are all multimedia, meaning that they are made of more than one component. These components include visuals, audio and sometimes graphics, titles, animation and other features. The difference is that with film and video, you have tangible raw elements. With digital, it is all put onto the hard drive, so the ability to manage your material, to keep track of all your elements, is extremely important.

One of the most crucial responsibilities in the logging stage is naming the tapes. It might be of interest to you to know that some entry-level jobs in postproduction require an assistant to log and name tapes and shots. Although this might seem a simple job, appropriate naming can save much time in the digitizing and editing process. Names should be simple, unique and easily recognizable.

The Paper Edit

When you have finished logging all of the clips, you are ready to go back through and become even more familiar with the footage. You should know it so thoroughly and have such a good feel for the end goal and the audience needs that you can create a paper edit. A paper edit can be accomplished in any number of ways. There are spreadsheets and software packages to guide you through the process, but the easiest (and cheapest) way uses simple index cards. On each card is a written description of a shot (including both image and audio), mit out sound (MOS) image (a shot with no accompanying audio) or wild sound (audio with no accompanying sound such as ambient audio or voiceover). Then, with the card in front of you representing each shot or sound, visualize the film before editing. This paper edit stage allows you to make some basic creative decisions without spending a lot of time and money in an actual edit suite. The log sheet allows you to create the next stage in the editing process, the edit decision list. This written form of your upcoming edit choices will be discussed in Chapter 10.

Footage must be accurately logged in detail. The organization of these digitized clips can be tailored to your specific editing preferences so that the information is logically laid out and easy to locate. Management of your media (whether it is video clips, audio tracks, animation, titles, or some other item) includes shooting for the edit, dealing with the digitization of your visuals and audio, storing your clips, deciding how clips of information are viewed and organized on the screen interface, effectively sorting information and accessing backup sources of information (footage, titles, and other items on removable drives, etc.). The key to any edit is to organize in production and organize in postproduction before you begin the actual edit.

Where Media Go on a Digital Nonlinear System

There is a certain hierarchy of activity in most nonlinear editing systems, and understanding the basics of this and how computers work is important to your successful navigation of the equipment. Each nonlinear system is different, however, and for you to understand your equipment fully, it is imperative that you go through the user manuals and any other supplemental support materials you may have. Nevertheless, in many cases, nonlinear editing software interacts with the hard drive and other equipment in fairly specific ways. Your edit is best accessed *not* from the desktop but only after opening the editing software and then opening various folders and bins to find the "true" version of your edit timeline. We mention this here because in several digital nonlinear systems, it is tempting to simply open your edit from an alias or referential icon on the desktop. However, this is often not the best way to get to the material and its accompanying bins, alternate versions, transition windows and other materials.

Some other very important concepts for you to grasp are what are often called clips (or shots) and media files. In Chapter 6, we discussed how to get your footage from a videotape into the computer, but for the moment, understand that once your footage has been input, you can see little thumbnail photographs of the first frame of each shot that you can double-click on to see the footage. This photograph (or shot title and description) is called the clip. And this is where it gets a bit tricky. What you see on your desktop is *not* the footage. It is simply a reference to the footage, which is stored somewhere else in the system, as illustrated in Figure 7.5. The media file is the footage. And the media file is *not* stored on your desktop. It is stored on some kind of storage device connected to the computer monitor. For this reason, you could take your actual footage off-line (meaning remove it from the computer by unplugging the storage device or taking home the disk) and still see your thumbnail clips on the desktop. However, when you went to play a shot, the computer would tell you that the media is off-line, meaning that it looked for the file but couldn't find it. There are different ways of thinking about this; one is to think of the clip (or shot) as an entry in a library card catalog. It is not the actual book, but it tells where the book is, what is in it, where it was created and so on. The media file (or the actual footage) is like the book. If the "book" isn't there, the "library catalog card" isn't going to do you a lot of good.

When you digitize or input footage into your digital nonlinear editing system, the computer and other equipment do two things: They create media files, and they create a clip at the same time. Remember that the media file is the actual footage and the clip is simply a pointer or reference to the actual video and audio. The reason the system handles it this way is because media files are huge. Motion video and audio take up a sizable amount of space. We almost always store these media on some other storage device, not on the hard drive that the editing software is stored on. Therefore, the computer must have some way of easily referencing our interactions with the actual footage—thus the clips.

The most basic areas of action within many editing software interfaces are covered in Chapter 9 but for the moment let's mention three of them:

1. The project folder: This folder holds all of your clips, bins and editing sequences. You might have more than one project folder if you are working on different versions of a project or if there is more than one editor working on a film.
2. Bins: These are simply files that hold your clips and sequences.
3. Sequence or timeline: This is your working edit or the final version of your edit. It is a series of clips, transitions, graphics and so on.

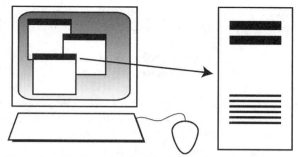

Thumbnail clip seen in bin is a reference/pointer
to the actual footage file on computer system.   **FIGURE 7.5   Where Media Go**

These three items don't take up an enormous amount of space in the computer because they are all simply referencing actual material elsewhere. The project folder, bins and sequence can be thought of in the same way you approach clips; they are what you interact with on the desktop, but the real media they are referring to are somewhere else within the system. So your main goal in media management is making sure that you constantly evaluate what media files you have on-line and determining whether you actually need to access that material. Because media files take up so much space, unless you have unlimited amounts of storage (unlikely!), it will behoove you to be methodical in removing what you don't need.

Remember that you control what is on your various computer drives. It is your responsibility to keep on-line only what you truly need. Otherwise, you are wasting space and possibly slowing down the system. There are often various software packages bundled into systems or integrated steps that can help you manage your material and effectively move or delete media as needed. You might choose to maneuver material because you are running out of drive space and/or because having large amounts of material on-line uses a lot of RAM (random-access memory) and can slow down the workings of the nonlinear system.

Tips for Managing Your Material and Saving Space

Following are a few steps that you might want to consider as you decide how to best manage material on your particular system.

1. Digitize your material at a high compression rate and at low resolution to allow you to access larger amounts of your footage during the rough-cut stage. (Note: If your footage is already digital, you are simply inputting material via Firewire, so this is not a concern.)
2. Once you have made the decision in the rough-cut stage, delete your media and batch digitize only the needed footage at low compression/high resolution. This was covered in Chapter 6.

3. Alternatively, digitize small portions of your media at high resolution and then output to tape, being sure to save the project file that contains this final partial version.

4. Always save a backup version of this project file (remember, this is a pointer to the actual media) on some kind of removable media such as a CD-ROM or an Orb, Jaz or Zip disk.

5. Methodically delete media files that you don't need. Be sure to delete both visuals and audio if they were digitized onto separate scratch disks. If you think you might need that footage again in the future, do not delete the associated clips for this footage. Keeping these clips on hand will allow you to quickly digitize or input the material again because the accompanying time-code will already be referenced in the computer.

6. Get rid of precomputes. These are rendered graphics, transitions and the like that are taking up space in the storage device. They will remain there even if you have subsequently deleted the related shots. Every time you render an effect, it takes up space by creating a file that stays on the drive. If you have too many of these, your drive can become full much more quickly than you expected, and having to keep track of them eats into your RAM.

7. Consolidate your media files. When you digitize or input media, they are often spread over various parts of the designated drives. You can copy the media files associated with clips and sequences onto a different drive that you specify. This is like moving the library book but keeping the catalog card where it was. The catalog card (or the clip in our case) will still be able to point to the book (the media file).

8. Never totally fill your drive. Each drive, no matter how big, needs at least 250 MB of empty space left over in order to best access the footage sitting on it. Some editors go so far as to leave the last gigabyte free. Think of the space as maneuvering room for the drive.

9. Create several different bins for storage—one bin for each tape or each section of your project. This doesn't save space on your drive, but it can make your clips and edit sequences more manageable.

Managing your material in an organized and thoughtful manner is an extremely important responsibility of the digital nonlinear motion picture editor. These systems are complex and powerful, and an orderly and systemized process for storing, naming and accessing your footage, audio and other editing elements will prompt successful editing sessions and allow you to sleep well at night.

8 Storage of Media in the Digital Nonlinear Environment

Storage Devices for Digital Material

Storage of your digitized material is a critically important (and cost-intensive) part of the nonlinear editing system. In general, two types of storage are used: tape-based and disk-based systems. This is where your digitized and compressed material resides in the nonlinear system. There are many different options to consider, and sometimes you will incorporate combinations of storage solutions.

Simply put, storage is the amount of data capacity space there is available. It is stated in computer terminology: kilobytes, megabytes, gigabytes and terabytes.

The most obvious starting place is your main hard drive or a **RAID** (redundant array of inexpensive disks) system. A RAID is simply an interconnected stack of storage disks (see Figure 8.1). Remember that the more storage space you have, the more footage you will be able to digitize and/or the higher the resolution at which you will be allowed to digitize your source footage. You have many options in storage device sizes, from 9 GB to 32 GB to 60 GB and on up. On a basic RAID system, material is "striped" across several disks, and bits of consecutive data are recorded on these different disks. This is called *RAID 0*. The work of one drive is shared over several drives. Without going into elaborate technical detail here, a RAID device promotes faster access to your material and a higher data transfer rate, meaning more megabytes per second (remember the saying "Time is money"?). Another type is *RAID 1*, which provides something called **disk mirroring.** This simply means that information is duplicated as a copy elsewhere on the array as a safety device.

There are now fiber-based disk arrays, such as the one shown in Figure 8.2, that are designed for the needs of data intensive applications such as animation, full-motion video and special effects. These new fiber arrays incorporate increased bandwidth, are multistream (so more information can go through at once), can allow several users to access footage on a main image bank (this is the way most campuses utilize storage space), and are hot-swappable, meaning that the drives

FIGURE 8.1   RAID Storage
Device with Removable
Drawers

can be removed and replaced without powering down your entire system. The storage capability of these improves almost monthly, and what seemed an unbelievable (and unaffordable) amount of storage space last year is attainable today.

What you need to look for when considering a RAID device is quick "seek time." Remember that RAIDs scatter footage all over the array, so the speed of finding footage (seek time) when you need it is critical. You might also want to examine expandability options; some RAID devices allow additional and/or removable drives.

The term *hot-swappable* means that you can remove a storage device without rebooting your entire system. These are large high-end disk drive storage solutions incorporating Ultra-SCSI transporting mechanisms.

The same goes for digital audio tape (DAT) or digital linear tape (DLT). Figure 8.3 shows a DAT deck. The tape is fairly cheap (around $20), and each tape holds about 7 or 8 GB, but the time it takes to access the material directly off of the tape is much longer than most of us want to wait in an edit session. As we mentioned in previous chapters, when exploring any system component, you want to find out about technical support from the manufacturer in case anything goes wrong.

Certainly, if a production has the money, large servers can be used to store footage. Servers are often used in a situation in which multiple editors are working together on a footage-intensive production. Various editors

FIGURE 8.2   Fiber Array

FIGURE 8.3   DAT (Digital Audiotape) Deck

have access to the footage from different computer stations and sometimes even from different parts of the world.

When dealing with storage devices, you must also consider the interface between various pieces of equipment. Simply put, this is the connection from the computer to the storage device—a pathway through which the data move. There are three basic ways to measure the effectiveness of the storage space and disk drive combination: capacity, throughput and access time. Capacity is easy to define. It simply refers to the amount of data the storage device can hold. Throughput is the amount of information a drive can read or write in a given time. Access time is the amount of time required for the hard drive to locate stored information, and is affected by drive fragmentation.

Removable and Portable Storage Devices

Another option is removable storage technology or media backup devices. These let you move between different editing systems with your material or take important files away with you at the end of the day, either as a safety backup of your material or so that you don't have to take up hard drive space with your media. This is an area of particular interest to student nonlinear editors who have to share systems with several other students. Each student saves to his or her own personal storage device at the end of an edit session so that there is enough room on the main hard drive for the next student editor to digitize footage and perform editing functions. If you need to spend several days on an edit or if others are using the same system and the same hard drive, you will most likely need to dump your material back to an additional, removable storage system at the end of the day so that the others can use the hard drive space on the system for their own edits. These removable storage devices are used quite often, and what you need to consider when comparing various devices are speed and portability. Since removable media devices are often used to transport very large files of information from place to place in multimedia production, you must take into consideration how easy it is to install each drive in typical computer systems.

There are currently around thirty different devices available to choose from. These small, removable and portable devices are sometimes referred to as *near hard disks.* They perform in the range of low-storage hard disks and can be used as additional storage or even your primary storage if necessary but are somewhat costly and don't offer a huge amount of storage space; one of Iomega's Jaz disks holds about 2 GB of information. The Jaz drive can also come in the form of a "magazine" holding several removable cartridges, like the one shown in Figure 8.4. Iomega also distributes the Peerless 20-GB portable storage device. Like the Jaz, Syquest's SyJet is a magnetic hard disk; it holds 1.5 GB. Most of the other removable storage disks are magnetic optical devices. As you research disks and drives, remember that in utilizing two-sided drives, only one side can be accessed at a time. If you need to incorporate two pieces of information together, they must be on the same side of the disk.

Digital tape drives (DTD) currently provide the fastest and most cost-effective way of backing up media for the nonlinear editor. Several companies now offer a variety of digital tape drives that can store around 42 GB on each tape, uncompressed.

The tapes themselves cost much less than a removable drive and hold more gigabytes of information. The other critical difference between digital tape back-ups and removable drives is that information on the drives can be accessed in a nonlinear manner. So if you chose to, you could access your source clips directly from a removable drive (but remember that there would not be a whole lot of source material to choose from). Digital tape, by its very nature, is a linear medium. Information is laid down sequentially and can be accessed only in this same manner. However, digital tape backups are used not as an editing access device, but as a storage device holding about 8 GB of media information. This information is then transferred to the hard drive for accessing during the edit. Also included in remov-

FIGURE 8.4   A Jaz Removable Storage Disk

able media options are DVD-ROM, DVD-RAM and CD-R/W technologies. Panasonic offers its PD/CD-ROM, which provides fast access and large storage.

Capture Cards

Capture cards and interfaces are perhaps the most rapidly evolving areas of editing systems, and you should always read the technical specifications and capabilities of them before purchasing. We mention some current transfer rates here, but note that these may have improved by the time you read this. The capture device (the interface that accepts the analog material and begins the digitization process) in nonlinear systems are able, at this point, to take only about 8 or 9 MB per second. This is one of many examples in which one link in the entire nonlinear and computer chain is evolving more slowly than its surrounding links. **Capture cards,** which use dual-stream playback, have begun to catch on, and capture cards in several systems are able to incorporate uncompressed video. Of course, as with all equipment, changes and improvements are rapid, and specific research on high-performance RAIDs and SCSI drives relative to your specific needs is recommended. It is important that you understand the concept of bottlenecks in any computer system. These are various components within the entire system that simply can't transfer information as quickly as other parts of the system. Your goal is to have a computer editing system that either eliminates or minimizes the possibility of these bottlenecks.

Three Types of Interface

Let's talk a bit about these various interfaces between equipment. **SCSI** buses (standing for small computer systems interface) are reliable standby cables. There are various levels of SCSI devices, beginning with SCSI-1, which has a fairly narrow-bandwidth pathway. SCSI-2 can move about 20 MB per second, and an Ultra-SCSI-2 or SCSI-3 can move 40 MB per second. If you need to transfer uncompressed video in real time, you will need to incorporate an Ultra-SCSI-2 drive. Many nonlinear manufacturers allow for the possibility of two SCSI drives (or buses), allowing you to move even more.

Of course, more and more video producers are shooting with the new digital video cameras. Some of these cameras and some of the nonlinear editing systems incorporate a direct digital output/input device called **Firewire** or IEEE 1394. IEEE 1394 is the industry standard name, and Firewire is the brand name Apple Computer gave it for marketing purposes. Firewire is an interface, just like the SCSI drive discussed earlier. Like the SCSI, it is a connection device (see Figure 8.5). However, because the Firewire interface routes digital information (instead of the analog information carried along by SCSI and other similar drives), it doesn't require a separate drive because this particular interface requires a uniform protocol. This setup allows you to go directly from a digital signal to a digital editing system for editing and other image manipulation and back out to digital with virtually no loss in picture or sound quality. This signal could then be broadcast digitally, minimizing any loss in quality. However, many editors and producers using digital cameras as acquisition

**FIGURE 8.5   An IEEE 1394
(Firewire) Cable and
Input/Output Port**

devices go back to analog at the final broadcast or distribution stage, since television sets and VCRs in the United States are still primarily analog.

The best qualities of the Firewire protocol, in contrast to SCSI serial connectors, are speed, ease of use (plug and play, no drives required) and keeping media in the digital domain. Many producers and editors consider Firewire the missing link in the low-cost digital world. This digital interface technology allows you to transfer digital information using inexpensive cables and simple connectors. Sony, Panasonic and many other companies have introduced Firewire export/import devices on their digital cameras. Firewire is now a firmly established protocol. Microsoft, Compaq, Texas Instruments and IBM have jumped into this interface by supporting IEEE 1394 technology. With Firewire or similar future interfaces, digital video brings cameras and computers into full integration. Beyond that, Firewire is now used to connect digital video disk players, digital still cameras, digital satellite systems and web browsers. Industry experts predict that in the near future, it will also be used to connect home theatre components, audio systems, telephones, security systems, consumer electronic devices and computers. Eventually, Firewire may compete with Ethernet in carrying information. What makes Firewire even more inviting is that devices connected through the Firewire port can be hot-swappable, so the computer doesn't have to be rebooted to connect or disconnect a peripheral device. This eliminates the downtime required by rebooting using the SCSI interface.

For more information on Firewire, point your Internet browser to www.apple.org and search for "firewire," or go to http://www.adaptec.com/firewire/1394.html.

The **universal serial bus** (USB) is another interface you might want to consider (see Figure 8.6). The USB is similar to the Firewire protocol, but while Firewire can pass data at a rate of 400 MB per second, the USB calls for a maximum bandwidth of just 12 MB per second—a big difference. However, USBs are stable interfaces and ideal for devices that do not require a high rate of date transfer. In other words, a USB connection is perfect for connecting your mouse or personal organizer to your computer.

Because digitization and compression so radically alter the video signal and because your goal is to output the highest-quality broadcast signal possible, many nonlinear systems now incorporate internal color bars, waveform monitors and vectorscopes. These are all measuring devices used by engineers and other video operators for test and set-up purposes. **Color bars** are reference colors produced by a color bar generator and include red, green, blue, yellow, magenta, cyan, white and black bars. A **waveform monitor** measures the luminance or brightness of the video signal, and the **vectorscope** measures the parameters of the color within the signal. Figure 8.7 shows a waveform monitor and vectorscope. Using these devices, with the color bars as a stable reference, the footage and the equipment are calibrated. This is important so that you don't end up with footage in your system that is washed out or off-color. Your goal is a clean, sharp, appropriately colored image.

These devices are not extremely difficult to use, but let's talk about one of the biggest complaints about the huge popularity of desktop nonlinear editing. One of the great things (and one of the only great things) about analog linear editing was the final, on-line edit. During this on-line edit, you hired a postproduction house and an on-line editor to produce the final, broadcast-quality version of your edit, complete with all of the graphics, transitions, sound mixing, and so on. Such an on-line edit is expensive, but the result is a professional edit. You paid the money and got a very slick product. The money paid during an on-line session went not only toward the high-end equipment, but also toward the expertise of the on-line editor, the tape loader, the sound mixer, the graphics artist and others. Their individual

FIGURE 8.6   A USB Port and Cable

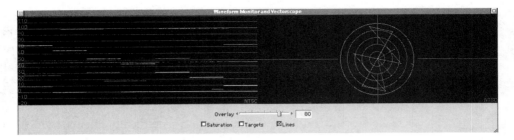

FIGURE 8.7   A Waveform Monitor and Vectorscope

expertise in the various areas of a professional video edit were incorporated into your final master video. They are professionals at sound mixing and equalizing, **timing** (color correcting), and so on.

So let's jump now to your scenario: a new nonlinear editor who is excited about the equipment and its possibilities, ready to follow your calling as an editor. But maybe you weren't trained in video engineering. Maybe vectorscopes and waveform monitors are still alien devices to you. Maybe you prefer to just eyeball the color corrections and hope no one has tweaked your monitors. So you do just that and begin your edit. Maybe you will get lucky, and everything will look great when it is laid back to tape. But maybe it won't. Maybe you will have wasted a lot of time because you didn't want to take on all of the jobs required by a nonlinear editor in actually performing a final, on-line nonlinear edit. You wanted to do only the fun parts—in other words, the editing and fancy transitions. This is one of the biggest downfalls of nonlinear on-line editing. You are required to perform many, many jobs, most of which demand that you spend time training to fully understand functions and outcomes.

If you hire an on-line digital nonlinear editor, that person (or someone working with them) will be an expert in encoding and compressing the material. For example, under the MPEG umbrella, there are two ways of encoding: real time and non–real time. Real time encoding and compressing is faster, eliminates human intervention and results in higher data transfer rates. The engineer doesn't really manipulate the process but instead just lets things run. The source material and the equipment through which it is running determine the picture quality. On the other hand, non–real time encoding gives you lower data delivery rates but a higher-quality image. In this case, human intervention into the process occurs at every step. So the final quality is based not only on the source footage and equipment, but also on the talent and ability of the engineer (the title for this position is *compressionist*). This expert-assisted encoding is expensive but gives you a highly skilled engineer who controls the compression at every phase, ensuring a high standard. So remember, if you are performing your own footage compression and final nonlinear edit, you can't sit back and rely on the expertise of others. It's your baby in many ways. You must become a technician, not just an artist.

CHAPTER 9

Graphic Interface, Areas of Action, Terms and Processes

Basic Areas of Action and Windows on the Desktop

Although each system may call them by a different name, there are certain common features you will address within the graphic interface. The most common areas of action within systems are the following:

> Please note that each system's manual names these windows differently. What might be a timeline for one system is the program window for another. In each case, the term refers to the place on the desktop interface where the film is put together. Be sure to learn the proper terminology for the system you are now using and be willing to relearn terminology when you move on to a different nonlinear system.

- The clip bin is where the source footage is located and can be viewed with frame-by-frame control and playback from in and out points (see Figure 9.1).
- The **preview window** or edit suites are where in and out edit points are set (see Figure 9.2). Many systems allow for full-speed previewing with the ability to compile only those sections of a preview that have changed, providing a significantly improved response time. The preview or monitor window allows you to preview edits and to watch the edited project. Just as in analog video editing, you should always preview your edits before rendering them. Although it's easy to change your edit using the nonlinear system, you may still save some valuable time by previewing first.
- The **program window,** construction window or timeline is where you assemble the film. Specifically, this is the window where the film is put together; all of the visual and audio elements are dropped into this window (see Figure 9.3). Additionally, you may deal with some combination of capture, clip and trim functions, and transition parameters as well as title and motion path editors and graphics layering.

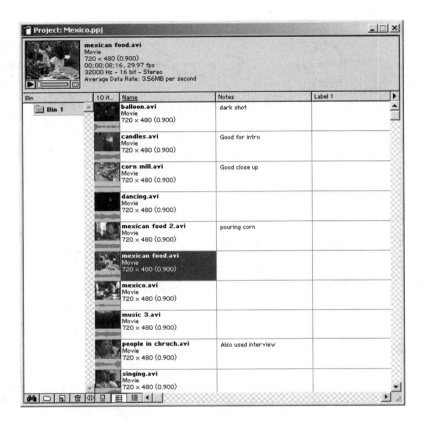

FIGURE 9.1   Bin with Clips

Becoming familiar with the specific areas of action and capabilities of your specific system will require dedicated time reading the manual and, if available, completing the system tutorial.

Work with the clients has changed in two profound ways. The first is in their personal exposure to our craft via television at home. They are very fluent in the look of what I call MTV-style editing. They walk in with that in their hip pocket already, and they have preconceptions about what they want. The second is that we now have the capability to do high-end graphics. They experience that for the first time and realize that they can make changes to the look of a show. There are advantages to this, because we can be more responsive to the client. Before, you might plant your feet a bit because with older technologies, it was more difficult to make changes. But now the editor and the rest of the team can be more flexible.

Dan Sparks, Director of Post Production at Four Square Productions, San Diego, California

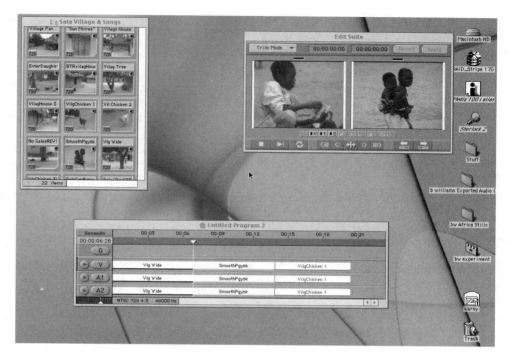

FIGURE 9.2   Preview Window

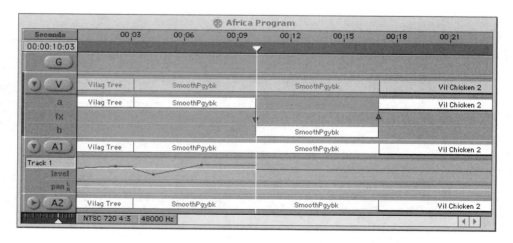

FIGURE 9.3   Timeline

A Few Examples of Visual Interface
Elements for Various Systems

Let's compare the visual interface of various systems in order to provide one indication of how various systems differ in layout and approach. While the basic interface varies some, Media 100, Fast's Video Machine and Sony systems incorporate an **A/B roll model** with two video tracks (A and B) and a transition track in between. If you want to dissolve between shot A and shot B, you must provide a physical overlap of these two tracks on the timeline. In other words, there is a space where track A "lies on top of" track B. In between this area, in the transition track, the editor inserts the dissolve transition icon (see Figure 9.4). When this section is then played in the timeline monitor window, the transition takes place. The Avid family of systems did not integrate this A/B roll model. Instead, on these systems, a single layer of video can be quickly edited together, with added transitions to bridge the cut points. Some editors prefer this method because it is slightly faster—first figure out what shot goes next to what shot and then go back to concentrate on your transitions.

The previous example hints at different design approaches. As you learn a new digital nonlinear editing system, be aware that you will be able to move with relative ease on to any number of other systems but that you will need to spend some time and effort to become familiar with the minor differences in layout and approach.

Within the timeline of nonlinear systems, there is a current time indicator arrow or slider that, if grabbed with the mouse, allows you to scroll through the current version of the edit (see Figure 9.5). For scrolling or regular-speed playback to be of real value to an editor, the playback rate of the image and audio must be precisely controllable, and during playback, the rate must remain perfectly steady. It is difficult to make precise editing decisions when the footage jumps and stutters. Seek out software and hardware systems in which efforts have been made to smooth out the motion.

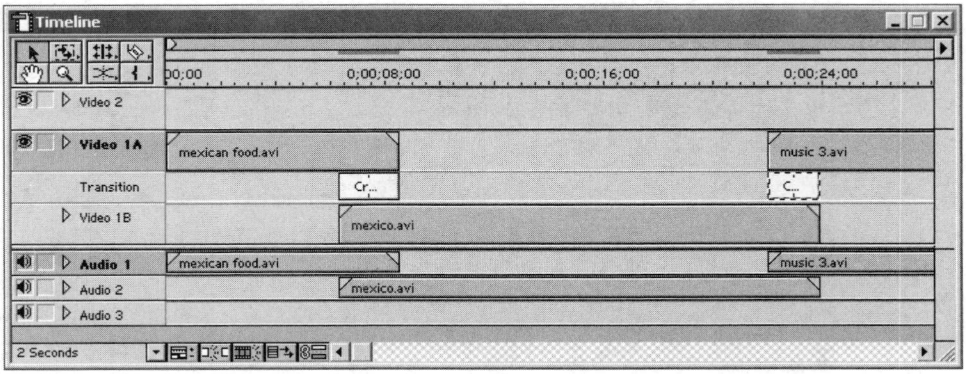

FIGURE 9.4   A/B Roll Editing

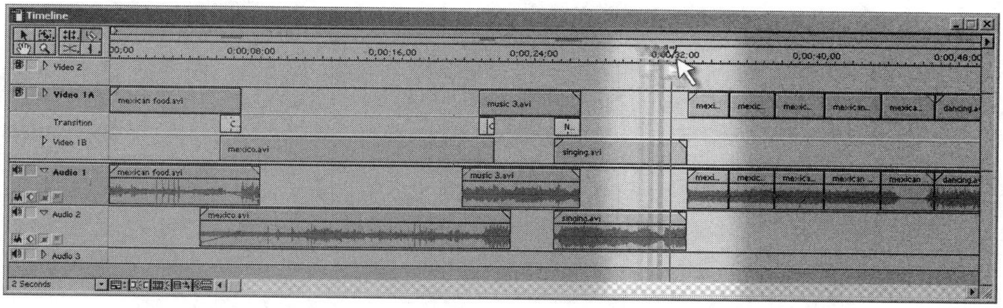

FIGURE 9.5   Scrolling through the Timeline

Various nonlinear manufacturers incorporate a wide variety of additional tool types into their systems including items such as ripple and rolling edits (if you insert a shot in between two existing shots in the edit, the material is rippled or rolled down to make room for it), visual/audio track locking and unlocking (allowing the editor to move only the visual or audio portion of a sync piece of footage while keeping other elements in the timeline in place) and trimming windows (supporting fine-tune editing and the addition or deletion of frames). Figure 9.6 shows locked tracks in a nonlinear system, and Figure 9.7 illustrates the use of a trim window.

Many nonlinear manufacturers have really gone for the "click, drag and drop" method of moving your video, audio and transitions around, while others encourage editors to make use of a simple keystroke method to accomplish various functions.

The Lightworks interface differs radically in many ways from most other nonlinear editors. The Lightworks system, which was recently bought by an American company, was designed by British film editors who recognized the movement toward digital editing but were unwilling to give up the film editing mindset that has been proven over the years. Software engineers incorporated their ideas and created an "electronic flatbed." *Flatbed* is the generic name of a film editing system such as a Steenbeck in which the various reels of positive film

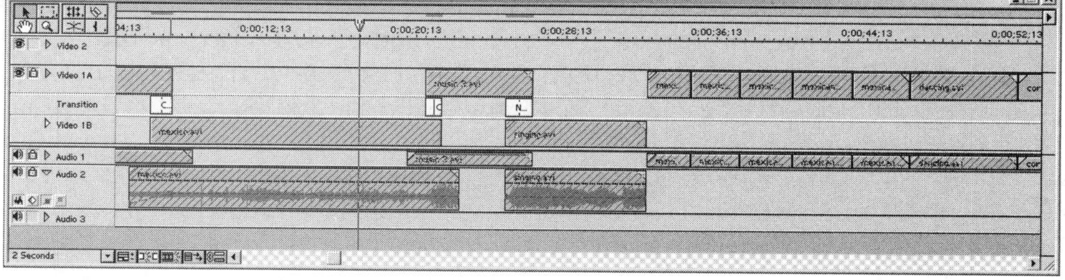

FIGURE 9.6   Locked Tracks

FIGURE 9.7   Trim Window

workprint and magnetic sound stock are cut and spliced together. In the Light-works system, "strips of film" are pulled by "sprockets" in a very responsive way using a simple lever. The lever controls the direction and speed in which the clips move on the screen. In addition to this large lever, there are only a few other but-tons for various functions. The Lightworks interface incorporates several visual icons not seen in other systems, including sprocket tape guides and a "metal" splicer. Various "doors" allow you to enter different scenes, which can be assigned to different people working on the same subject or even different edit versions of the same program. All in all, Lightworks is unique in that it truly caters to the film mindset.

In the various nonlinear systems, audio tracks differ in appearance and capa-bilities. The number of audio tracks differs, and the ways in which you manipulate the signal vary as well. Some systems offer an option of expanding the audio time-line vertically so that the editor can better "see" the audio levels. Several manufac-turers have incorporated what has come to be known as **rubberbanding** your audio (see Figure 9.8). Within the audio track, when expanded and enlarged verti-cally, the editor can mark key frames, and the audio levels can be dragged up and down visually.

On some systems, such as Avid, the editor can adjust levels at each cut point, and the system will remember when the level was changed. Audio crossfades are possibly a bit quicker on the Avid system, since a dissolve can be used to bridge two clips instead of overlapping the audio edit points and then rubberbanding the audio up on one track and down on the other (see Figure 9.9).

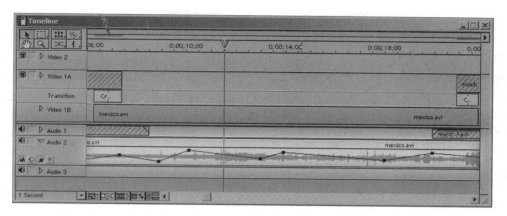

FIGURE 9.8   Rubberbanding Audio

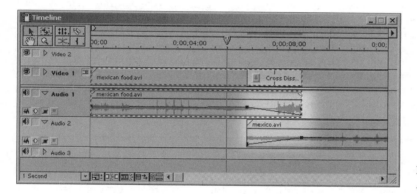

FIGURE 9.9   Crossfading Audio

We should point out the importance of wearing headphones when editing, whether on an analog video system or in the digital domain. Remember that editing is about telling a story, which requires not only the construction of visuals, but also the effective manipulation of audio. To perform truly critical audio edits, one needs to use headphones. How can you expect to make the precise cut when people around you are talking or a police car blasting its siren drives by?

In the early years of digital nonlinear systems, audio manipulation seemed to take a back seat to visual editing and graphic capabilities. Luckily, the designers of these various systems quickly heard the cries of motion picture editors who wanted just as much flexibility and support on the important audio side of motion pictures. At its most basic, nonlinear editing systems allow the editor to raise and lower audio levels from within the system. This is often accomplished by simply rubberbanding the audio line as discussed previously. However, as these systems are now often used to complete a final, broadcast-quality video or a digital edit that will then be transferred back to film, editors needed additional audio options. Many systems have internal audio-equalizing capabilities and audio filter integration (see Figure 9.10).

Among dozens of other options, such internal equalization and audio manipulation allow the editor to easily accentuate a female voice-over with the proper filter, clip out the high-end frequencies of unwanted wind noise or make a young child's voice sound metallic and robotlike.

Most nonlinear digital editing systems include many functions other than basic editing functions. Still store, 2-D and 3-D digital animation effects, titles, keyframing and multiple visual layering are areas you will want to examine.

Many digital cameras have menu settings that allow you to manipulate the video image as it is being recorded. These might include a strobing effect, color saturation, movement streaking and black and white. Although it is tempting to make use of these settings, it is much smarter to simply record your material, concentrating on clean and clear audio, proper lighting, appropriate composition and so on. If you are using a digital nonlinear editing system, you will have the option of adding these and any number of other digital effects to both your visuals and audio during the postproduction stage and will not have committed yourself to one look (possibly the wrong look) in the production phase. Your original footage should be as professional as possible and give you as many options as possible, not keep you tied down to one particular look.

The most important consideration in exploring a system's graphic user interface is how it works for your editing style. Are you a Mac person, a DOS person, a film-trained editor? Do you want to fully utilize an edit decision list? Are you in need of fancy graphics? All of these needs will affect the interface of your chosen system. Just make sure it is clean and easy to navigate.

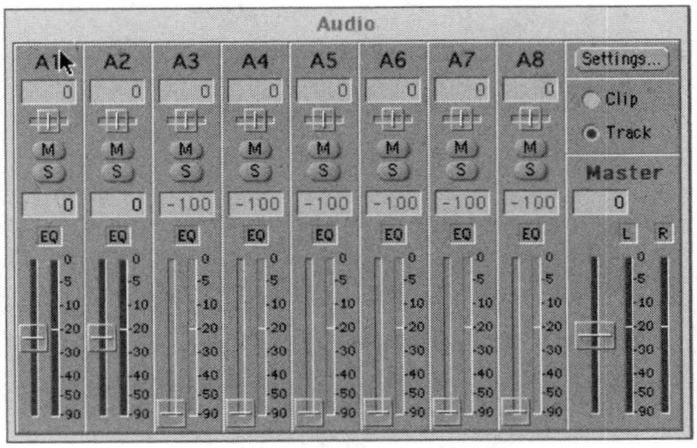

FIGURE 9.10   Audio Equalizing

One or More Monitors

As you become familiar with various systems and with the working styles of different nonlinear operators, you will notice that some setups incorporate two monitors. This option is discussed in Chapter 5, "The Digital Nonlinear Workflow and Work Environment," and Chapter 13, "Choosing the Right System." Whether to use the dual-monitor option is ultimately a personal call and depends on whether you prefer a visually compacted work space or like to have various windows spread out. Some interfaces are simply cluttered, requiring the user to constantly rearrange various windows on the screen to see the ones needed. Instead of simply using a large 20-inch screen, some editors opt for two separate monitors. Using a graphics board interface, the mouse functions and so on can move across the two screens, with bins on one side and the timeline on the other. Figures 9.11 and 9.12 show a single-monitor setup and a dual-monitor setup, respectively.

FIGURE 9.11   One-Computer-Monitor Setup with Added NTSC Monitor

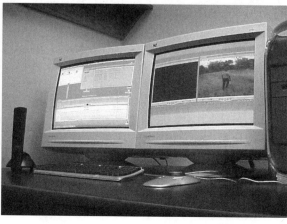

FIGURE 9.12   Two-Computer-Monitor Setup

Some Tricks of the Digital Nonlinear Editing Trade

Because you will probably soon be editing on a nonlinear editing system (if you aren't already), let us take a moment here to give you a few tips or tricks of the nonlinear editing trade. We cannot emphasize enough the importance of discipline and methodical working.

1. Make sure all of your peripheral hardware, including external storage drives, speakers and separate monitors, are turned on. Then after all of these pieces of equipment are fully up to speed, turn the main computer on. This will allow the master hard drive to recognize everything it is connected to and to communicate with each piece successfully.

2. Perhaps the easiest way to edit on a nonlinear system is to take advantage of the fact that you can go back into a program and fine-tune it. This doesn't need to be done on your first attempt. So work on being methodical, and follow these steps: Choose the footage you want and input it into the storage space, edit by putting it in the correct order, thus creating a rough cut; trim the shots, paying attention to pacing and tension; adjust and manipulate the audio; import graphics, and add effects and titles.

3. Make sure that if you are using a system with other editors, you open your own project and footage bins and not theirs. Each nonlinear system is set up differently, but usually you will access some type of user name and then a master program document that holds your own bins and program (edit). Most systems allow you to set specific user preferences and settings for each user.

4. Save various versions of your rough cut edit so that you can compare and get a feel for the different stages.

5. Many editors create a new bin for each tape being input. Call the bin the same name that you labeled the tape.

6. Remember that for broadcast-quality resolution, you can only have 2–3 minutes of full-motion footage per gigabyte. Bear this in mind when you are close to filling up all of your storage space. You never want to completely fill up a drive.

7. Use the vectorscope to set colors in the system. You should have carefully calibrated color bars laid down. Pay special attention to the colors red and yellow, as they make up the basis for many skin tones.

8. Make a bin on the desktop with bars, tone and countdown for easy access.

9. Don't have too many windows open at a time. Take care not to clutter your visual interface. You should have a relationship with the footage and the edit, and too much visual clutter can detract from the editor's mindset.

10. Remember that an excellent editor is one frame off of the perfect edit, a good editor is four frames off, and beginners are often ten frames or more off. Make one frame (or no frames off!) your goal.

11. Consider making a sequence that simply strings out all virgin shots from the bin so that you can review them all together.

12. Keep your sync locks always turned on unless for some reason you need to unsync visual footage from its accompanying audio.

Most digital nonlinear editing systems allow you to lock or unlock the various visual and audio tracks in the timeline. Why might you be concerned with this? Imagine that you are in the final stages of your edit and you have synced your music with the various other audio and visual elements. If you need to make a minor adjustment in the length or placement of one small visual shot, you might inadvertently alter the placement of other elements within your timeline. Maybe the music has moved over as well or you have caused another shot to get shorter. Problems may abound. However, if you have kept all of your other tracks locked, the only thing you will be moving is within the unlocked track. You can move your one shot and then lock that track back down to keep all elements safe and in place.

The Time Factor in Nonlinear Editing

One word on the time factor in nonlinear editing: These systems allow you to make quicker edits and come out with multiple versions of rough edits before making final decisions. However, what you need to consider is this: Are you truly saving time? Or are you merely trying more cuts and spending just as much time—if not more—as you might on a linear analog system? Although this may seem to be a setup question, it deserves to be examined. Nonlinear editors are not necessarily faster editors, even though they have easier access to footage and ease in manipulation of materials. In fact, nonlinear editors often take longer to complete an edit simply because there are so many options to consider. As we mentioned in Chapter 7, "Management of Your Material," this is where planning, logging and editing with a goal in mind can help immensely.

10 The Edit Decision List

Definition of the Edit Decision List

The **edit decision list (EDL)** is a listing of all the edits and transitions in chronological order and their relationship to the original source material. This list is necessary if you are editing first with an off-line system and then finishing on an on-line editing system. It is also important if you are planning to complete a rough edit on a nonlinear system and then go back in and batch digitize only the necessary footage for a fine cut on the same system. If you have edited on a nonlinear system and then plan to complete the original cut on film, the conformer or negative cutter must have an EDL. In this particular case, the EDL will include the film edge numbers. (See the Chapter 11, "Shooting Film and Editing on a Digital Nonlinear System," for an example of a film EDL.)

Sometimes a new master print or videotape of the project is required months and even years afterward, and the EDL will enable a new master to be made from the source material. This ability to make accurate new video masters was almost impossible before the 1972 invention of timecode. (See Chapter 7, "Management of Your Material," for more information on timecode.) Since the mid-1990s, all nonlinear editing systems have incorporated timecode to identify source material and to develop the EDL. The system keeps track of your source in and out points and the transition types and shot durations, and it produces the EDL on your instruction.

Off-Line and On-Line: What Do They Mean When You Are Shooting and Finishing on Film?

If you need a review, go back to Chapter 7, "Management of Your Material," to refamiliarize yourself with the off-line and on-line editing processes. Remember that these terms actually have two meanings. The definition we will use in this chapter refers to the various stages of postproduction: the initial editing of the production that is often a rough cut and usually uses duplicates of the original source material and the final stage of editing the production that results in a final and professional edit. However, remember that *off-line* can also refer to material that has not yet been digitized in the system. Sometimes when you are editing with digital

FIGURE 10.1   An Off-Line Analog Video Editing System

nonlinear equipment, the system will indicate that an edit can't be performed because the footage is off-line.

Figure 10.1 shows an off-line analog video editing system. In an off-line edit for a project that originated on film, the duplicates of the master footage will have timecode incorporated on them. And in the case of film, the edge numbers (numbers placed on the film by the manufacturer to be used as reference by editor) are usually burned onto the video transfer as a visual reference. In this situation, the editor often makes a handwritten EDL to double-check against the EDL produced by the system. The negative film conformer will also visually check the edge numbers against the original film. See Chapter 11, "Shooting Film and Editing on a Digital Nonlinear System" for more information.

Another reason for off-line editing is that broadcast-quality (on-line) systems such as the one shown in Figure 10.2 are usually very expensive to rent by the hour and many offline systems are less expensive to rent and/or own. In off-line editing, the editor can select the best shots and performances, cutting the visuals and the sound together and easily making revisions. Most off-line nonlinear systems can output up to Digital Beta and D2 (see Figure 10.3).

However, owing to restricted memory capacity, these systems usually compress the signal. The digitized footage is not the same as the original source, and some image quality in this digitized edit version is lost. Therefore, ordinarily, the output from the off-line edit is not broadcast quality. In addition, because of this compression, the output projects poorly in larger-screen formats and venues.

Ordinarily, the online editor doesn't make radical editing changes in the off-line cut but instead assembles the master from the offline EDL. The editor might do some video noise cleaning and some other formatting necessary to complete the master to broadcast standards. It is a good idea for the editor to be present at this online session, as some decisions may be necessary in the final master edit. In the

FIGURE 10.2   An On-Line High-End Video Editing Suite

FIGURE 10.3   D2 and Beta SP Videotapes

past, some off-line nonlinear systems inadvertently added or dropped some frames from the EDL and this did not show up until the master was viewed on the more powerful on-line system. Sometimes a transition might look different on the on-line system, and its duration must be adjusted for the final master. In high-end postproduction facilities, where these on-line edits are usually carried out, the on-line editor is a staff member of the facility, and the editor of the production and possibly others involved, including the producer and director, are in the editing suite as this final edit is carried out. Even with a written EDL that notes all of the editing decisions, it is a good idea for the editor to be available for any questions the on-line staff may have.

The EDL Format

From one system to another, the EDL is the method of transferring the edit data. If you know you are going to finish on an on-line system, you need to determine the EDL format that the on-line system you are going to use can read. Some EDL formats such as CMX and Sony are similar, but small differences can make them incompatible. However, computers usually have no problem converting one format to another if this is done in advance. Many EDLs are ASCII files using alphanumeric character and/or text-only. Ordinarily, whatever disk type they are saved on, they can be viewed with a word processor and edited if the disk can be opened.

Communication with the on-line editor will help you to know what EDL format the on-line system can read and the capabilities and limitations of that system so that you can create readable information. This communication will aid you during the edit when you are assigning reel names during digitization and editing and creating and saving the EDL. Past experience has shown that it's a good idea to try to keep your reel names five to seven characters in length. These reel names are assigned during digitization. Always remember that finding out about the on-line system's format needs before you begin to digitize will avoid time-consuming and costly trouble during the final master edit. It is a good idea to send your on-line editor a test EDL so that the editor can check for things such as format problems. This can save time, headaches and money in the on-line session.

Preparing for Editing and the EDL as Production Begins

When you are editing a video project, it is a good idea to ask the video cameraperson to use preset hours so that an editor can easily distinguish between tapes. The first tape could start with 01:00:00:00 and so on as the production progresses. When the production passes 24:00:00:00, it must restart at 01:00:00:00 because timecode is related to the number of hours in a day. This means that each succeeding tape will need a unique number or name so that the source material can easily be found in the editing and final edit stages. Another way in which many productions label source material with timecode is to have the first day start with 01:00:00:00, the second day start with 02:00:00:00 and so forth, as shown in Figure 10.4. Documentary productions and sporting events can also assign different timecode for different phases of the production. Assigning different timecode numbers to each tape speeds up the editing process and saves time during the final edit.

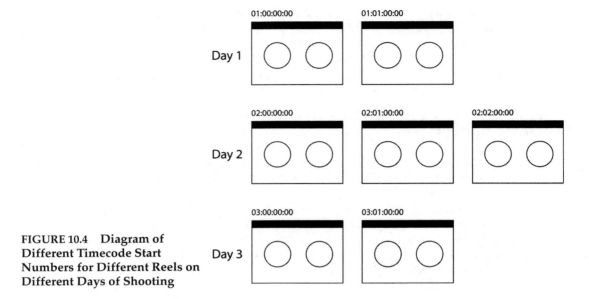

FIGURE 10.4   Diagram of Different Timecode Start Numbers for Different Reels on Different Days of Shooting

Timecode Burn-In

In editing a film project, timecode can be placed directly on 16mm or 35mm negative film by using an Aaton, Arri or Panavision film camera that has the capability of burning the timecode. However, most productions forgo this method and have the transfer lab place the timecode directly onto the video transfer as it is being copied from the original film negative (see Figure 10.5). This also works because most high-end editing software has the capability to make up for the difference in frames between the film edge numbers and the created timecode. This discrepancy will be compensated for on the final EDL negative cutting list (see Chapter 11). In lower-end nonlinear systems, additional software such as Slingshot may be needed to help generate the EDL with compensation for the keycodes and timecodes.

EDL Elements

The following elements are ordinarily included in a normal EDL. Format differences mentioned above may cause the element names and positions to vary, but the information will basically be the same. You should be familiar with these to understand the value of the EDL.

1. At the top of each EDL is the *title* and whether or not this list is recorded in drop frame or non–drop frame timecode. For various reasons, the source timecode will sometimes change from non–drop frame to drop frame. When this happens, the list will be interrupted and will denote that the timecode mode has changed from non–drop frame to drop frame and vice versa.

00:44:31:10

**FIGURE 10.5   Timecode
Burn-in on Video Dub**

2. An *edit* or *event number* is an identifier that begins with the number 1 and increases with each event until the last one. Edit numbers are simply a single edit, and event numbers are used in the final edit to call up an individual edit. Edit numbers cover an entire cut from the in point to the out point. When there are split edits, they can take up two lines on the EDL but will only have one edit number.

3. The *source ID/reel number* is the number of the tape, video disk or other storage site where the source material for that edit is located. Other sources such as digital effects are auxiliary sources, and the Source ID/Reel number will have an "X" after the number.

4. The *mode ID* tells you if the edit takes place in picture or sound or both and will identify this usually by the use of "V" for video, "A1" and "A2" and so forth for audio, and both "V" and audio channel(s) if the edit includes both.

5. *Source in* and *source out* are the timecode numbers for the beginning of the edit and the end of the edit.

6. *Keycode in* and *keycode out* are the industry names for the edge numbers taken from source film materials. Some nonlinear systems can track these by using the FLEX file provided by the lab that made the transfer from film to video. In some systems, the keycode and its identifying timecode may have to be logged by hand in the initial digitizing. The keycode or edge numbers are very important if you are going to finish on film, and they are the only way the film negative conformer can cut the negative and match it back to your nonlinear final edit. (See Chapter 11 for more details on editing a film production on a nonlinear system.)

7. *Transition* tells if the edit is a cut ("C"), a wipe ("W"), a dissolve ("D") or a key ("K"). Other than cuts, transitions are followed by a duration time, which is

usually noted in frames. Some keys and wipes may have additional letters indicating what type of effect is being used. However, these codes are not standardized from system to system. You might want to make an additional handwritten or typed note of this edit number to indicate which type was used.

8. *Record in* and *record out* indicates where the source shot is to be recorded on the master. This enables a change of duration in one to occur without changing the source in and source out points of any edit on the list, but all record in and record out points change for every edit number following the one that was changed. The nonlinear system effects these changes automatically, which eases the work on the part of the editor.

Figure 10.6 shows a video EDL, and Figure 10.7 shows a film EDL.

Another EDL for the audio tracks and sweetening of the audio should also be made before the audio finish. See Chapter 11, "Shooting Film and Editing on a Digital Nonlinear Editing System," for more information on sound.

The edit decision list is one of the most important parts of the editing process. It is sometimes the only means of communication between the editor and the online editor and, with film, between the film editor and the negative conformer. An incorrect EDL will result in an incorrect final product with perhaps disastrous

```
Text: D:\MEXICO.PPJ.EDL                                              _ □ ×

TITLE: MEXICO
FCM: NON-DROP FRAME
FCM: DROP FRAME
001   001   AA/V   C           00:00:59:28 00:01:06:09 01:00:00:00 01:00:06:09
FCM: NON-DROP FRAME
001   002   AA/V   D      067 01:00:00:10 01:00:16:01 01:00:06:09 01:00:22:00
EFFECTS NAME IS CROSS DISSOLVE
REEL 001 IS CLIP MEXICAN FOOD.AVI
REEL 002 IS REEL B.REEL AND CLIP MEXICO.AVI
FCM: DROP FRAME
002   001   AA/V   C           00:03:25:13 00:03:25:13 01:00:22:00 01:00:22:00
FCM: NON-DROP FRAME
002   002   AA/V   D      058 01:00:16:01 01:00:17:29 01:00:22:00 01:00:23:28
EFFECTS NAME IS CROSS DISSOLVE
REEL 001 IS CLIP MUSIC 3.AVI
REEL 002 IS REEL B.REEL AND CLIP MEXICO.AVI
SPLIT: VIDEO DELAY= 00:00:01:28
FCM: DROP FRAME
003   001   AA     C           00:03:25:13 00:03:32:05 01:00:22:00 01:00:28:22
003   001   V      C           00:03:27:11 00:03:32:05 01:00:23:28 01:00:28:22
REEL 001 IS CLIP MUSIC 3.AVI
=>
=> CONVERTED CMX 3600 EDL.   REEL NAME CONVERSIONS:
->   B.REEL  =002
```

FIGURE 10.6   Video Edit Decision List

Optical List:

Lethal Seduction Picture	6 optical units all counts are inclusive (inside/inside) all colors are specified as RGB

OPTICAL #1   Assemble Event #1   total length: 24+13

Optical Footage	Sequence Footage	Desc	Length	+- A side--------------------+ First/Last Key	Cam Roll	+- B side--------------------+ First/Last Key	Cam Roll
0	0	Leader	6+00	LEADER			
95	95			LEADER			
96	96	Fade In	3+00	LEADER		KU 72 0704-5703&16	8
143	143					5706&03	
144	144	Normal	15+13			KU 72 0704-5706&04	8
396	396					KU 72 0704-5718&16	

FIGURE 10.7   Film Edit Decision List

results. Therefore the editor must take time to ensure that he or she understands how the particular nonlinear system will generate its EDL. Communication with the on-line editor will help to ensure the proper format for saving the EDL to a floppy disk, which the on-line editor can use in their system. This will speed up the input for the final edit and save time and money.

Other disadvantages of these nonlinear systems are what I call "blink of an eye." If you are using either film or analog video, you have to shuttle through the footage. You have the ability to go through it and become familiar with it. Even though I am a believer in nonlinear technologies, I kind of agree with those who lament the going away of these older systems that force you to look at the footage over and over as you scan through material. Nonlinear editing is murderous on people who don't label and log well. They can't find anything. This is critical. Organization is so important. There are really only three aspects of film editing. I call these the "Three L's": labeling, logging and lugging. Do these carefully and well, and you'll be okay. Because with digital you don't have the physicality you have with film. You can't look for "the small roll with the blue leader" if you are missing a shot. There is no physical bin to look down in to see if the shot is there. You have to know what the shot was called and access it via the computer.

Jonathan Mednick, Founder and President of Other Picture Production Company and Co-Producer and Editor of the "American High" Television Series, New York City

CHAPTER

11 Shooting Film and Editing on a Digital Nonlinear System

With the rapid changes in image capturing, why be concerned with film, a technology that is over one hundred years old? Digital video is developing rapidly and has come a long way toward looking as good as film. The images from digital still photography, digital enlargements and higher-end video are getting closer to the quality of film and, most of the time, are more convenient than traditional film recording methods. However, many motion picture producers still choose to originate on film.

Digital versus Film

Despite the claims of the HDTV sales and rental companies, digital video hasn't yet quite achieved the quality of celluloid images and projection for larger audiences. Using identical lighting and filters and comparable lens tests, digital video doesn't hold highlights, it averages the light (thus causing a color shift when underexposed), it muddies shadow detail and it still has a problem accurately representing skin tone. The color red bleeds and blurs with many digital cameras.

Film has a texture and depth that digital video hasn't been able to duplicate. Digital shooting has not yet reached film's image range. Having said this, however, we suggest that you look at digital video and film as different and equal rather than seeing digital video as some cheap substitute for film. There are certainly situations in which form and content would indicate a preference for digital video over film. And, of course, there are situations in which your budget will make the same call.

Another Reason You Might Consider Originating on Film

Another reason to continue to use film is that it is used worldwide in the same formats. Because of this, film is still the primary origination format for feature films, many television shows and most commercials. In today's world market system, a feature film, television show or commercial can be sold for use in many different countries. Television standards vary from one country to the next. Some use NTSC, some use PAL (phase alternate line), some use PAL M, some use PAL N and some use versions of SECAM (sequential couleur á memoire). But film is film. Every country uses the same few available options (width difference, film stock difference, etc.).

There are some technical problems in shooting on film, which normally runs at twenty-four frames per second, and then editing on a digital nonlinear video system, which (in North America) reads information at NTSC video's standard thirty frames per second. Some in the industry are working on dealing with these by developing HDTV twenty-four-frame digital video.

However, twenty-four-frame high definition with separate equipment for twenty-five, thirty-, or sixty-frame video is currently not economically practical for most manufacturers and production/postproduction companies. Some manufacturers, such as Panasonic, are taking the approach that only multiple-use systems and production devices will lead to the extensive and lasting success of HDTV.

Several methods of scan conversion exist to try to overcome some of these problems, such as real-time scan conversion. This procedure converts the original format's time into the same time in the new format.

Many distributors choose to transfer directly from the original film negative to NTSC (U.S. standard for video), PAL (many European and other countries) or SECAM (many Asian countries) video, thus keeping the rich film image and avoiding the artifacts in transferring from NTSC video to PAL/SECAM video or vice versa. To prepare for this process, many producers are editing their film projects using nonlinear systems to create the EDL for the negative cutter and conformer. They conform the negative to the list, and a low-contrast print is struck to transfer to PAL or NTSC.

On some nonlinear systems that output to Digital Beta, D2, Beta SP and/or PAL broadcast quality, the producers are going directly to the tape from the nonlinear system. The finalization of American and European HDTV standards may bring an end to many of these transfer problems in the near future.

Feature Films on Digital

At this writing, George Lucas has just finished shooting Episode II of the Star Wars epic series on a special digital experimental camera developed for him by Sony. The production crew adapted many different film lenses to the camera to improve its image-capturing capabilities; this also caused the equipment to be quite large, bulky and somewhat difficult to move around. However, the same Sony 24P cameras are used without the special lenses on A&E's "100 Centre St." production with excellent results.

Lucas apparently chose this approach for practical and economic reasons. He knew that he was going to have computer-generated images in nearly every shot of the film. Rather than shooting it on film and then having to digitize the whole movie for the computer imaging, he is shooting it digital. It will be directly input into the computers. When the editing is complete, he will have the first completed digital feature for theater projection. Spike Lee shot the low-budget movie "Bamboozled" using "prosumer" digital cameras, and it was distributed in the theaters

on film. And of course, many independent and short documentary projects originate on small-format digital media.

One can shoot a project digitally, edit in the digital nonlinear domain, add
the graphics and transitions, complete the master edit and transfer the project to
film for a projection print. However, one must light the original footage well, use
a high-end professional digital camera and understand that although it will still
look better transferred and projected on film than projected by video, it still may
lack the quality of film. In the case of narrative films, one still has to overcome
many distributors' prejudice against narrative products shot in video/digital
video. In ultra-low-budget films, it seems that it would be the way to go, and
perhaps the distributors' attitudes will change as digital video's image keeps
improving.

I would give two basic pieces of advice. The first is either have and/or develop social
skills. Of all the people I've met in this business, those who achieve the highest level of
success have social skills. Most people in an editing room are shy and retiring and comfortable in a dark room. But having social skills, an ability to schmooze, express your
interest, having diplomacy, and the ability to articulate your intention is important. Going
along with this, I try to emphasize that you have to get on the phone and call people. Be
good at taking rejection and coming back. The thing that motivates that is your passion to
do something. In this case, it is editing and filmmaking. Those who are motivated
develop the social skills if they don't already have them.

Bennett Goldberg, Vice President of Editing Services at Digital Symphony, Los Angeles, California

Why Edit Film in the Digital Nonlinear Environment?

Film editing has been around for a hundred years. The basic skills and methodolo-
gies are pretty easy to understand. Why mess with a good thing? Editing on film is
nonlinear, so why edit film on a computer-based system? Tony Buba is an award-
winning documentary filmmaker who screened his feature documentary "Struggles in Steel" at the 1996 Sundance Film Festival's American Spectrum. When
asked this question, he said, "For myself, nonlinear was a savior for 'Struggles in
Steel.' Because of all the different formats we were working with—Hi-8, 3/4", Beta
SP and 16mm film—the nonlinear system (D-Vision) become the common denom-
inator. Also I have never been fond of video editing and the linear approach you
have to take with it. I was never comfortable editing video, but digital editing gives
you the film approach even when you don't shoot in film."

Another reason for nonlinear film editing is time. The physical process of cutting and splicing film takes seconds or minutes; in the digital domain, cutting and
splicing take just a few seconds and can be undone just as quickly. With film, the stor-

ing of trims, frames and shots requires a great deal of attention to detail in labeling, logging and remembering where you put them. Most nonlinear systems have some built-in trim, frame and shot storage as well as labeling and logging features that, if done correctly, speed up the process and help in organization. Saving time translates into saving money on most low-budget feature films. This makes nonlinear editing attractive to producers and investors alike.

As with documentaries, the integration of many types of media into feature films began in the late 1980s and has continued to increase. Some features have material originating on a variety of formats, including 65mm, 35mm, 16mm, D2 video, Mini-DV and others. Figure 11.1 shows some film widths.

Special effects are developed and composited in the digital domain and brought back to film. This technological manipulation for film, along with the many advances and improvements in the digital domain for this manipulation, gives nonlinear editing the edge. For example, a film set in the 1600s might have an airplane in a location shot; the editor can send the shot to a graphics department to have the scene digitally altered and the plane removed from the image. The film is transferred to the computer graphics program, and the airplane is literally painted out in the digital domain. The manipulated shot is then transferred back to film negative, and the film and digital correction are returned to the editor to be logged and placed in the nonlinear system and later conformed for the final projection print.

The manipulation in the digital world is not limited to image. Audio manipulation has evolved as rapidly in nonlinear editing as video and film manipulation have. All of these digital systems have made changes in the filmmaking process. It will no longer be limited by linear/analog systems. In the future, the different artists involved in all of the production and postproduction crafts will be working in harmony at the same time, instead of using the step-by-step progression of the

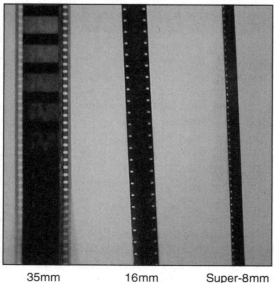

35mm   16mm   Super-8mm

FIGURE 11.1   Different Film Widths

linear/analog world. This requires some thinking and decisions about how this integration functions best.

> With all this new technology, it seems that every project should be edited on a digital system. But this is not so. For low-budget projects that are shot on 16mm film and are going to be finished as a projected print, I don't think digital nonlinear editing is cost-effective. By the time you do the transfers and all the headaches involved with the sound mix, I think you really have to think twice about digital nonlinear editing and just go out and get a used flatbed.
>
> Tony Buba, Award-Winning Independent Filmmaker, Pittsburgh, Pennsylvania

Why not just transfer the film to video and edit off-line in video? That way, there is no need for an expensive nonlinear system. For years, some filmmakers have been editing with video, developing an EDL, conforming the negative and striking the projection print. James A. Sullivan, an independent filmmaker in Dallas, Texas, for over forty years, used to have the lab transfer the film to video with the Telecine machine, with the edge code number and video timecode burned in (window dub). He edited linearly with the video transfers and made his own hand EDL with the edge code number and the timecode, and from that list, he cut and conformed the negative.

"When I first started," Sullivan says, "film was transferred locally by film chain at WFAA-TV, the ABC affiliate in Dallas, Texas. Timecode only was used, as there were no film edge number readers then. I had to guess which video frame was close to the real film frame. Later when Kodak came out with Keycode, Keycode readers were attached to Telecine machines, and this made the job a little easier. But still you had to be careful when matching back the video to conform the negative."

Sullivan was very good at this and, because of his experience and developed skill, overcame many of the technical problems that video and nonlinear systems cause for film editing. These problems are of the utmost concern in using nonlinear systems to edit a feature film that requires a print for projection. Understanding the problems and the relationships between film and video will help you make your decision on the best tool for editing your film project.

The Video/Film Relationship: Frames per Second and Timecode

In the United States, video runs at thirty frames per second (30fps), and video timecode counts from frame :00 to frame :29 before rolling over to the next second. However, for several electronic and technical reasons, 30fps is really 29.97fps. Timecode is not measuring real time; it is precisely identifying every frame of video with a specific number. Because the timecode may say 00:29:00:00, one would think that the film was 29 minutes long. Actually because the videotape is playing 0.1 percent slower than real time, the film is really 29:02 minutes long. The old timecode, called *non–drop frame timecode* (see Chapter 7, "Management of Your Material," for a more in-depth discussion of drop frame and non–drop frame timecode), is inaccurate by 0.1 percent because it never drops any frames while it is counting. To overcome this problem, drop frame timecode was developed. By skipping some frames that do not affect the video pictures, this gives a running time that is closer to the actual real time of the film. Drop frame timecode does this by dropping the :00 and :01 frame every minute except the tenth minute. In this way, the source and record times are real time and can be used to determine length. This is calculated by subtracting the in timecode from the out timecode. There are special calculators for this purpose, and higher-end editing systems do the calculation internally. Through the use of algorithms, drop frame timecode allows conversion of timecode into film edge code numbers in the final EDL.

Keycode Numbers

When you look at a piece of 65mm, 35mm or 16mm film, you can see small numbers on the edge, as shown in Figure 11.2. These edge numbers are preprinted on the negative stock and are called **keycode numbers.** When a positive work print is struck, the original key numbers from the negative are printed on the work print, and after the location sound is transferred to magnetic film stock, the editor places those same numbers to the magnetic stock to aid in syncing the picture to the sound. Another method is to code the film and magnetic stock with the same code numbers by running them through a machine that prints the same numbers on both stocks.

   The edge numbers usually consist of a prefix composed of letters and followed by numbers that in 35mm are footage counters and in 16mm are frame counters. Shots are logged by counting the edge number and adding or subtracting a certain number of frames (up to 23) if the cut doesn't fall directly on the edge number.

   Kodak developed a film edge numbers for its film stocks early in the 1990s. These edge numbers (known as Keycode) are in machine bar code and are easily readable. For nonlinear editing, this has reduced a large amount of the human

KM 25 2345 6778

Keycode Numbers

FIGURE 11.2   Film Stock with Keycode Numbers

error in logging film numbers into databases and aids in the conforming of the digital work print to the negative.

Video is not recorded in the same manner as film. Each video frame is slanted because the tape runs across the play/record heads at an angle. Unlike film, each video frame is identified by its own timecode number but consists of two approximately identical video fields known as field 1 and field 2 (see Figure 11.3).

The image in field 1 is the odd half of the image. Remember that current video images are made up of 525 lines of video per frame. Field 1 consists of the odd-numbered lines, and field 2 contains the even-numbered lines. As the tape is playing, the full video frame occurs because of the interlacing (weaving) of the two fields. Owing to this interlacing, one sees only half of the complete video image when freeze framing the videotape.

Knowing these relationships and differences between film and video is very important to the nonlinear editing of film projects that are to be completed on film.

Let me give the following as another downside to digital nonlinear editing. I directed a film called "Dita and the Family Business." This is a documentary about the Goodman family, who owned and operated the Bergman's department store in New York City. Most of the film is constructed with home movies in 35mm, 16mm, S-8 and regular-8 film as well as still photographs. 16mm film is usually shot at twenty-four frames per second, but some is shot at sixteen frames per second or even eighteen frames per second. This was hard because when we wanted to do a film finish, we had to go back to the original reversal film. In the Avid, we could make things any length, but in our optical film, we had to have it all done in the lab. In the Avid, we could speed this up, change the color, and so on. It was hard and expensive to do all of these things on film that we could easily do on an Avid. The folks at the film laboratory said that my editor had "Aviditis." She was trigger-happy on the effects. Anything she needed to stretch and slow down to make it work, we did. But in going back to a final film print, any dissolves or fades that were other than standard laboratory length, we had to do it as an optical print. The lab was delighted. They made a lot of money on us because of it. You just do these things on the Avid without thinking, but if you have to go a film finish, you pay for it. But you ask (about the editing), Was this really rigorous? Maybe it is often better to just want straight cuts, don't do all of these effects. They are so easy to do on most digital nonlinear systems, but they may take away from the "purity" of the footage.

Jonathan Mednick, Founder and President of Other Picture Production Company and Co-Producer and Editor of the "American High" Television Series, New York City

Transferring Film to Videotape and Videodiscs

Transferring film to videotape is the function of a Telecine machine. The original negative or a positive print is placed on the Telecine machine and recorded to one's

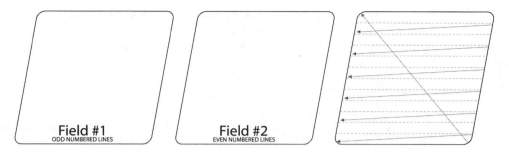

FIGURE 11.3 Fields of a Video Frame

choice of videotape format. Remember that film runs at twenty-four frames per second and video at thirty frames per second. So how is this difference handled by the Telecine machine?

The 3:2 Pulldown

Film moves at the speed of 24fps, which means that each frame moves at 1/24th of a second. Video moves at a speed of 30fps, which means that each frame moves at 1/30th of a second. Video is moving faster than film. Location sound recorded on quarter-inch analog tape or DAT (digital audio tape) has no frames and is recorded in real time and plays steadily. When the 2:2 direct transfer is being done, the action is speeded up by 20 percent, and this throws the audio out of sync with the picture. This type of transfer is called a 2:2 transfer (or pulldown). If one wants the video to record and play at the same speed as the film was shot, somehow every four frames of film has to be placed into five frames of video.

The Telecine machine does this by doing a **3:2 pulldown** (also known as *2:3 pulldown*) transfer. It makes every other film frame a little bit longer by copying it into one extra video field (see Figure 11.4). The 3:2 pulldown originally started

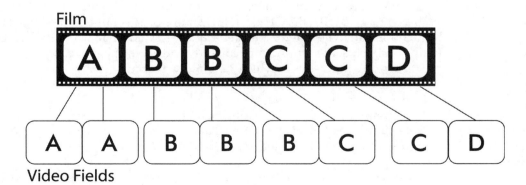

FIGURE 11.4 3:2 Pulldown

with three fields, but the industry soon discovered that starting with two fields was better. However, the name was never changed. Still, at some labs, it is a good idea to ask the lab's definition of 3:2 and make sure it is really a 2:3 transfer.

The 0.1 percent slower rate becomes very important in the handling of the soundtrack when you go back to a projection print for film. Otherwise, your projection print will be out of sync. See the section entitled "Sound and Film Rates" for more on this extremely important aspect of digital nonlinear editing of a project originated on film.

This means that certain video frames' fields will be made up of two totally different pictures. It also means that some film frames have been transferred to 1/30th-of-a-second video frame two fields long and other film frames have been transferred to 1/20th-of-a-second video frames three fields long. By doing this, the Telecine unit creates an even proportion of film frames to video frames. Because NTSC is really running at 29.97fps (frames per second) and not 30fps, the transfer is 0.1 percent slower. This transfer speed is applied to film, making the film rate during transfer to be 23.9976fps slower than the original 24fps. Another way to look at these relationships is as follows:

12 film frames of 2 fields = 24 fields
12 film frames of 3 fields = 36 fields
24 fields plus 36 fields = 60 fields of video
60 fields of video = 30 frames of video

The 3:2 transfer is a continual figure that takes place every four film frames. Every four film frames occupy the space of five video frames, all playing at 1/6th of a second and remaining in sync with the audio. These four film frames are usually given the letters A, B, C and D. This pattern ABCD occurs six times a second.

Sometimes, the video fields are further identified with their field indicator such as A1, A2, B1, B2, B3, C1, C2, D1, D2 and D3. This pulldown relationship can be identified anywhere in the transfer sequence; it aids in matching the video back to film and helps the conformer in correctly cutting the negative.

There are four ways in which 3:2 pulldown occurs:

1. Beginning on field 1 alternating 2 and then 3
2. Beginning on field 1 alternating 3 and then 2
3. Beginning on field 2 alternating 2 and then 3
4. Beginning on field 2 alternating 3 and then 2

Whichever way is used, only four types of transfer frames are created. In editing both film and video on the same system, the editing system must know the precise association between the film and the videotape. A database (log) has some interlock point between the film edge code numbers and the video timecode. Some version of the 3:2 pulldown is usually required. Knowing which version of the 3:2 pulldown was used becomes important. For example, if the edge code number was KJY 1216-12 after a Telecine of the first 3:2 pulldown method, the video timecode would be 1:00:00:01 and the key frame would be an A frame. If it was transferred using method 2, however, the video timecode would be 1:00:00:01 but the key frame would be a B frame. Knowing where the key frame is becomes very important when the nonlinear system does not have software to aid in this calculation. We will explain how to deal with it later in the chapter.

30fps and PAL

When it is known that an NTSC video postproduction will be done for creating visual special effects and recorded to film, that part of the film may be shot in 30fps. The film is transferred at the same rate as video's 29.97fps, and no pulldown is created in the Telecine process. The film is slowed down by 0.1 percent to attain the speed of 29.97fps. Some modern film cameras can be set to shoot at 29.97, creating a 1:1 association in the transfer without having to use the 0.1 percent slowdown.

If a film is going to postproduction on video or nonlinear why not just shoot the whole project in 29.97fps? This has been proposed but is usually abandoned because the added cost of the additional six frames per second can substantially—over the length of a feature, for example—raise the cost of the film stock (negative) and the processing. Some thought has also been given to shooting the film in 23.9976fps, which would allow film to be transferred with no pulldown and digital audio during the entire postproduction, but most film cameras are not capable of 23.9976fps.

PAL Telecine pulldown happens in two ways. In the first, the film is pulled down at the same rate as the video, creating a 1:1 relationship (one frame film to one frame video). If the original shooting speed is 24fps, then there is a speedup from 24fps to 25fps of 4.1 percent. No pulldown relationship is introduced in this type of transfer, and tracking the edge code number to the timecode is fairly simple.

Keeping the film rate at 24fps and the video rate at 25fps introduces a pulldown. This second type of transfer is not the standard 2:3 pulldown found in NTSC, but the frames are still numbered A, B, C, and D. In this transfer, film's 24fps must equal PAL video's 25fps. This is accomplished by duplicating only one video frame with two identical fields. Remember that this is not one exact film frame that is copied on two fields but two different film frames, numbers 12 and 24, each of which is extended by one field each second.

Most modern film cameras have the capability of shooting in 25fps, and some of the midpriced to expensive nonlinear systems and digital audio workstations have the capability of working in 25fps. It would seem that it would be easier to shoot in 25fps using a camera that can lay twenty-five-frame timecode on the negative and on the location sound tape, creating a true 1:1 relationship in the transfer. In Europe and other countries that use PAL, this is not a problem, as their postproduction systems work in PAL's 25fps, but in the United States and other countries where NTSC's 30fps is standard, it could raise the cost of postproduction because of the more expensive Telecine transfer and the renting of PAL players to digitize the video into the nonlinear system. It could work, but one would need to investigate the cost and compare the time savings and the possible frame inaccuracy for a production that is to return to film for final exhibition.

Editing Film in the Nonlinear Video–Based World

The Telecine machine is built to transfer film to video, so the process is straightforward. If the project is finishing on video or digital, you don't have to worry about the fields and frames relationships and frame accuracy. When the film project is going back to film for a projection print, then you have to be concerned. The problem becomes one of "Where is the cut? Is it between A and B or between A1 and A2?" Remember that when video is in freeze-frame mode, you are seeing only one field. With most videotape nonlinear editing, the EDL does not account for which field you were seeing when the cut was decided.

Frame accuracy in the film-to-video-to-film process has a couple of loose definitions. One is the 1:1 association between the film frame and the video frame that can be seen (*visual accuracy*). Another definition is manipulation that makes 60 minutes on video 60 minutes on finished film (*temporal accuracy*).

Nonlinear editing systems deal with the question of frame accuracy differently but from the same fundamental: They all are editing timecode. Timecode lists (EDLs) are created and take those numbers and relate them, through a database, back to the film edge code numbers (matching back). In the 30fps world, there is no 1:1 relationship between film and video. The only way to have true frame accuracy is to edit 1:1 with the videotape at 24fps. If you have access to special tape decks and special edit controllers, it is possible to edit frame accurately from a 2:2 Telecine pulldown.

24fps film to digital may be available very soon with the development of digital 24P editing systems. Perhaps the development of the 24fps Telecine is not far behind, making this problem obsolete. In the meantime, however, it is critically important to be aware of these differences.

Some nonlinear editing systems digitize video using only field 1. They do this to save storage space, and it gives only half the resolution. It then appears as shown in Figure 11.5.

The A frame is duplicated, and the five video frames now look like four film frames. It has an almost direct film-to-video relationship as long as one remembers not to cut between the A frames. In effect, you have twenty-four frames and the machine duplicates the fields during playback, but it is the root of digital skipping during editing and playback.

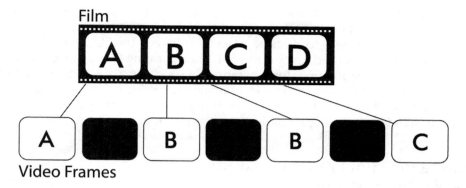

FIGURE 11.5   Video with No Fields and One Film Frame Duped

Lower-end digital systems can sometimes digitize video at 30fps or 24fps if they are using the suitable software and hardware. The most common of these systems digitize at 30fps but identify 24fps with individual numbers. This requires more space and contains some motion artifacts but is just as accurate as real 24fps digitization.

Most of the video and nonlinear systems that claim frame accuracy are not exaggerating. But film is not 30fps videotape. In the 30fps world of video, there is no edit cut on the tape or nonlinear system, except as mentioned previously, that is an exactly identical cut on the film. All the video and nonlinear systems try to give the preferred edit in both the visual and temporal frame accurate definitions.

The only true way to achieve both types of frame accuracy is to have a nonlinear system based on the same frame rate as the format in which the final product is to be delivered. All these systems use a mathematical algorithm in the video-to-film conversion. Because the least unit of film is one frame (1/24 of a second), the least error and the least unit of video is one field (1/60 of a second). Therefore, it is more forgiving to convert 24fps film edge code numbers to a frame-accurate EDL than it is to convert 30fps timecode.

The same software that Avid uses for its Film Composer system (a system designed for projects originating on film) is now available for its DV Express. For a project that is going back to a conformed negative, this gives a more accurate nonlinear edit and EDL on a less expensive system.

Some systems digitize only one field in order to save hard-drive space. The system duplicates the fields during playback and can have some digital skipping problems. The Avid Film Composer and Lightworks use a similar but more accurate approach. Avid digitizes the first video field, and Lightworks use the second field. Every third frame in Avid and every fourth frame in Lightworks becomes a duplicate. The systems do not read this duplicate frame, allowing for true 24-frame capture and film editing.

One sure way to check accuracy is to convert the EDL into a film work print and correct frame accuracy errors before conforming the negative. Most nonlinear systems have provisions for generating a negative cut list directly from the final cut on the system. This of course saves money and time. This list uses temporal frame accuracy, keeping the sound and picture in sync. The changes in the cuts made by timecode calculations on these systems are hard to notice.

Preparing the Film Project for Editing in the Nonlinear World

For projects shot on film and finishing on video, all of the above is nothing to worry about. If the project is shot on film and finished on film or, as most feature and TV shows in today's market, finished on both, some details must be handled before and during the Telecine process to aid in precisely cutting the film.

For almost twenty years, some Aaton cameras have had the technology to apply timecode to the negative while filming. Arriflex also has developed in-camera timecode. The in-camera timecode identifies each film frame by exposing timecode data onto the negative between the perforations. The running speed of the camera sets the timecode rate. A camera running at sound speed (24fps) has a twenty-four-frame SMPTE timecode. Aaton uses a dot matrix system, and Arriflex uses a barcode system.

Aaton's system provides readable information on the negative. This system also encodes production number, camera number, camera magazine ID, date and roll number. Arri's Film Identification/Sync system, currently available on the Arriflex 535 (35mm) and some of their 16 SR cameras, writes all the information with barcode for each frame. Using the Arri FIS reader head at the Telecine transfer gives instant access to all the timecode and machine-readable edge number information, such as Kodak's Keycode. The data with both the Aaton and Arri systems are correlated and/or can be used individually and placed into data disks and/or can be printed onto reference lists.

One of the best reasons for using this technology versus the transcribing of edge number/slate information is the reduction of errors in the digital domain. Still, the current state of the art of the 3:2 pulldown and the conversion available on most nonlinear systems make using in-camera systems unnecessary and not cost-effective for smaller productions.

Sound and Film Rates

When shooting **double system** (audio and image are recorded on separate pieces of equipment), there is usually some confusion about which speed and timecode (frame count) to use for recording audio elements. The sound speed, timecode and film speed need to work together with the Telecine process so that it can be correctly set and used during the entire postproduction process for all elements to remain in sync.

The Aaton Keylinker can link the 24fps timecode on the film to 25fps on the audio recording, giving exact sync at the beginning of every second. Although the practice is not common at this writing, in the future, most postproduction houses that are using digital audio workstations will be using 24fps timecode audio for keeping sync in the postproduction process. A current common practice is to use 24fps timecode for PAL (25fps) transfers when film is shot at 24fps. This yields a frame-to-frame connection between each film frame and the audio synced time. Whatever speed you use, be sure to tell the lab so that they can Telecine the picture and the sound correctly.

It is not necessary to have in-camera timecode. By using Nagra IV-STC stereo or DAT machines with timecode and a Denecke slate, a visual timecode is recorded on the film (or video) at the same time as the clapboard marker at the beginning of each take. The audio is slowed down (resolved) by 0.1 percent during the Telecine process and then digitized into the nonlinear system. The editor then inserts audio edits, syncing up the dailies by matching the slate timecode and audio sync for each take.

Alternative Location Sound Sync

Many low-budget producers and student filmmakers cannot afford the latest technology. SMPTE timecode on the audio track that matches timecode on the picture is great but not essential. To save money, many television shows in the past did not use timecode when recording location sound on their 4.2 Nagras.

Using no timecode on the audio is handled in the following manner. The picture is put through a Telecine and digitized. The audio, if recorded on a Nagra or similar 24fps recorder, as it is digitized is resolved (slowed down 0.1 percent) through the use of an electronic device (black box). This black box takes the sound recorder's 60 Hz signal and slows it to 59.95 Hz.

The editor finds the clapboard marker of the picture start and marks the in point and holds that spot. The audio is pulled to the clapboard slate and marks the in point. This is all done by visually noting the slate clap and listening for the clapboard on the audio. Locating the sound of the clapboard slate hitting (or the beep of an electronic flash slate) is aided by using the waveform monitor found on the nonlinear system. The clapboard marker will be easy to find on the waveform monitor, as it will look like a tall mountain. After a few syncs (*popping the tracks,* to use the film term), the editor should be able to sync the dailies as fast as using timecode.

Will it stay in sync? It will because of the nonlinear system's internal timecode. Most in-camera/audio production timecode is not continuous, so the nonlinear's continuous timecode is used in the editing process anyway. The production timecode is used when matching back to the film negative.

One must also remember that without production timecode on the location sound tapes, you cannot match back to the original audio. The sound in the nonlinear system is CD or better quality anyway, so the necessity of going back to the original tracks should not be necessary. The nonlinear system's sound is fine for going on to postproduction sound mixing and sweetening.

Digital audio tape is different than analog tape recording mentioned in the above paragraphs. Most of the time, since DAT is in real time, it can be digitized directly, and the editor follows the same procedure for popping the tracks as above.

Remember, if you are finishing on film, the sound has to be changed back to 60Hz. If you are using a mixed track out of the nonlinear system at 29.97fps, just tell the lab, and they can speed it up to put it back in sync with the finished film projection print.

Remember also to record a 1-KHz tone at the head of each of your location sound tapes and on your synced edited nonlinear system sound. The lab will set their equipment to these levels and will not change them during the process. If you do have a problem and need some adjustment, be sure to give it to the lab in writing and know that it is going to cost some money.

Making a Flowchart

It can be very helpful to make a flowchart for the entire production/postproduction process. In this manner you can see exactly where the film is at any moment. Figure 11.6 shows an example of such a flowchart.

Planning for the Telecine Process

If the film is to be finished on video, there are no such special problems encountered, and the Telecine transfer is fairly simple. The negative or positive film is transferred, and sound is synced at transfer or in the videotape recorder before digitizing or afterward in the nonlinear digital editing process. However, if the project is to be finished on film, some caution and planning should be observed to ensure accurate results.

Because in the Telecine transfer, the machine has to be stopped to sync up each picture scene with the audio, there is a danger of the operator making some mistakes that can hinder the editing process. Some ways to ensure the accuracy of the film and audio transfer are as follows:

1. Put the film into reels of the exact lengths needed for the sound tape. These reels should not exceed 1,200 feet. Be sure to place separation leader between each camera roll. This leader allows the colorist to maintain the continuity of the edge code and timecode numbers from one camera roll to the next in the assembled roll. The Telecine operator can transfer each reel without having to stop, reducing the chance for mistakes in the 3:2 pulldown.

2. Request that all the Telecine edits start on an A frame. The film edge numbers will not be in order and have to be logged each time as a new entry in the database. With the Telecine edits at the beginning of an A frame and :00 timecode, it means that every five timecode frames make up an A frame. Most Telecine systems now

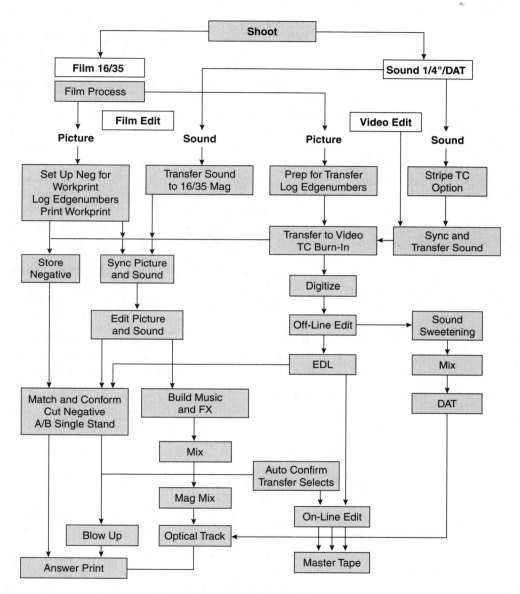

FIGURE 11.6 The Process of Editing for Film Release or Video Release When Editing on Film

have readers that can read the film edge numbers, such as Kodak's Keycode and produce an EDL machine-readable list that has the edge number, timecode and 3:2 type pulldown for each Telecine edit. When using a reader, such as the Evertz, to develop this data list, the stops in the Telecine transfer process can be followed and aid in syncing and film negative conforming for the final print.

Another device that tracks the edge numbers during the transfer process is a Time Logic Controller (TLC) box. A punch is made at the key frame at the beginning of a film reel, and the edge number is entered into the TLC. As the film moves through, the TLC shows the film edge number of the frame displayed on the LED display. When a Telecine edit occurs, the TLC keeps tracking the edge code numbers. At the end of the reel, the last key number is punched and compared to the TLC read-out, giving a good check for the accuracy of the edge numbers in each Telecine edit. If in-camera timecode has been used, then the Telecine transfer is even more reliable.

Following are more planning and preparation tips:

1. If you are finishing on film, the video picture quality might not be that important. However, if you are going to finish on film but want to use the video dailies for a final video "print," then good-quality in the dailies will be necessary. In this case, you might want an original transfer to D2 or Beta SP. If you are planning a video off-line rough cut before going to a nonlinear system, you will want to make VHS 1/2-inch dubs no more than 30 minutes each in length. This will save hours of time shuttling back and forth looking for takes. Using timed transfers can be expensive. If you don't need the dailies to be color-corrected, the one light or best light transfer is the cheapest method.

2. As was stated above, don't forget to record a reference tone at the head of each location sound tape. Be sure to let the lab know whether or not you want to transfer all the footage (usually the cheapest transfer) or selected takes only.

3. Be sure to let the lab know which aspect ratio you want them to use during the transfer. Do you want the standard video aspect ratio of 1.33:1, or do you want a different one, such as 1.85:1? Most labs recommend that you shoot a framing alignment chart at the beginning of the first day's dailies. This is very helpful to the lab in identifying possible camera and Telecine framing problems.

4. Video dailies are usually transferred with continuous non–drop frame timecode unless you ask to change.

5. The lab can usually give a specific timecode for each camera or assembled roll at your request.

6. Be sure to tell the lab where you want the video burn-ins displayed, since these can vary. Most prefer them on the bottom of the screen, but these can be cut off on the monitor during the editing process and not be seen. Checking this out beforehand will aid in the placement of the burn-ins.

7. Even if you are not going to cut the film right away, be sure to get the film transfer logs (FLEX or FTL files). As was explained above, these are created by manually entering the information such as keycode, camera roll number and scene number into the computer and saving it to a disk and/or hard copy. This process does cost extra and could be compiled by the editor while digitizing into the nonlinear system. Compare the cost savings with possible errors when you make your decision.

Nonlinear Editing of the Film

Many nonlinear systems are currently available on the market. If one has access to a system such as an Avid Film Composer, it is possible to edit in a 24fps environment, and that environment is the best for editing film that is to be conformed back to film. Some lower-cost systems with 24fps environment are coming onto the market. In addition, digitizing the footage at 24fps instead of 30fps saves about 20 percent of disk space. Twenty thousand feet of 16mm film digitized at 24fps uses around 16 gigabytes of hard-drive space. The footage at 30fps uses around 21 gigabytes. Another advantage is that the footage as seen on a nonlinear 24fps system is identical to the physical film frame. This leads to more accuracy in conforming the negative.

Not everyone has high-end nonlinear systems to use or can afford to rent them and therefore must use a 30fps nonlinear system. Here are some suggestions that, when followed, should lead to a more accurate conformed negative:

1. Always edit on the A frame. By looking at your visual burn-in of the edge code number, you can see which frames were designated A. Editing on any other frame may be editing on a frame that does not exist on the negative. Remember that to achieve 30fps, some fields are duplicated in the video.

2. The film log files (FLEX or FTL) need to be converted to a compatible format for each particular nonlinear system. Avid Media and Film Composers use Avid Log Exchange (ALE) to convert the FLEX or FTL files. Other systems, such as D-Vision, Video Cube and Media 100, need to convert the film log file to their specific requirements. Contact the manufacturer of the system you are using to get the correct conversion software.

3. When your editing is complete, you need to generate an EDL for the film conformer. This is done by converting your 30fps cuts to 24fps using special software developed for that purpose. Contact the nonlinear system's manufacturer for the correct software for your system. Your lab may be able to do this for you for using your 30fps EDL and FLEX files. Using the lab takes time and money but may be more accurate than some of the aftermarket conversion software.

4. Your film scene numbers are your ultimate safety net if all else fails. Be sure when you are editing in the nonlinear system to put them in by the scene number and take number as your clip name.

5. When you develop your final EDL, be sure to provide the edge code numbers, using in and out numbers, foot and frame count, and camera roll for each edit and a cumulative foot and frame count. Some of the nonlinear systems will generate this for you, but a good backup plan is also to make one by hand using the timecode and keycode burn-in.

6. Effects, such as dissolves, need to be of a duration that your lab can work with. Check with the lab to see what the requirements are for their minimum and maximum film frames. For example, a dissolve could be as short as 16 frames or as

long 96 frames or longer. This translates to 20 and 120 video frame rates, respectively. Please remember that many effects that can be done on the nonlinear system can not be done on the film. Some effects, such as dissolves, fades and wipes, can be done on the film, but you must have the correct number of film frames on the negative for it to work. Do not be fooled by the nonlinear systems effects. The nonlinear system can generate video frames where they do not exist to create a dissolve or other effects.

7. If you have used the same scene twice in your rough cut, be sure to note this in your EDL so that a duplicate negative of that scene can be made to be used in the conforming process. A **dupe negative** is printed from the master positive or original negative film stock.

Besides conforming the film negative in the usual manner, another method is to single-strand the negative—a technique that is sometimes called *no cut*. Your cuts are spliced together with several frames left on either side of the cut and then optically printed to a projection print or, in the case of Super-16, blown up to 35mm. Of course, this costs money, but it could save some time and cost in the end, depending on your final film format.

Planning and communication with your lab will help to ensure a successful nonlinear film edit that results in a successfully conformed negative and an accurately synced projected film print. Best wishes for your completed film!

CHAPTER

12 Interviews with Film and Television Editors

Mark Block, Editor at Crew Cuts
Postproduction House, New York City

Tell us about what you do and what kind of work your postproduction facility brings in.   Probably 95 percent of the work done here is national commercials, and we are usually hired by the ad agency. The dailies get dumped on our doorstep, and unlike in feature filmmaking, the director is often out of the picture at this stage. Sometimes the director has a hand in hiring us to do the postproduction, and sometimes top directors will insist that an editor of their choice gets the cut. In that kind of situation, the director may come in to do the edit, but it is unusual. Generally, the ad agency hires us as well as the director. They may as a courtesy let the director into the editing room, but sometimes they want him a thousand miles away.

What kind of equipment do you have in-house?   We are all on Apple Macintosh–based Avids. Because drive space has gotten cheap and plentiful, we digitize every last frame of film for our commercials. For the first few years of nonlinear editing, we would go through tape dailies and pick selects [selected shots] and only digitize the shots we knew we wanted to use. When I started editing on nonlinear systems, a 2-gig drive was about $5,000. Now we have a tower that holds eight 9-gig drives. We're exploring what should be the next step. We may go to one huge server and have everyone share it. We have twelve edit rooms here at Crew Cuts. For us to buy new 36-gig drives for each is expensive. We now make do with these 9-gigs but will soon be upgrading them.

What about the art of collaboration in editing? You must do a lot of negotiating while editing commercials for these ad agencies.   Yes, I like to have the producer, director and art director there with me while I digitize the footage. I go through the dailies with the clients, and we create the selects while they are here. We talk about why they shot a particular image, why it was shot this way and what is important to communicate to the viewer. Part of my job is to give my clients what they want, so I like to get their input. Some editors seem to think that they are making "Citizen Kane" and that they are the auteur of the piece. They want an unimpeded first cut and no one in room while they do it. I think instead editing commercials or any project is a craft. It is cooperative, and I want ideas from those involved. Then I give them the choice to go away and let me cut or to stay on while

I edit. I find that clients used to want to stay more than they do now. More and more now, they usually go back and work at the agency while I begin the first edit. We all have more work to do these days. Productivity is higher, we all have more to do. So often, they are happy to have me do a first cut so they can get their work done. Generally, I can easily cut a 30-second commercial in one day, and they come back next day to view it.

With any kind of motion picture editing, some type of consistent organization is important in keeping track of shots. What are your methods?   Yes, labeling shots properly is critically important. My own system is based on the fact that I started editing film on both Moviola and KEM systems. I would use bins to hold my strips of film. So I label like I always have, by scene and take number according to the slate. This makes it easier to look back at the script notes and get information about the shot. If one of the clients in the room says, "How many takes do we have of that shot?," I can look at my bin, and look at the various takes to tell them. With the Avid, you have columns you use to give additional information about a shot. The next column in my bin is my description of the shot, which I keep to a minimum. The scene and take number, a description and the timecode start and end numbers are all I really need. I keep descriptions to a minimum. If something is shot with wide shot, medium close-up, and so on, I will mention this. I also try to somehow distinguish one take from another. If it is a faster pan, I will mention this. If the creative director is Dan and there is a note that Dan likes this shot in the script notes, I will write that in. Later, when Dan is sitting there with me and he asks, "Are you using the take I like?," I can answer. Some editors don't use scene and take numbers at all. In the column called scene, they'll practically write a novel describing the shot. These are typically young editors who don't know any better. When I pick up a project from other editors, I go back in and fix this. You don't need all of that information there. There are better and easier ways to label your shots.

With the ad agency coming back in, we make multiple cuts. It is easier to try multiple versions and compare them. In old analog video editing days, if someone had what I considered a bad idea, I would spend a long time trying to talk them out of it so I wouldn't waste time editing something I knew wouldn't work. Now we just do it. And besides, sometimes a bad idea leads to a good idea. Someone will say, "I told you this wouldn't work," and someone else will say, "Yeah, but it would if we made this other change." It opens up creative possibilities. I think one of the reasons that the editing of commercials has become much freer than feature films is that the commercial editors got Avids first, and it became easier to try things out. Some old film director friends of mine, the Coen Brothers, are still screening takes on a Moviola and cutting on a KEM. This is how they cut "O Brother, Where Art Thou?" Some feature editors have been slow to change for whatever reason.

Also, in commercials, they shoot many more takes than in features. In a commercial, we have twenty or thirty takes per setup, so I have much more material to work with. It is also a one- or two-day shoot. On a feature film, the director has his way and that is it, but with a commercial, you have more people giving input. And also you have only 30 seconds to tell the story. So you want to try things. With a feature film, if someone says that you need to re-edit a 10-minute chase sequence, that is a lot of work. But with a commercial, you are more willing to try everything every which way. The problem with the process is that I will put a cut together, and it is maybe close to perfection. But it may take a week to get back to that, because it is human nature to want to try things out and make changes. No one realizes you tried it that way a week earlier. It is also like a committee when editing commercials. The producer, writer and art director try things, then the creative director tries things, then the account people try some changes, and then sometimes it even goes to the president of an agency. Finally it goes to the client. Sometimes just getting a cut out of an agency is torture. So many people have input. The nice thing is that usually they have air dates, so they can't torture you forever.

How are entry-level jobs changing at high-end postproduction houses? My entry into the postproduction world was as a foot messenger. Usually it is still like this. Or you might start out as a receptionist in the building. Nobody gets out of film school and gets a job here as an editing assistant. We've had some stupid people turn down jobs as a receptionist. They say that they didn't go to school to work in that kind of position, but that is simply oftentimes the way you get in. In terms of moving up, it is just being lucky. But in my experience, if you are good, it takes about six months. Usually you are then a second assistant or a floating helper. The greatest skill you can have is organization. I think the role of an assistant editor has changed a lot. They used to have to have certain skills. They would sync up dailies, know how to get a release print out of the lab and so on. They don't usually do these things anymore. The assistants now have a very undefined job description. The problem for me is that sometimes you don't have the communal learning that there used to be. When I was an assistant, I had an editor who was very firm on how to do things. He would tell me, "This is the way you label trims and put them in the bin." He was very specific about teaching me the proper steps to take. Now, except for learning very simple things like how to dub a tape, how to work a patch bay, the job often includes such mundane tasks as filling out FedEx bills, ordering lunches for clients. It is that kind of thing. What I like to see in an assistant is someone who, on their own time, learns things that can come in handy for me later. They will take it upon themselves to learn Photoshop, the Avid and Aftereffects. With the really good assistants here, I can say, "Can you animate this title in Aftereffects for me?" They will go off and do it, and I appreciate this so much. Otherwise, it would either cost us money to hire it out or it would take my time to do it on my own. The really good assistants have a graphic ability. The bad assistants simply do what they are told, and that is the end of it. Another thing assistants used to do was hang out in the edit room. You had to be there. You were required to be at the editor's side all day. That is not the case anymore. I don't need anybody near me when I am cutting on the Avid. So I would say to new assistants that if I have clients with me, hang out in the room with us if you don't have other duties at the moment. It is rare that I can convince them this is worthwhile. But just simply hanging out shows you how a commercial is put together, and you might pick up something that will help us out later. Ninety percent of an editor's job is handholding. The assistant will learn this by being there. They will learn the bedside manner. I sometimes wish that handholding wasn't such a necessary part of it, because I think I'm better at cutting than handholding. But your personality is very important to repeat business. It is like cocktail party chatter. Some people are good at this, some are not, but by watching and doing it, you will get better. It is the same with working with clients. If an assistant spends time in the room, they will also get to know the clients and may work with them eventually. When you are with someone for awhile, you gain a general impression about whether they are someone who "gets it." You should let the client know that you get it.

If they hang out with us while we edit a commercial, they will get a feel for the huge amount of control the ad agency has on the final product. Sometimes you can have final approval from everyone, and then you'll hear, "Oh, the Fox Network thinks the graffiti skull and crossbones on the back wall in this shot are threatening, and they won't air it." So you have these last-minute changes.

What are some of the typical clients Crew Cuts brings in for edits?   We do most of Pepsi's work. I do toy commercials for Hasbro. This year I had a package of six spots for them. These are a lot of fun to work on. They have special effects all the way through. There's lots of fast cutting and humor, so you can really go wild with them. These commercials air on Nickelodeon. We also do Charles Schwab, Visa, Doritos, Cingular and GM corporate stuff. These are not all done in the New York facility; we also have branches in San Francisco and Los Angeles, so it is spread around. But we do a lot of big-name commercials.

Of course, for a long time, we were cutting on film and then on videotape. During the transition from film to video, there was a point where half of what I was editing was cut on a KEM and half on 3/4-inch tape. I said many times to many clients that if I had nothing to do but tape editing, I would quit the business. Having to edit video is not fun. Cutting film is fun for me, but cutting tape isn't. They are different skills. But it was hard to talk clients out of having their commercials edited on videotape. I remember the last couple of film jobs I did, I literally talked the client into film. I said I could cut dialogue better on film, and it is cheaper for you anyway.

Luckily, at about this time, nonlinear systems came along. Nonlinear editing is like cutting film but more flexible. Crew Cuts got Beta systems with E-Pix [double laser disk-based storage system] and an Avid. The bad thing was that it was on a DOS and then a Windows system, and it was very hard to learn. If anything went wrong, we really had problems. Where you put scenes on which laser disk would determine how it played two weeks later. So you had to plan out music, sound effects, dialogue, voice-over, and all of the other elements of the project to determine in advance where they went. If you mislabeled your laser disks, it would play the wrong scenes. I used the system for six months, but every day I felt like I had been run over by a truck. It was still more fun than cutting videotape, but it required the utmost concentration. After this system, we got in a complete Avid as a test. Basically, nobody took more than a day to learn it, so on day 2, you could do paying work. On the early Avids, the picture was so bad in the output that you had to go back and use every assistant to conform the original videotape for the spots. But we really like Avid. For the most part, they are really stable.

How have nonlinear systems changed your editing aesthetics?   One thing I think has really changed is a more sophisticated use of music. I think some of this change is due to these nonlinear editing systems because it is so easy to try things out. Also, compact disks are so easy to use. We don't use LPs anymore. You used to have twenty or thirty LPs as your music library. For 10 years, if a commercial needed music, you cut without, and after it was over, you sent it to the composer. Now, choosing music for the rough cut is critically important. Knowledge about music is a great thing to have for an editor. Getting the right music in a rough cut is crucial now. When I started, it wasn't even an issue.

This is how it usually works when using music for a rough cut and then hiring a composer. You say to the composer, "We cut this to Rage Against the Machine, and that is the style we want." Most of the time a composer will "copy" what you used. All he or she has to do is stay in that style. Some composers complain that this takes away their creativity. But in my opinion, it narrows down their choices so that they can be even more creative in composing without ripping the first piece off.

In fact, I have never put a piece together in the past few years without adding music in. Usually I'll get to a point where I say, "I really need to know what kind of music is going through these pictures." So my assistant and I go through hundreds of CDs to try music out. It seems pointless to go further without knowing what kind of music is going to be there.

Another concerns the sound processing we can do on rough cuts. Our rough cuts not only look more finished than they used to, they sound more finished. I put EQ, level riding and time compression on every cut I do. My favorite sound plug-in is time compression. It used to be a great concern when I'd get a script that required 32 seconds to read (even when going like a bat out of hell). Now instead of cutting copy or reading the script too fast, I just speed it up digitally. Huge speed-ups (like 20 percent or more) sound perfectly natural. I tell announcers not to worry about timing; just give me a good reading and I'll make it fit. Having time compression available to me is an absolute life saver. I use it all the time and don't know how I'd work without it. The old business of cutting a spot long and "lexiconning it" later is history.

How have computer-based nonlinear editing systems changed the job your are expected to do?   I think the biggest changes are special effects and compositing. With the Avid, it is easier to do special effects, so more get done. In the past, if you had a couple of blue or green screen shots, it was a big deal for the lighting and wardrobe crews on the set. Now, these are minor concerns because the red, yellow, green removal is so easy with the computers. Rotoscoping and tracking are so much easier now and are done in post. Big-name directors give us a hard time and say, "Oh, you editors are all the same. You just want me to make your job easier." It used to be that if you didn't shoot it right, you really had problems in postproduction. Now, if you have the time and money, almost anything can be done. And it is.

So almost every commercial has special effects. They are everywhere. And lots of times you don't realize they are even there. Ten years ago, even the best composited picture was identifiable. It never fooled you. Nowadays, if it looks fake at all, you can tell it is bad production. You can't get away with it. It is not good enough to have animation look pretty good; it has to look perfect. Because of technology, it is done more. With Avid, I can do chromakeying, compositing and matting.

This has caused clients to expect the rough cut of an edit to look really good. You end up knowing whether the composite is going to work, whether you have an issue that has to be addressed later, if you have to put blowups or moves, if you have to combine two different takes where it should have only needed one. You know all of this because the equipment lets you know. I even put final titles and the copyright in the rough cut. This used to all be done on the final version. Now, nine out of ten times, I'll make sure the titles work in the rough cut. This first draft looks almost finished. The only difference is that they have a few flaws, but all of the elements of the final commercial are there. It used to be days of tests and getting approval, cutting the film in, going back and making changes. There is less than that now This all changed for us when Avid's title tool became sophisticated enough to look professional. Titles used to be an on-line finish thing, and now they are a rough-cut thing. You can check the timing [color] of the footage with the systems as well.

I think a lot of the thinking and planning that used to slip through the cracks is prompted for you by the systems because they are so sophisticated.

I also finish a lot of spots on the Avid. I think on-line editing is an occupation that is going away. Now, either the graphics company will finish it visually on a Flame, or I will finish it on an Avid.

Wayne Derrick, Director and Camera Operator for "The Real Miami Cops" (Discovery Channel, USA, and Channel 5, UK), London, England

You work a wide variety of positions in documentary film production, from producer and director to camera operator and editor. Right now you are in the process of editing your series "The Real Miami Cops," for which you served as director and camera operator. As you sit down now with your editor, tell us what goes on for you at this stage.   Editing is telling the story. Or figuring out *how* to tell the story. You work together to find the *best* way of telling it. This is the final step.

In your career, you have edited on both film and analog video. Now you work in digital nonlinear technologies. What changes do you see occurring for editors with these systems?   The main thing that lots of people have mentioned is that when people were physically cutting on film, you could watch an assembly together and you could make detailed notes when you watched it about what should happen. It would take a fair amount of time for the editor to go through and find shots and talk with their assistant. While this was occurring, you had time to think about the film further. You had time to digest the footage and what edits had just been made. I think nonlinear machines in general are now so quick that it can take a lot of time to get to assembly stage, but once you've got that, you can do a massive amount very quickly. This would be fine if you had the same amount of time, but with budget crunches and current television schedules, you are forced to work much faster to get the film to a presentable stage. At the moment, I have two and a half weeks to get a rough cut of this program I am now cutting. It takes several days to get a long assembly, and then you've got to get it in presentable form in two or three days. I've got my boss saying, "Can we come in and see it?" I've only just seen it myself! And in order to show it to others, I also have to write commentary [narration]. So even though it is very fast, the system allows us in two days to take a very rough film and transform it. But it is very pressured. People want it out very quickly. If I show the rough cut to someone two days before I should, it will be so rough that I can be out of a job. But if I hang onto it for those two days and work it, I can make a good film. You are invariably really up against it timewise. In the older days of film, you could do some rough splices and get the rough assembly. But there was plenty of time for thinking between this version and the fine cut, because it took time to do the physical labor of cutting. I think, from my side of it, that is the main effect of these digital systems. You suddenly get these three or four very intense days when you are trying to get the rough cut finished with commentary and get it looking really good, and then I may have to show the rough cuts to my producer or others before I've really seen them myself. There is always a period where I really wish I had another week. You seem to lose time to just view things. You lose time to think about it after viewing.

I am currently in the editing room at Atlantic Productions, Limited, in London. I'm working for Channel 5 in the U.K. and the Discovery Channel in the U.S. It is called "The Real Miami Cops," and it is a series of six half-hours. I served as director and camera operator. At this stage, it becomes a collaborative effort with my editor, Giles Llewellyn-Thomas. "The Real Miami Cops" is a docu-soap type of series and focuses on personalities, characters and action scenes. I bring to Giles the scenes I want to include and an idea of the order they could fall in. But there is quite a bit of movement once we really start cutting the scenes. It is really a dramatic type of cutting. It is the people and what they say that are important. So once we've got those scenes roughly assembled and ordered, then we start looking at what the script needs to do to put the right emphasis or to help the audience follow the story.

In this collaborative process, who really makes the key decisions about the editing?   Well, I like to log all of the footage. This forces me to go through all of the rushes. I begin to think about how different scenes can go next to each other. I often think this way while shooting, and when you go through the rushes, it goes to another stage. This is one of the big advantages of working with another editor who has a new eye and looks at the scenes in a new way. Because I was there and shot the footage, I have an emotional investment with it. You can get locked into how it should go together. It can be useful to have a fresh eye on all that. I would like to say, though, that the choice of the editor is crucial here, because two heads are not always better than one. Luckily, Giles is probably the best editor I have ever worked with.

The kind of programming I do, it is not scripted out in advance. It can't be. We are talking about real life and real people. No one really knows what will happen. You get to cutting room and see what happened, and you can begin to work out how to tell the story.

What changes do you predict will happen as the technology evolves?   The technology is advancing so quickly now. The quality of the cameras is getting better for the size, and they are able to film in even less light now than they used to be. In

Britain, you find more and more series where they give cameras to directors with no real camera training to shoot. In terms of editing systems, the storage space is so much cheaper. And now there are home editing systems you can use professionally. I think it wouldn't surprise me if we start doing rough assemblies in the field. And then come back with this rough cut already done before we enter the editing suite. I don't think editors would be pleased with this, however, because they want to see all of the footage.

A lot of decisions in technology and shooting and editing approaches are being made on financial grounds rather than creative grounds. I am actually quite lucky here at Atlantic because Anthony Geffen, who runs the company, tries to ensure we have enough time to put the programs together so that they are very successful films. He is into making quality programming. That support is really crucial. There are lots of other companies in London that wouldn't be giving me the time I need to do the best job possible.

The problem with not having enough time is that you can come in and very quickly throw out a type of film that is a very controlled, very predictable style of filmmaking. This is quick and economical but not very good filmmaking. I would suggest that nonlinear technologies could well be helping a lot of financial directors of companies make more and more of that kind of program. It is like a factory style. It is putting a lot of film through very quickly.

How does this affect the viewer?   First of all you've got to give the viewer a choice. They prefer more creative films. I think it is important for places like the Discovery Channel and the A&E Network to make and market these beautifully crafted programs. They need to support that brand and need to give the filmmakers the time to do it well.

What advice would you give people who want to pursue motion picture editing as a career?   I would tell them to be prepared for several years of doubts. You are going to have a period of "Am I going to get there?" It is those who don't give up who will end up making it. It is about sticking to it. It is very much a world of who you know. And really, personalities are crucially important, and people have to get on with each other. Some editors are brilliant editors but quite difficult to work with. Others are great editors and brilliant to work with. With them, you make the film you want to make but made even better. The films I used to shoot and produce in jungle environments, where you have your hammock strung up next to someone in the jungle for six weeks, you have to get along. Now it is Giles and I spending 12 to 14 hours a day together with the pressures of the job. You need people who can deal with that pressure and that stress and don't develop egos that get in the way of their careers.

Your work is often commissioned by large television networks and cable stations. What is that like? What kind of input do they have at the editing stage? Working with Discovery, I've got some flexibility. But you do get very strong encouragement to take the film in certain ways. With the television market as it is at the moment, so competitive, they are keen for it to be popular and get good viewing figures. You are encouraged to include scenes that will be enjoyed by a wide section of the viewing audience. There is a clear lack of enthusiasm if you try to be too, what we call here in England, "BBC 2." This is an informative, factual, old-style filmmaking. I think there is definitely encouragement by my producers and others at the company to keep it enjoyable. And that is just part of what happens when you have fifty channels and people surf around to see what they can see.

What about the editor's mindset? What happens when you are in the editing room working with all of this footage?   In this three- or four-day period that I was talking about, you've looked at assembly and it is dreadful, and you know that in three days you have to start showing this program to several people. At that point, you don't know what will come into your mind. Will you see the way? There is a leap of faith that what does come into your mind is the right way. If you go down the wrong road, you won't have time to go back and fix it. I don't know where the ideas come from, but sometimes you think, "Let's try this or that," and trust that it will work. Time and time again, it is like writing a song. It just pops in your head. You don't know where it comes from. The great fear is that one day it won't pop in your head. I am thankful when it happens, but I don't know where it comes from or if it is going to work each time. I'm just thankful when it is there.

Bennett Goldberg, Vice President of Editing Services at Digital Symphony, Los Angeles, California

Talk about your background. Where did you start out?   I actually did not start in this industry. I graduate from college and went to work in employee benefits at some major companies. Having remained single then was an asset. At thirty-two, I decided to do something different and took a year leave from my job. I had some money saved up, and I just wanted to try some other things out. Having grown up in Los Angeles, I wanted to try filmmaking. Within a year, I had a staff position at a UHF television station. I became the inhouse technical director, live director and producer. Because of these other duties, I learned video editing. I was given an opportunity to be trained on the CMX 6000 [an earlier editing system]. I offered to teach some CMX 6000 classes in order to get additional time on the machine. I was then hired and sent down to Disney in Florida. I worked on episodic TV, a television series called "Superboy." For me, it was a tremendous opportunity. With limited experience, I was sitting in the editor's chair. It was very clear to me early on that nonlinear was the way to go. When I came back from Florida at the end of the season. I had no connections in Los Angeles and couldn't sit in an editor's chair that following year. I literally went to work for a cable company again but kept pursuing opportunities in nonlinear editing. I met a few people working at Droid-Works, and they offered to train me. They started referring work to me. My first work as an assistant editor, the editor was not happy, and the director turned to me and said, "Here, you edit." I had unprecedented opportunities. Shortly after completing that film, they asked me to run DroidWorks. George Lucas seemed to have no interest in going digital with the Droid, he was more interested in selling this newly designed software to Avid. There was movement to turn the Droid project over to J and R Company [a film supply company]. But at the time, George wanted to keep the Droid going and didn't want to pink-slip all of us. They wanted to start a nonlinear department at DroidWorks, and Lucasfilms wanted to keep the staff working. He decided just to rent the Droid system out for a while to keep all of his editors in a job. It also gave the company more opportunity to continue discussions with Avid. They eventually entered into a royalty with J and R Company, and I became the operations director there. Eventually, I started working with Avid and Lightworks. I have been doing this ever since. I am the vice president of editing services at Digital Symphony, which is owned by Liberty Lightwire. I am involved in marketing and operations. I also serve as an advisor to the Board of American Cinema Editors. It all revolves around nonlinear for me. Avid specifically.

How has digital nonlinear editing changed the editor's job?   Well, let's start with editor's perspective. I've worked with video and then film. When I was editing on the Droids, I was responsible for one channel of picture and two of sound. My intention was to move people emotionally. Dealing with the aesthetic of the story. Today this is usually still the film editor's intention, but now they also have had to make a transition technically. New editors are much more grounded technically and still have an aesthetic feel. They can deal with equipment and also be sensitive to the emotion content of the end result. Over the course of seven or eight years, editors all of a sudden have a higher demand for what the are responsible for. They have maybe ten layers of video, twenty tracks of audio or more. It can detract from the primary focus or responsibility, which is performance. The demands and distractions created by nonlinear equal the good things about it. A much more skilled editor is required to deal with this.

The other thing is, before, people *became* editors. They didn't know what it was before they walked into a cutting room. It took time to be trained and mentored. Today people have a much clearer indication of what editing is before they ever walk into an editing room.

But I would say that regardless of the toolset, an editor is an artist and an integral part of the creative team. The demands are great to stay on top of technological changes. However, it is important to remember equipment is a tool to accomplish something artistic. Editing is now attracting a different type of person. Before, people said, "I want to be an editor." But now, my children of seven and nine know how to edit. Editors are really worried about no longer having the opportunity to mentor assistants. This mentoring used to bring them along over a period of a year and teach them the craft. On the other hand, there is a whole group of children who know what editing is on the same level that Steven Spielberg knew what filmmaking was at the age of ten. These kids will have ten years of experience by the time they get to college. We'll have a whole new world. Film will take on an entirely different appearance. It will be something we can't even recognize today ten years from now because these people have their hands on it so early. Instead of mentoring, we'll have people coming into it with a pretty broad knowledge, and maybe we can help hone that for them. It used to take six to ten years to train to become an editor. Now, if you are lucky and skilled, it can take about two.

My children have a different understanding of the toolset. Part of the evolution is because of computer-based editing. And it will evolve again into some other form after this. I can't conceive of it now, but thirty years ago people couldn't conceive of what we are working on now. That said, children of today, they will take these tools and apply them differently. Because of that, the art form will change The expectation of the viewer will evolve. My neighbor can do things on his computer for under a thousand dollars that I couldn't dream of ten years ago. He will stumble onto it. But it will take the dedication of an artist to exploit the technology. My children will have a better sense of the possibilities with the technology than I will have, and I am at the leading edge of this field. I never envisioned as little as a year ago what I see today, and my children absorb it as routine and matter of fact. They consume things very intellectually. We will see a different viewer in ten years. They will be much more demanding. As a result, the artist will be very different in what they create.

I think in a few years, you won't have an Avid. It may be called an Avid, but it will be entirely different. I think we'll have servers at various places in the world, and say, "I want these functions at my terminals today." Some company will provide it for you almost the way the phone company does. It is just an issue of practicality. We will figure out stumbling blocks like encryption for security. I fully believe that in five years, we will work this way. And as consumers, we will manipulate what comes into our house, going beyond what is offered by TiVo. All of the issues of advertising will be forced to change.

Some editors talk about going "into the zone" when they edit. Have you ever had that experience?   When I sat in the editor's chair on "Superboy." The first director I dealt with was Jackie Cooper. I had tremendous anxiety. I don't know how to describe it, but I had a sense of "you are going to come out of this glowing or you are going to come out of it looking for work." But Jackie was as gracious as anybody I ever met. And that was episodic TV, so he hadn't seen anything I had done before. After 30 seconds of rolling the film, he said, "Why did you do that?" And I thought, "Oh no." I explained to him why, and he said, "You know, I hadn't thought of that." And we went on. I got better and better also at picking up what he wanted. We began to communicate well, and he was gracious about it.

My own editing preferences have always been toward action and dramatic. Comedy strikes terror into me. That sense of timing is so critical. That fraction of a second is so crucial. I love to make people cry. I want to work on things that have enough heart and meaning that it has the capability of creating some type of epiphany for the viewer.

I want at every cut to do two things. First, it should disappear. Second, it should affect the viewer emotionally. And I mean every cut. So that was my primary focus. I don't want to make a cut if I don't have to. That is my approach. How can I minimize cuts? If I do cut, it should affect them emotionally. I concentrate on the tonality and cadence of the scene.

Let's segue into that. The pacing and timing of a scene are so critical. How do you approach these as an editor?   When I worked in UHF TV, I did foreign-language programs. I had to serve as studio switcher on shows based on a pacing or rhythm I would see, because I didn't speak the language. I would look at what was coming as opposed to what was going on. The editor's biggest job is pacing and sense of timing. I will play scenes back with the sound off or with my eyes closed and try to feel the rhythm. I got into this because of my love of music, and I think I have a very good sense of rhythm. The emotional context of the music and other sounds can change things.

Dealing with this cadence is one of the biggest things an editor does. If you look at film, the editor is the first one to deal with the material. You are given a huge block of film, and you are asked to make a small statue out of it. Something that could reside on your desk. You have two tons of film, and artistically you look at it and say, "Yeah, I see a small statue in there." The editor decides on the length and order of the shots. Over 95 percent of the decisions you make in the editing room stick and become the final film. Even when directors and producers change things, so much of it is still your decision. You do the final rewrite of the script. And get relatively little credit for it. Most of the greatest directors were first and foremost editors. The directors I have great reverence for can communicate with editors as well as actors.

What other advice can you give to those interested in motion picture editing?   I would give two basic pieces of advice. The first is either have and/or develop social skills. Of all the people I've met in this business, those who achieve the highest level of success have social skills. Most people in an editing room are shy and retiring and comfortable in a dark room. But having social skills, an ability to schmooze, express your interest, having diplomacy and the ability to articulate your intention is important. Going along with this, I try to emphasize that you have to get on the phone and call people. Be good at taking rejection and coming back. The thing that motivates that is your passion to do something. In this case, it is editing and filmmaking. Those who are motivated develop the social skills if they don't already have them.

The second piece of advice is to always hold onto the artistic concept of what you want to do. Walter Murch is one of my favorites editors. He is a soft-spoken gentleman. He lights up when he talks about editing. The artist just jumps out. Bear in mind that the technology is a tool. Like any other tool, it is what you do with what you have. Many successful editors don't fully understand the technical side, but they do understand the art form. Regardless of money and politics, it is an art form. I'm fond of saying it is about emotional survival, not about anything else. If you believe in what you are doing, you will do okay.

Jonathan Mednick, Founder and President of Other Picture Production Company and Co-Producer and Editor of the "American High" Television Series, New York City

Jonathan, to start out, give us your personal definition of what motion picture editing is. What place do you come from in approaching the material?   For me, editing is the selection and arrangement of sounds and images. Like a musical composition, editing provides the basis for the language and structure of the art form.

Let's talk about to new digital technologies. Do you have any pet peeves about these nonlinear systems? Are there things you actually don't like about them?
Well, it is certainly a drag when the system crashes. However, because I know that computers can have the tendency to crash, especially when you are up against a deadline or when you have a lot of material loaded in, my experience is that I rarely have experienced being left high and dry by a crash. I back up my media files and sequences frequently. We had this very brilliant first assistant director on "American High." He developed a system to keep it from crashing. He absolutely wouldn't let us use digitize clips longer than 2 minutes in length. Some of the shots we needed to pull information from were 20 to 30 minutes long. The editing assistants who were responsible for inputting the footage into the system would have to log and break these shots up into many smaller clips. The assistant director's feeling was that if there were many smaller pieces of media, it wouldn't overwhelm the system. And he was right. We had eight Avids networked together. All editors had access to the same media files on an external storage device, so I imagine that the possibility of a crash was greater than ever in that kind of situation. It only happened once in the year and a half of editing "American High." The system was down for a couple of days. Some media was lost. It is a tremendous disaster when you can't work and you lose footage, but it could have been much worse. We had 1.5 terabytes of media online. So if it had all crashed, that is about 700 hours of footage. It would have taken many 24-hour days to get the media back on-line. For us, we had beginning-of-year, middle and end-of-year interviews with all of the kids in "American High." We wanted to have this stuff on-line all the time because these interviews provide so much of the structure of the show. We needed access to it at all times. It was the well that we drank out of every day. We had all second unit [B-roll] stuff on line all the time as well. You need that footage to go to as cutaways. This included crane shots, tracking shots and exterior tracking shots of every place we shot at. We had the outside of the school, the Burger King the kids hung out at, and so on. We needed this all the time. So we were very careful to back up media. We had an assistant whose job each night was to back up every editor's media.

Other disadvantages of these nonlinear systems are what I call "blink of an eye." If you are using either film or analog video, you have to shuttle through the footage. You have the ability to go through it and become familiar with it. Even though I am a believer in nonlinear technologies, I kind of agree with those who lament the going away of these older systems that force you to look at the footage over and over as you scan through material. Nonlinear editing is murderous on people who don't label and log well. They can't find anything. This is critical. Organization is so important. There are really only three aspects of film editing. I call these the "Three L's": labeling, logging and lugging. Do these carefully and well, and you'll be okay. Because with digital, you don't have the physicality you have with film. You can't look for "the small roll with the blue leader" if you are missing a shot. There is no physical bin to look down in to see if the shot is there. You have to know what the shot was called and access it via the computer.

The other thing people say is that editors make lightning-fast decisions, which is bad. They don't necessarily take time to think and linger over where the best edit is. They just do it. The lack of cumbersomeness encourages quick action.

In some ways, the limitations of both film and analog video editing helped to create discipline and rigor. On the other hand, you can think of the editing system as a personal instrument to communicate. The digital nonlinear systems are easy to use, like an extension of your mind.

Let me give the following as another downside to digital nonlinear editing. I directed a film called "Dita and the Family Business." This is a documentary about the Goodman family, who owned and operated the Bergman's department store in New York City. Most of the film is constructed with home movies in 35mm, 16mm, S-8 and regular-8 film as well as still photographs. 16mm film is usually shot at twenty-four frames per second, but some is shot at sixteen frames per second or even eighteen frames per second. This was hard because when we wanted to do a film finish, we had to go back to the original reversal film. In the Avid, we could make things any length, but in our optical film, we had to have it all done in the lab. In the Avid, we could speed this up, change the color, and so on. It was hard and expensive to do all of these things on film that we could easily do on an Avid. The folks at the film laboratory said that my editor had "Aviditis." She was trigger-happy on the effects. Anything she needed to stretch and slow down to make it work, we did. But in going back to a final film print, any dissolves or fades that were other than standard laboratory length, we had to do it as an optical print. The lab was delighted. They made a lot of money on us because of it. You just do these things on the Avid without thinking about them, but if you have to eventually go back and finish the production on film, you pay for them. But you ask (about the editing), "Was this really rigorous?" Maybe it is often better to just want straight cuts, don't do all of these effects. They are so easy to do on most digital nonlinear systems, but they may take away from the "purity" of the footage.

But in the end, I love working on these systems. It's crazy. You don't have to lose anything. I guess one of the downsides is that with the equipment, the industry has the tendency to exploit the editorial department. To some extent, it makes them work longer hours. It is like comparing a typewriter to a computer. With a typewriter, you did two drafts instead of one hundred. I don't know if the result is better with a computer, but you certainly spend more time. Here is an example of what can happen in the industry. Say you have a postproduction house who uses an Avid to edit commercials for their clients. The editors see edit decision list and assemble the edit based on that. The clients look at it and consider it good but not quite right. They want to know if the editor can make some changes. The editor says, "Sure, come back tomorrow, and you can see what we have done." The next day, the same thing happens. Once the client likes the edit, they have the opportunity to look at multiple versions side by side. Digital nonlinear editing gives tremendous power to clients once they realize they can demand multiple versions. They can exhaust the possibilities of the footage. But to make these, it is very time consuming. The editorial department has to stay late. They can do it faster, but it takes more time. A friend of mine at ABC makes ungodly amounts of money in overtime. But I consider it good to want to exhaust the artistic possibilities of the film. Don't settle for the first or second pass. Somebody said, "Films are never finished, they are just abandoned." That's it. That is perfect. Nobody ever says, "Alright, it is good enough now." And these nonlinear technologies forestall the abandonment even further. But at some point, the editor will say, "I've got to move to another project" or "I have to finish this because it has a firm broadcast date."

One of the good things about the incorporation of digital nonlinear technologies into postproduction houses is that there are fewer and fewer people doing simple "library" functions like syncing and coding rushes, reconstituting trims and outtakes and just looking for things. In the past, the assistant to the editor would often spend time hunting for shots. Since that is basically unnecessary with digital nonlinear systems, now they may spend time assembling the first pass of an edit following a script. The lead editor might say, "Here's the outline, try it out." Or get them to do montages, things like that. The assistants do less mind-numbing things, more creative things. They spend more time trying to help get the *edit* right instead of other things.

Do you see new technologies radically changing motion picture editing for you?
I don't see radical structural changes, I just see improvements. Refinements to what we have already. People will get more storage, and the resolution will get higher and higher. I think ideally that we can start to put more things on-line on the Internet. I edited a music video two years ago. The band was in L.A., and we were in New York. We emailed them a QuickTime of their music video. We were excited at the ability to do that. We got instant feedback. None of us had to wait for a FedEx shipment. We didn't want to have to wait one and a half days for feedback. By then, you have gone through five more versions of the edit. The ability to stream video and audio at full screen across the Internet will be really nice. The structures exist; we just have to make things faster.

We had eight Avids networked together in Los Angeles for "American High." Maybe in the future, these eight Avids could be in different places in the world and the material would be shared over the Internet. I don't know what the advantage of that would be, however. With "American High," it was difficult that production was going on in Chicago while the post was going on in Los Angeles. We vowed never to do that again. We wanted the producers, shooters and editors in same room. The editors wanted to be able to quickly ask things like, "Is this true to the character?"

What about music? Talk about how you use music in your own work.   I find it helpful to use music early on. I use scratch tracks for my rough cuts. The danger of this is falling in love with music you can't get permission for. But music does give you a feeling for rhythm and for the mood of the scene. We used so much music in "American High," sometimes I felt it was a crutch to communicate what we didn't have visually. Maybe it was sometimes a bit weak filmmaking. This can be particularly dangerous for documentaries. People will say, "What is that music doing there, what does that have to do with the world we are watching?" You can alienate people very quickly by using music to try to make up for your lack of visuals or a story. I think we see this a lot in current television programming. When MTV's "Real World" series came on, I found it appalling. The music was so omnipresent. I guess we can forgive it in some ways because it *is* Music Television! Their audience willingly goes to television to help them make decisions on music purchases. But in my mind, it was bad editing, bad filmmaking.

As an editor, talk about how you develop creative tension in your films or television shows.   For me, it has to do with setting up an expectation and delaying the payoff. That is what Hitchcock said. He called it suspense. You have two options. The first is to show the assassin planting the bomb. We watch the hero going about his business totally unaware the bomb is ticking. Will he be there when the bomb goes off? That can give 15 minutes of suspense. Or you can simply have the bomb go off. That gives you a minute of surprise. Any time you have a choice between surprise and suspense, go with suspense. I think it has to do with the omniscience thing the audience feels. We know something the character doesn't know. We gain a certain narrative pleasure in this. So for me, as an editor, it has to do with withholding the payoff. It is about concealing and then revealing information. Don't immediately gratify the viewer's desire. That is what tension is.

Some editors really feel like they are constructing a film, while others approach editing as chipping away at the footage to *find* the film. Talk about how you use either or both of these approaches.   Well, in documentaries, I look for the film all the time. You chip away, move things around. For fiction, it is interesting and usually different. In this class I teach with a Hollywood editor, we have the students first do a rough cut, to make sure all of the info is there. We say, "Don't worry about pacing or rhythm; just make sure the shots are in the right places." I mean, we have them work it a little bit to give it some life, but I think you should just get it all together first. In fiction, I tend to like just following the script. I would consider narrative fiction requiring of this more additive approach, while documentary, even with a script outline, usually requires a more subtractive approach.

There are ongoing discussions about the ethics of motion picture editing. Tell us about some of your most recent experiences with having to make decisions about how to edit images and what challenges you had with concealing and/or manipulating the footage.   I can think of a lot of situations that we had in "American High" that were very tricky in terms of moving things around. We often had to do this in order to tell a coherent story. However, it makes you nervous. Sometimes it doesn't matter to the telling of the story, but it hurts your credibility with the people who served as your documentary subjects. They see the finished version and can tell if you have moved things around in time, if you used an actor to speak a line that someone had actually said but your recording was too low. They see your chicanery. And this can undermine you as a producer. You have to be very careful.

We got into problems in editing with people wanting to change their mind about your showing an aspect of their actions. As an editor, you make decisions about what the theme of the show or episode is. You create characters with dimension. We did this with the Spring Break episode of "American High." The cool, rich kids went to the Bahamas, rented hotel rooms, drank alcohol, since the legal drinking age is eighteen in the Bahamas. A bunch of them got romantically involved. For them, it was a great, unchaperoned trip. The other Spring Break trip we taped was the band trip to the People's Republic of China. This was a very regimented tour of a communist country. We made an episode intercutting these two trips. So you see the "nerds" in the PRC and the rich kids hanging out on the beach and drinking. There was one girl who was feeling alienated in the Bahamas. She didn't like drinking, didn't have a boyfriend and wasn't really interested in casual sex. We built the Bahamas part of the episode around her. Her point of view was "I just want to have a good time with my friends and hang out in the sun." In the episode, it appeared that she was just not into the hedonistic pleasures her classmates were enjoying. However, in real life, it turned out that while she didn't like to drink, she did smoke pot. But we were forbidden to show smoking pot by the Fox Network, which commissioned the series. So in reality, she did an illegal activity we couldn't show. After seeing the edited version, she said, "I look like a loser." We told her that we wanted to present her as the hero who follows her heart. And in editing, I don't think we showed anything incompatible with the truth. We simply didn't show certain things. But she thought that showing all of her activities was essential to telling her story. She said, "I'm not one of those retro-alcoholic kids, I'm one of the hip kids who smokes dope."

So with ethics, you have to just do your best to selectively show parts of the footage to tell stories. We selected one story to tell about her, not her preferred story. This is what editing is. This can be unethical in that they may see themselves in a different way. Sometimes you conceal the truth in order to tell one big truth.

Let me give you another example of an ethical quandary in editing working as second unit photographer on this film called "A Perfect Candidate" about Oliver North running for the United States Senate. There is a conversation that goes on and extends throughout the full length of the film. It is in a car and occurs between the campaign manager and the communication director of North's campaign. However, this is a conversation that never actually happened, at least the way it is specifically presented on film. We had one interview with each of these two men. Both of these interviews took place in cars, but not at same time. We cut it to make it seem like they are talking to each other. They had many conversations in many cars, but not this one. This "conversation" is absolutely the spine of the movie. It wouldn't be a film without this. Neither of the two men objected to the way we edited it, however. There was logic to the things they said, a flow. It is a little lie to tell a big truth. They did have these car rides and talk about Oliver North. This is a distillation of these conversations. Maybe there are people who would think this is a terrible thing to do. Suppose it were Oliver North and Idi Amin, and we were intercutting their interviews to make it appear that they had a conversation that they really never had at all. In my mind, that would be bad. But in the case of this particular film, the reality was there.

Can you comment on the collaborative nature of editing? Well, the collaboration in editing "American High" was huge. We assigned people characters to edit instead of episodes to edit at first. They made stringouts of what they thought was interesting. The scenes would get passed around and used in various episodes. We would decide to use particular characters in particular episodes and go to these stringouts to figure out which footage to use. There was a lot of negotiating about who got to use what. Somebody would cut the scene, and we would fight about who would get to use it. We would of course have to recut it to get the pacing right It was fun later in the process, but there was tremendous fear and anxiety early on because we didn't know the form of the show yet. Once the first episode was locked in, we then knew what the form was, and there was comfort in that. You have the open, title sequence, Act One, Act Two, climax and show end, and so on. It got easier once we could see how the structure flowed with this kind of footage, and we worked within that. Our job became massaging the footage in. I edited the prom episode. It was a kind of tag-team effort. I am a good editor but not really fast. I came in late at night to do it and worked for two weeks. Then my other editor came in and was fast and finished it off. He was good at montage, and so if we needed a scene to lead into what he was working on, I'd go onto another system and cut the intro. We worked together to put the episode together, and for the most part I liked it. It was a little weird at times, but it is just a matter of labeling shots and sequences well so we could both easily find them. Sometimes there was some headbutting among editors, but I don't know if that was really because we were all editors or more simply because we were just people with different tastes.

Do you like to get feedback from others when you are editing?   Yes, constantly. I look for it all the time—at the end, after I have made my first cut, anytime. With "American High," we'd lay it to tape every other night to get feedback from executive producer and director. We wanted their feedback. We'd send the edit to the Fox Network once a week. During the last week of editing we sent it every day. The feedback might consist of notes that could be from any network department—legal, artistic, standards and practices, any department. I showed a rough cut of an "American High" episode at an academic conference the week before the show aired, and I found it really helpful. It was good not so much for what people said, but because I could tell when people were bored, when they missed something and when we nailed it.

Shortly after this interview Jonathan Mednick passed away. We, along with many colleagues and industry professionals, mourn the loss of this talented producer, director, editor and friend.

Lisa Riznikove, Editor and Co-Owner of Absinthe Pictures, Los Angeles, California

What you do on a daily basis?   Everything! I co-own the company. I edit, I look for clients, everything. We are a two-person company, so we have a lot to do.

What systems do you work on at Absinthe Pictures?   We use Avid as our primary editing system. We do our graphics on a G-4 Macintosh with a lot of different software loaded on, including Aftereffects. 3-D programs, Commotion and so on. We do visual graphic effects. We commission our sound design out of house where they use ProTools. This allows us to communicate between Avid and ProTools.

What kinds of clients does your company bring in?   Some examples are our Universal Interactive Studios [games and graphics], Guess Jeans, Apple Computer and website startups like Evolution TV. We did their branding video when they launched the company. We've won fourteen different awards since July 2000 on that piece.

What is your personal definition of motion picture editing? Editors work with directors and other people to tell stories. This is an aspect that a lot of editors don't seem to grasp. I learned with old-school editors, and they taught me that we are visually telling something, whether it is a 30-second commercial or an hour-long show. There is now a tendency for people to skip a lot of steps in their knowledge as an editor. They are learning how to push buttons. They are getting caught up in the technical aspects of it. They are hung up in various programs, systems, knowing how to rewire machines. That is wonderful and increasingly a larger part of our job, but if you don't know the fundamentals of visually telling a story, then you aren't an editor.

With Final Cut Pro becoming a prevalent force in the field, you can take a relatively small investment in the system, a weekend class, a tutorial on the computer, and think you know it all. So there is a glut of people who call themselves editors. They are missing the big picture. There is a trend to do it all yourself. It used to be that a producer and an editor would collaborate to craft a spot. Now editors are being asked to write and produce their own material. So if you don't have the experience to tell the story, you will have a really hard time writing and producing. This is also causing a trend now for writers and producers to take a class and think they have become editors. They have now lost the collaboration and don't have the background.

The collaborator has another sensibility, another set of eyes. It is short-changed on both sides. Most writer/producers who also edit don't craft as well and are not as strong visually as are editors who are forced to write and produce. They certainly aren't as technically proficient. They just didn't have the background. Being an editor is more than cutting and more than running a machine. We like to joke and call them these producers who think they can edit "preditors."

People are being asked to wear an awful lot of hats. It is scary for them because they do not have the background.

What are client expectations with nonlinear digital equipment? The digital age in general has changed the patience level of clients. Everything is available on the fax, cell phone, Internet, email, all the way around in communications. So no one plans anymore; they expect things to happen at the drop of a hat. I also see directing executives who don't have experience in media, so they don't know how long things take. They don't understand the steps. Even after a picture is locked, they want to make changes. Certainly the expectations in terms of time is very different. They want it fast.

Also, when we were all linear editing, when you did a rough cut, it was rough looking. If you did titles or graphics, it was a black card with white letters that said, "Graphics go here." Today's executives expect to see almost a finished spot with a rough cut. They'll get hung up on graphics and hung up on scratch tracks. The executives have gotten spoiled. Because the technology now lets us do graphics and transitions that look very professional, it is now expected that these are included very early in the editorial process. The bar is raised year after year. The exciting thing is that you as an editor can design a graphic look for your spots. You define it now, instead of sending it out. The downside is, it is a lot more work. It is another hat, now you are a graphic designer. Okay, so you could barely pass finger painting in kindergarten, and now you have to have a graphic sensibility. I would encourage anyone learning to edit to learn the basics of design. You should know where things should be on the screen, flow energy, colors, all these things. You can consider an editor a painter. They have a lot of tools to work with. Paint, paint brushes, canvases of different sizes and textures, they need to learn how to use all of these tools.

What advice might you give to new editors or to those wanting to change careers?   I would caution them that it is a very packed marketplace. Don't expect to find a job right away. Don't expect to edit right away. Be willing to pay your dues. Spend time in tape vault, as a runner, as an editing assistant. I get a lot of resumes from recent graduates with some internship experience or classes, and they want a position as an editor or assistant editor. You can expect to become a runner, production assistant or to work in the tape vault. Those are your first steps. In a smaller market, you might be able to work as an assistant editor. You are not competing against only people who went to film school, but also people changing careers. There are lots of producers, scriptwriters and directors who think they want to become editors. You need to be realistic about the time period it takes to become an editor. It can take two years or more. In long-form filmmaking, that is an even longer process. There are lots of things you can do to help yourself. Take internships in school. Not just classes. We want to see you have worked in a professional broadcast environment. The college television station even. They want to see you have been on a set, in an editing room. I want to see people who have been around clients, even at an ad agency. It is all valuable experience to help you land a job. Internships are a great way to step into a job. They often turn into jobs. I'd much rather hire someone who I've worked with, seen their experience, watched them work.

Tell us about the steps you like to go through with a client when editing.   I like to first meet with them to get the feel for what they are looking for. Then I like to have at least a day to sit with the footage, go through it, come up with my own ideas. Much of what we do is not storyboarded out. We are given a lot of creative latitude. They want our creative input. So I'll have multiple music choices. I like to do a first cut without the client. I think it is good to have a couple of different cuts to give them some choices. Then they can give input about different things. I find giving a couple of choices gives them the satisfaction of making the decisions and that you are more open to working with them.

What are your thoughts on the ethics of editing as you work with clients?   It is a tricky thing. Ethics change with every client. We do advertisements and promotional pieces, so the ethics line is very blurred. We are held up to broadcast standards, meaning Standards and Practice rules set out by the FCC. We can't show cause and effect. For example, we can't show a gun being shot and then show somebody being shot. We can't show children in jeopardy. In terms of ethics beyond those standards, there is very little. Shots are cheated all the time, and we are not in the business of making news or documentary. There is no claim that all the shots are correct. We are attempting to entice the viewer. So it is making no claims beyond truth in advertising. And this is perfectly okay to do this. Quite frequently, you use a shot in another place and make it seem it fits in, you make a line that someone says, you take it out of context to support the copy you've got on the spot.

As an editor of advertisements and promos, it is very hard to let your personal ethics get in the way. Some editors have a problem with violence in movies or with sexy commercials. That is fine. But they also need to realize they are limiting their career. I've seen it happen. It is difficult if your client or boss has to tailor what they can bring you. I've seen careers stall.

I guess ethics does come into play if your client has specific concerns. NBC doesn't want to be associated with certain things. They won't do ads that cross those lines. Procter & Gamble has different ethics, more stringent. And Fox might be considered different from these two. Every client is different.

Dan Sparks, Director of Post Production at Four Square Productions, San Diego, California

As an editor, what do you consider your job to be?　I hate to use the cliché, but it comes down to this; it is visually telling a story, conveying a message. The ultimate goal is to connect with your audience, with the corporation, whoever the piece is for. There are varying degrees of skills that editors bring to the table in order to tell the story effectively. But the ability to tell a story is the most important.

Four Square Productions works with a wide variety of clients. Tell us about who you work with and what their needs are.　Yes, our clients are quite varied. We are a company going into our twenty-eighth year, so we have a lot of repeat business. I would guess that maybe 60 percent of our work is high-end corporate work, including new product releases, training videos and so on. That has opened up even further with the advent of multimedia on the web. Before, we were narrow in what we produced as a product. The client wanted video with music, and that was about it. Now we have to be more broad-based and service all of their needs. We address questions such as these: Is their print collateral? Should the product also live on CD-ROM and DVD? Should it have an accompanying website? All of these are under the digital media domain. We can produce them. In addition, we've been groundbreaking with high-definition television, DVD production and widescreen. The balance of our work is broadcast, commercials, and DirectTV spots. We do sports packages, NFL, ESPN Game Ticket and other similar programs. We also produce the spots that market these programs.

We have government defense agencies and other federal clients which have new technologies or new areas of concern they want to address. They need some kind of media presentation to take to Congress or state agencies to try to get support or money for research. Since we are a full-service production house and not just a postproduction facility, they come to us for the full package. One case in point is cyberterrorism. Federal agencies come to us for visual media to try to raise money and awareness. These projects are high-end pieces. They are drama-based.

We call them "visioneering" pieces. We showcase the technology, even though it is not yet developed. Our graphics team helps to visually design these technologies to show what they want to produce. Therefore these kinds of projects are very effects laden.

Work with the clients has changed in two profound ways. The first is in their personal exposure to our craft via television at home. They are very fluent in the look of what I call MTV-style editing. They walk in with that in their hip pocket already, and they have preconceptions about what they want. The second is that we now have the capability to do high-end graphics. They experience that for the first time and realize that they can make changes to the look of a show. There are advantages to this, because we can be more responsive to the client. Before, you might plant your feet a bit, because with older technologies it was more difficult to make changes. But now the editor and the rest of the team can be more flexible. We have a little bounce in there, if you will. If the product name changes at the last minute for legal reasons, we have flexibility we didn't have before. It is simply a different skill set than when we were working in linear editing systems.

You have been in the industry for a while. What equipment did you start out on early in your editing career?   I've been in the business so long that I edited back when we were literally cutting videotape [laughs]! So, I've gone all the way through. I don't know why I tended to swing to the postproduction side of things. I have directed and produced, but I favor postproduction. I guess I like gadgets deep down inside. I'm comfortable in that world. What has kept me involved and kept it exciting is that it is constantly evolving. We are using Media 100s here. This is because we are a production company and not just a postproduction house. The work is our own product. Therefore we don't have to sell the Avid name. And that is more about attitude than anything. In Los Angeles, it is Avid everywhere. When you are your own production company, you can make choices about the system that really fits your need. And we definitely prefer the Media 100 system. The picture quality is better, and they are consistent with upgrades and releases. We also have a traditional on-line bay, and we keep it updated and maintained, but I don't foresee putting any more money in that room. Other than maintaining it, I don't see reason to put money into it much longer. It is used to dub off of D2 tapes and for compositing off of D2.

In terms of storage, we have a high-speed server, so all of our media files are moved back and forth. All of the rooms are linked, so you can control anything from any other room. The editors no longer really have to focus on final mix of audio or graphics. They focus on telling the story, working with the client. Audio issues are handled by our sound designer in a separate studio mix. He cleans up the audio, equalizes it and sends it back to editor. It is the same for visual effects. Depending on the editor's skills, if they can do effects during edit, that is fine. But if they are not graphically skilled but still a great storyteller, they send it out to graphics department, and the editor drops into the show. In the old days, a lot of this was done in the on-line room. In the nonlinear world, it can be spread out.

Obviously, the job market has changed in the postproduction world in the past few years. What are entry-level positions like at Four Square Productions? One of the biggest things I see happening is that students are learning the technology but not the theory behind the technology. When you have to go through that process, it sticks with you. What I see is younger students who have been taught computer-based editing and graphic design but no heart and soul. They often haven't developed their style. If I see that they have this already, they get hired. I get a lot of resumes on a daily basis from technical schools. They promise people careers in multimedia. They may know the equipment, but they don't have a sense of style or basic storytelling experience. If they have style and heart, I am willing to forgo the lack of equipment experience and teach them that. We have them start out batch-digitizing to give them some hands-on. You can see if they have a good work ethic, if they pay attention to detail, are they really interested in doing this? And there is no faking it. Either you have it or you don't. It is a pretty grinding profession. They need an energy and drive.

To get this "other side of things," the heart and soul and storytelling ability, I would suggest that if they truly have it in them, they are already involved in student projects or they are talking with fellow students. They are already driven to do extra things. They do more than is required. They can't *not* do it. It does help me, when I am deciding whether or not to hire someone, to see something they have done. I'll look at student films.

Something I have noticed in my years of hiring is that there tends to be a gender bias in terms of who applies for jobs. A lot of the people who send me resumes in the postproduction end tend to be male. I find that interesting. In graphics, I do get more resumes from women seeking graphics employment. They often work in PhotoShop and Illustrator and tend to be oriented toward design. I seem to see more men interested in 3-D and Aftereffects and less in design. In terms of graphics, when I see people interested in graphics, I want to know if they have training in design, balance and color schemes. If they are just technicians with no sense of design and color, I won't hire them. I need multifaceted people, and that is whom I most often hire. They need to have a sense of design and an ability to collaborate in telling a story.

A piece of advice I would like to give to students or new editors is this: You have to be good at teamwork. In the past, there was a sense of editor on autopilot or in a solo role. They worked in a more privileged position. But because of non-linear quality and the nature of the digital systems, the editor and the client are interacting more. The editor needs to have people skills. It is different in that before, in the high-end on-line edit, you could give the client the back of your head. They had no clue what you were doing. They can now look over your shoulder and see you moving clips around, so you do need to converse with people. This helps them work through a problem or puzzle area with a project. If an editor can't fit personality-wise, I won't hire them. We can't deal with attitudes. If an issue comes up, even if it is nobody's fault, the client wants you to come up with a solution, don't cry about it. We are team players. Editing is being part of a big storytelling team.

Bart Weiss, Independent Film/Video Producer and Editor and Director of the Dallas Video Festival, Dallas, Texas

As director and curator for the Dallas Video Festival, you must view a huge amount of material each year. Based on current trends you witness and on your own role as an editor, give us your definition of motion picture editing.   Editing to me is the process of finding the right moments in the material and placing them in the right order. It is finding the best performances [whether they are actors or documentary subjects] and telling a story without losing your audience. You should always think about your audiences. Most television viewers [where a vast majority of film/video material is viewed] have a remote control in their hand. If you think about their thumb on the remote while you edit, you will edit differently.

I would also define editing as "falling out of love with your footage." The famous Soviet filmmaker and film theorist Sergei Eisenstein said something like "Editing is the ruthless suppression of the inessential." I would agree with that statement.

Going back to a more technical side of editing, with new technologies, the definition of editing or the job of the editor has also been expanded to include layering with appropriate graphics and working on sound design.

Talk with us about both the best things and the least preferable things about non-linear motion picture editing.   Well, let me talk about the bad things first. Tonight I have to edit a package program for a local PBS series I produce. All I have to do this evening is add an introduction, a lead-out and the credits to the program. I have the actual program on digital tape, and I have to now make sure that all of these additional elements are packaged in with it. If I were simply using a videotape-to-videotape non-computer-based editing system, this would be a very quick process. But because I am using nonlinear, I have to spend time capturing the program into the computer, then edit these elements into the program and roll it all back to tape.

Another bad thing about digital nonlinear computer-based editing is that you might not spend as much time really getting to know your footage, even though you have logged it. With tape-to-tape video editing or with film editing, you spend a fair amount of time rolling through the tape or film while looking for a shot. This extreme familiarity with your footage happens because the equipment forces you to scroll through it. You end up saying, "Oh yeah, that is good . . . . I had forgotten about that shot." With digital nonlinear, you don't have to look through things once you have captured the footage. Your footage is already broken up into shots, and you simply click on the thumbnail clip or the name of the shot in order to immediately access it. This efficiency can cause you to lose "chance." Chance and happenstance are very important to the creative process of editing, and the utmost familiarity with your footage allows you to consider all possibilities. This is why, with digital non-linear editing, logging your footage well is so critical. It may be the only time you see everything. If you know what to look for in your footage, it is there easily at your fingers, but you have to really know the footage in order to do this well.

I guess the only other bad thing about digital nonlinear editing in my mind is that editors are getting snookered. The time crunch and the expectations for speed because of the equipment are enormous. As an example, a feature film editor use to have several months to edit a film. Now he or she may be given weeks to do the same job. There is the expectation that because the equipment is so efficient, you don't need as much time. And it is this time that allows air into the piece. It is a work of art that needs time to be fully fleshed out. But with nonlinear equipment, the anxiety level and the expectation to edit quickly are tremendous. This ties in with the problem I mentioned above about familiarity with footage, but in addition, it directly relates to an editor's income. It is not like your daily rate has changed. Whereas you used to be paid over a few months to edit a film, you are now paid for a few weeks for the same work. This is good for producers, bad for the craftspeople. It is hard to make a living as a craftsperson in the digital age.

As for the good things about digital nonlinear equipment, they are many. You can easily find shots when you need them. There is virtually no time between the point when you think of an idea and its execution. It's like "What would happen if I? . . ." and then you try it. If you don't like it, simply undo it. There is no searching for footage. You don't have to stay up all night searching for two film frames in the bottom of your trim bin or why you are two frames out of sync. You just type in "+2" to fix it.

Also, if you've logged and labeled your footage well, you are halfway there. You can use the comment windows attached to each shot to discuss thematic value, characters, describe the shot and so forth. On that note, logging must include all of the potential themes that the shot might incorporate into the final project. You need to list how many ways the shot *might* be used. Label the shot mentioning these. This requires forethought, and that takes experience.

Another good thing about digital nonlinear editing is that *you* are the editor. On the flip side of that—*you* are the editor. Now you are responsible for everything. You now have to produce the final, finished product for your film. In the past, there were always several people working on various aspects of the project. And of course in high-budget productions, there still are. But if you are an independent or smaller-budget producer/editor, you must do it all. And you can with these systems. But now you must become a colorist or timer [manipulating the color, contrast and hue of your images if necessary], and this is a subtle art. Sound design is a subtle art. My prediction is that in the future, people who are trained as professional colorists will be hired to come to your editing system at the final stages and tweak it.

What changes do you see in the future for your type of editing projects?   The best change has already happened: I can edit at home. Last night I edited from 10:00 P.M. to 1:00 A.M. and then went to bed. I can also have a cat on the monitor and another on my lap. This may sound silly, but this kind of familiarity can be important. It brings calmness and tranquility to the process. And music. I like music playing while I edit. You can't do all of this if you are editing in a high-end post-production house. On another note, though, I predict that in the future, there will be even more cases of carpal tunnel syndrome and other maladies because people can sit at home and edit all day and night without paying attention to the needs of their body. The digital world allows fewer people to do more things. Computerization replaces workers. The nature of the work environment has changed.

Talk about music in the creative process of editing. How do you use music in your projects?   I find that a lot of good editors were at one time musicians. They look at the internal beat of a scene. They can tell the literal beat of the footage. An understanding of music is good to have as an editor. For any scene you are editing that will include music but you don't have the proper clearances yet, it often helps to add a scratch track of music while you are editing. The energy of the music will allow the shots to stay on longer. Otherwise, you will end up cutting the shots too short, and when you go back in and add the music to this edited version, you will often feel that the images are cutting too quickly.

I often give the following suggestion to beginning editors: Edit together some footage you have shot. Then lay it against various styles of music. Use rap, metal, classical, reggae, jazz, techno or whatever you want. Each time, you will get a different sensibility from the scene. This is the same with sound effects. They can make a scene more real or more unreal. And sometimes the soundtrack becomes absolutely integral to the unfolding of the plot. Take Mike Figgis' film "Timecode" as an example. Without the soundtrack, you might get lost in the film. But the music continually clues you in.

Talk about tension in motion picture editing.   In the digital world, you can see how quickly you are cutting by looking at the timeline. You have a visual representation of the footage laid out, and every cut or transition is represented. You can immediately assess whether there is equality or disparity in your tempo. This similarity or difference is what creates tension.

Do you consider yourself an additive or deductive editor? Do you find shots and begin adding bits and pieces together, lengthening as needed, or do you string out your raw footage and then winnow away at it?   It really depends on the project. Sometimes you are working from a script, so you build up the thesis within the film, using that as a basis. Sometimes, especially in the documentary mode, you chip away at the footage, almost like sculpting to find the best reality. Narrative filmmaking almost always seems to me to be more additive in the editing process, and nonfiction or documentary is most often deductive. Either way, it is easier with digital nonlinear systems!

What are your thoughts on the ethics of motion picture editing?   It has gotten to the point now where you truly can't believe what you see on television or films. Videotape produced as evidence is no longer acceptable in my mind. It can be so manipulated. If the President were assassinated today and there was a Zapruder-type film, we would all wonder if had been digitally altered to tell one version of the story or another. Yet video testimony is still being used. This affects public discourse, yet all videotape has a point of view. I believe if you want to use videotape for depositions, lawyers should be smart and have their clients lit well. If it is someone they don't want the jury to believe, pull the microphone back so they are harder to hear. All of these things, how someone comes across, can be altered by a skilled craftsperson in both production and editing. You can put one shot next to another in editing and radically alter the meaning.

Clearly, creating a production affects people. Images affect the way people think and act. As an editor, it is your job to put things together that didn't exist quite like that in reality. We do this because a lot of the time, life is boring. Your job as an editor is to manipulate reality. But let's all remember that that is what is happening.

As an editor, ask yourself, "Where do my personal ethics lie?" It is very important to think about this while you are in school or while you are new to your career. I know it is sometimes difficult when you need money to make a decision on taking a job based on your personal ethics, but if you are strong in yourself, it will be much easier.

Describe your experience with the collaborative process of editing. In the digital world, some storage systems allow you to easily share information with other editors, sound designers, graphic artists and others working on the production. Also, Firewire pocket drives allow you to edit, output onto these small drives, walk off with them and share the edit with people at another location. The footage all remains digital. Collaborating over the Internet is possible now, providing you have the lines fast enough to allow you to stream over the Internet. Writers and musicians do this a lot. It will start happening more and more with video.

How and why did you become an editor? I first started in school. But in documentaries, which I often work on, editing is the process where the film emerges, and I love this process. The role of the editor is valued. As both an undergraduate and graduate student, my experience was that the role of editor was a coveted one.

Editing is an intellectual challenge. There is a saying that goes "If you can't solve it, dissolve it." As a new editor, I would go to great lengths to think through an edit and not dissolve.

Shooting is very physical. It is very visceral. In editing, you play God with the material you shot. It is very intellectual. You find out how smart you are in telling the story well. It is an incredible challenge. You attempt to figure out what you can do with this footage, and you make it your life's work. If you do it well, nobody knows how great a job you did.

However, I was never just an editor. I continue to do work in other roles in production. As a student, it is critical that you also understand shooting and other production crew positions. It is also good for you to be shooting one project and editing another at the same time. You will learn more this way about both production and postproduction. The lessons will intertwine. As an editor, you will say, "Oh, I needed that cutaway here, or that establishing shot there, that I didn't get on location." Your production mistakes will inform your editing lessons, and your editing will inform your shooting. If you spend all of your time editing, you will become a hermit. You never see the sun, you drink too many Diet Cokes, you lose reality and you need this connection to the outside world. If not, you become too self-obsessed, too obsessed with the footage, and you have no framework within which to make your decisions. On the other hand, when you sit down to work, you must be focused. This is when the magic happens. Editing is kind of like driving.

You don't think about putting your foot on the gas, you just do it. In editing, your mind melds with the material. It is very intuitive.

Talk about the steps you take in editing.   I used to do paper edits [writing down your proposed edit on paper before actually getting on the equipment] but haven't in awhile because the digital system allows me to make changes so quickly. However, paper edits are invaluable if you have limited storage space on your digital system. If you can only input a small amount of your footage at a time, the paper edit can become invaluable. Also, if you have carefully logged your footage, this lessens the need for paper edits. But in student editing situations, they are often good.

Do you seek feedback from others during the editing process?   This is the bad side of editing at home! One of the great things about schools is the peer group you have around you. Sometimes the input of these peers is more valuable and helpful to you that that of faculty. It is critical to choose a film/television school by hanging out in the editing room. Do a site visit if you can, and get the vibes. The same goes for jobs. Listen to what the editing room is like. How do the editors communicate, and see if you agree. Peer groups are major resources for you as an editor.

In some ways, if one of you gets a job in the industry, all of you do. You have hung out with these folks, helped them out and watched their films. In the film and television industries, it is so rare to find people without self-interest. Of course, you can also ship edited footage to others and share comments over the Internet. You hook up with your colleagues at school and benefit each other.

As for showing footage to others while you are in the postproduction stage, the feedback can be invaluable. But there is something even more important than what they say. If you show your work to somebody and you watch it with them, you will see the project differently than if you watch it alone. All of the flaws will become obvious to you. If you find yourself thinking, "Just wait until the next scene, it is really good," pay attention to the scene you had this thought during. There is something wrong with it that needs to be fixed.

If you do decide to show your work-in-progress to others, make sure you have a good screen and that the sound is good. Don't talk during the screening in attempts to tell them where cutaways will eventually be. Just let them watch it. It may not be perfect, but make sure it flows.

Why do you like specific systems?   Well, I am going to be biased here, because I am a huge fan of Apple systems and absolutely love Final Cut Pro. However, Avid has a very elegant interface. The logging on Avid systems is very sophisticated, and that is good. But it is very expensive. You can buy one Final Cut Pro system for less than one year of Avid tech support. However, Avid tech support people will stay on the phone with you until you get it. I hate NT and Windows-based systems. If I have a problem on those systems and I can't fix it, it seems clunky and not intuitive at all. Discreet is nice for a Windows-based system. Adobe Premiere is okay. The title tools are easy to work with, and the motion tools are intuitive. It allows for a subtle manipulation of images and is similar to Adobe Photoshop. And by the way—anyone in editing should have a working knowledge of Photoshop!

Give us at least one suggestion for emerging or potential motion picture editors.
You should rent a DVD or videotape of your favorite film. Look at one scene.
Count the number of shots. Make a graph about the length, the screen direction
and all other elements of the scene. Then go out and shoot the scene. Then edit it
exactly the same way. This will give you a feel for the intricacies of how a scene
comes together.

For someone learning digital nonlinear editing, the sooner you learn the keyboard commands instead of using the mouse, the better. You will save time, and it
promotes intuitive work. It is like typing. You don't have to think of where the H
key is, you just hit it. In the work environment, I would also suggest only using one
computer monitor (in addition to the NTSC monitor). Most nonlinear systems have
or suggest two computer monitors, and you use one as the preview monitor and
one as the program monitor. This has a historical precedent, but it comes from studio production, not motion picture editing. It is unnecessary. Just edit using one
screen, and if you don't like it, undo it. You don't need a separate screen to look over
at. This generation of editors likes familiarity, so it will take awhile for this second
screen to go away, but I predict that soon systems will only have one monitor.

CHAPTER

13 Choosing the Right System

There are several things you must take into account when considering nonlinear systems. These concerns involve three basic levels of use: entry-level, intermediate and advanced. Choosing the nonlinear editing system that best fits your needs is a time-consuming process. There are dozens upon dozens of systems on the market, but there are specific questions you can ask to determine your needs and expectations in this exciting area of media postproduction. Figure 13.1 shows a complete nonlinear workstation, using some of the hardware and software discussed in this chapter.

Review of Choices: Five Areas to Take into Account Based on Your Needs and Level of Use

The first concern is whether you prefer a system that is *open* or *proprietary* in structure. An **open editing system** is one that can be used for multiple purposes. An example of such a choice would be Adobe Premiere software installed on a computer in a student computer lab or on your home computer. The computer can obvi-

FIGURE 13.1 Complete Nonlinear Workstation with Editor

ously be used by you or other students for many purposes, but when you need to edit, it becomes an editing system as you access the appropriate software. Such open systems are often utilized in student editing situations because they allow basic digital nonlinear editing while not requiring the purchase of a lot of expensive hardware. However, an open system can cause obvious problems in scheduling and system failure. **Proprietary editing systems** are usually preferable because equipment (both software and hardware) is dedicated as an editing bay and not used by folks for word processing, video games or anything else. However, there is some argument in the industry as to what *proprietary* actually means. We have defined it above in comparison to *open* as a system that is meant for nonlinear editing. However, most nonlinear manufacturers want to label their system open, to indicate not that you can also play video games on it but that it is capable of using widely accepted hardware and industry standards such as JPEG and Apple's QuickTime. So in a way, *open* can mean either "this is a setup on which you can accomplish things other than nonlinear editing" or "this is a professional system that incorporates well-established industry hardware, CODECs, applications, platforms and standards and interfaces with these to support your nonlinear editing needs."

The second concern is *image quality*. Digitizing and compressing analog footage is a complicated process, and many factors are involved, as discussed earlier. For the moment, suffice it to say that at one time, there was a wild variation of nonlinear edit systems in this important area, but things have begun to level out quite a bit in the midrange and high-end systems.

As you are now well aware, *storage* is a critical issue. There is a popular saying among digital editors: "You can never be too rich, too young, or have enough storage space." Suffice it to say that the amount of space available to you dictates how much footage you are able to digitize and at what resolution you are able to digitize. It is important when deciding what nonlinear system to use or purchase that you consider systems to which you can easily add storage space and whether funding is available to purchase additional gigabytes.

Audio is a critically important consideration. Obviously, most of us aren't making silent media productions, so the audio is as crucial as the images. This is a second area in which systems in the past few years are playing on an increasingly level field. Many systems have recently made great strides in this area, and most include some type of visual audio wave representations on the screen that your sound elements can be manipulated during the edit session. All nonlinear systems offer at least two channels of compact disc quality audio. Each has analog and sometimes digital inputs and outputs for audio.

Next, you must consider value and how much *money* you have to pour into a purchase, if that is your goal. Always save some of your funding to purchase additional RAM and storage space, and work from there. There are good entry-level software packages and editing systems for three to four thousand dollars. The higher-end systems obviously cost a good bit more, and as the saying goes, you get what you pay for. In this case, what you pay for includes resolution, direct digital input, real-time rendering, layering of text, transitions, image manipulation and other features. When weighing your budget, also consider technical support and software upgrade programs.

Review of Additional Options
for Your Consideration

Obviously, *system capabilities, hardware* and *software* must be judged. Again, money
is the deciding factor in most cases. These are exciting areas. Because image and
audio qualities are highly competitive in most systems, the marketing push is on
which software offers the most bells and whistles. These additions are what set
many systems apart. The argument over image quality comparisons coming out of
various systems is more or less a dead one. While there is still some minor discrep-
ancies between the higher-end systems, it is negligible at this point; they are all
putting out images whose signals conform to broadcast specifications. Although
this argument is sure to heat up again, especially as the United States moves into
the high-definition television arena in the next few years, most editors realize that
this is not the place to make your nonlinear system choices anymore. As more and
more systems incorporate digital inputs and outputs, this area will become even
less a point of contention. First and foremost, your objective is editing, and you will
need to consider common editing tasks that enable you to perform your edits with
ease. Most editing systems include such functions as splice, lift and extract, trimming, rearranging shots, audio manipulation and crossfades, entering timecode
numbers, setting in and out points, footage logs with thumbnail images and space
for you to add information (great shot, take 3, etc.) and edit decision lists. If your
intent is to add flashy animation and titles, you will want to consider options such
as compositing layers of video information and graphics. You should try out different systems and get a feel for what intuitively (and financially) feels right for
your editing needs. Spend the time sitting in on a demonstration of different editing systems; compare how long it takes to perform specific editing tasks. Most systems also allow for various ways of performing the same task. For example, if you
are used to using a mouse to move information around a screen, do you want a system that emphasizes typing in information via a keyboard?

Next comes the *visual interface.* You gaze at it all day long. The visual interface, or the workspace on the computer screen of your nonlinear desktop, is for
many people a very important part of the system to consider. As editors, we are all,
to some extent or another, aesthetic beings, and our aesthetic preferences carry
over onto the computer screen. Manufacturers invest a lot of time and money trying to figure out what you want to look at. Think of it like the layout of your
favorite local hangout or the inside of a new car. The arrangement, navigability,
colors and comfort of the environment are extremely important. The graphic interface of nonlinear editors is a big selling point. When you think about it, this makes
sense; you will be spending hours interacting with the interface, so you want it to
be easy to understand and aesthetically pleasing. Those who speak true comput-
erese refer to the graphic interface as "real estate." This makes sense in an interesting way; you want as much "real estate" as possible, and you want it to be pleasing
to the eye and easy to maneuver around.

When considering nonlinear systems, you also need to think about *monitors.*
Most system manufacturers of editing systems recommend that a monitor be at
least 17–21 inches. Many editors like to add a second monitor that, with the addition

of a special video card, can become a simple visual extension of your graphic interface. Once you move the mouse to the extreme right side of your left-hand monitor, it appears suddenly in your right-hand monitor. By using two monitors, you can spread your various windows and bins out so that you can work with ease. Single widescreen flat monitors are still relatively expensive, but we predict that they will become the norm in a few years.

Several systems are now incorporating hidden but accessible *vectorscopes* and *waveform monitors* as part of the graphical user interface. The usefulness of these video signal measuring tools on a computer has been debated in the past, but as the systems gain continued input from true video engineers, they are becoming more accepted.

In the area of system capability, hardware and software consideration, you must also decide whether you are aiming for a *PC-based system* such as DVision or an *Apple Macintosh–based system* such as Final Cut Pro. Some systems are applicable to both; many are one or the other. Currently, more people are familiar with PC systems, but for many people Apple remains the leader in graphic technologies. Of course, with the sharing options between Apple and IBM, nonlinear system and compatible software choices have opened up.

As a student or new editor who may be looking into purchasing a low-end system, you have several things to consider. Many editors prefer the installation of what is called a **turnkey system.** This term basically means that the system is easy to set up and, in most cases, all of your technical support concerns are handled by just one company. This can be a big help if your system goes down in the middle of an important edit.

Your Genre, Postproduction Preferences and End Goal

What is your goal? When doing your own research on various nonlinear systems, you will quickly discover that all companies say they are truly on the cutting edge of digital editing and way ahead of the competition in all areas. Many manufacturers also claim that one size fits all and that their system supports your needs, no matter what your needs are. You need to understand that this is not necessarily true.

Some editors are much more supportive of off-line editing or nonlinear editing when the final goal is going back and cutting the original film negative. Others work well for shows with large amounts of source material such as documentaries, and some for multicamera broadcast shows. Some offer multilayer effects and fancy titling capabilities, and others offer limited transitions. Some are meant to be used as simple off-line low-resolution systems, and others are truly on-line, broadcast output systems. Although even low-end systems include some of the following, if you need multiple fancy transitions, image layering, multiaudio channel audio, extensive titling and keying, you might need to look at higher-end systems. Also remember that the more sophisticated the software is, the longer is the learning curve and the more likely you are to buy features you will rarely, if ever, use. The kind of program and the type of editing you intend to do, along with an idea of what your audience expects, are the most important factors to consider in rating various nonlinear systems.

Remember that you need to specify your own needs and goals when considering the dozens upon dozens of nonlinear options in the field today. Specific pieces of hardware and software are better for certain end results and are beginning to be marketed to niches within the industry. For example, there are some systems designed specifically for the needs of the news broadcast market, enabling producers, journalists and editors to contribute simultaneously to the creation of a broadcast news story. Others provide an environment for writing and editing scripts and linking audio and video clips to specific points in the text. Although a Hollywood feature film editor might not be interested, a broadcast news editor might make tremendous use of these tools.

Some digital nonlinear editing systems are very popular with editors who originated as film editors because the controls and graphic interface most resemble those on a Steenbeck flatbed film editing table, thus supporting the film mindset. So as you consider your options among the various nonlinear systems, it is essential that you understand your editing and distribution goals.

Working with a System Integrator or Engineer for Installation

If possible, you may work with a reputable dealer and integrator or engineer who will help you put the system together. Many students, colleges and independent producers have suffered time-consuming and costly experiences with suppliers who did not properly install software or configure hardware or who took extraordinary amounts of time to do so.

Warranties and Support Packages

Most companies offer various support packages that include warranties and different levels of technical support. You might want to consider an editing system that is easy to upgrade; some support packages, which you pay for on a yearly basis, include automatic software upgrades. Usually, you can opt for just this software upgrade option if you don't require extensive technical support. A nonturnkey system such as Adobe Premiere software may be more financially accessible, as long as you are able to mix and match and verify different hardware and software components. If you have a computer at home, you might want to purchase such a software package that installs onto your existing hard-drive. This option can get you into the digital domain relatively inexpensively, utilizing equipment either you or your institution already has.

As systems become more refined and the competition between various companies becomes stiff, what is becoming increasingly important to editors is the total packaging of your investment. If you can get into a system whose arrangement includes many variables, all the better. For a digital nonlinear editor, especially a new one, there is nothing worse than feeling like you are in a black hole somewhere with no one to help you out. Training and support of your choice are important considerations in looking at various nonlinear editing systems. In any large metropolitan area, there is usually at least one of each industry-established editing system and therefore at least one editor who considers this the best system on the market.

Your Own Research

If you are in the market or simply curious about various systems, it would behoove you to seek out experienced users of these systems for input and advice. In addition, systems manufacturers worth their salt will provide basic as well as advanced training courses and will provide tutorial tapes that will walk you through the system. Also, most companies offer on-line help via websites and email, and they have warranty and technical support options as well as software upgrade options once you have purchased a system. Given the vast number of nonlinear editors out there these days and the current fluctuations of the digital industry, it should come as no surprise that most of the major systems have Internet mailing lists devoted to the ins and outs of the equipment, software, applications and so on. It is in cyberspace where you will often get some of the best—if the most blunt—information (see Appendix A).

Digital nonlinear editing is by no means the end-all for every fiction or documentary editor. Lots of editors are quite leery of this digital domain, noting the tendency to facilitate quick and sloppy work. These artists strongly believe that this new technology is breeding a type of editing that is not committed to the art of effective communication and storytelling. It has been said that digital nonlinear systems are being used simply as a means of applying fancy graphics and cut-and-paste mentality without thinking through the ramifications of various editing choices. Tim Robbins's film "Dead Man Walking" included a credit at the end claiming that the film was cut on good old-fashioned film editing equipment. This statement was not necessarily a statement against the new technologies per se but was directed at the industry's current mania for high-tech equipment. Editing is an art, not a game, and you should choose to work on a system that will support your creative abilities, not simply offer you flashy style.

We have included here various considerations you should take into account when looking at diverse digital nonlinear editing systems. It must be pointed out, however, that you need to pursue current information on various systems. Equipment specifics may change subtly and sometimes radically at any point in time. This is the nature of any computer-based art. One easy way to begin your research is to look into what systems are being used professionally. Editors in Hollywood, New York, New Delhi, Beijing, London and Tokyo who likely have more money to spend and more at stake than you do have undergone some real nuts-and-bolts research before plunging into specific systems. Therefore the systems that are in heavy use in the industry are usually stable and proven.

When choosing a specific system for your needs, you should always remind yourself that as an editor, you are a visual storyteller. This is your first and foremost goal. Given this, you need to ask what role does the editing system play in supporting visual storytelling and at what point do all of the possible bells and whistles become just that: shiny toys that possibly go overboard relative to your needs. As editing systems have evolved, they have provided us with a wide range of new tools. In some situations, these tools (such as dozens of different transitions, multiple image layering and extensive audio manipulation) aid in getting the job done effectively and powerfully. At other times, they simply muddle the editing process and waste time. The choice is yours, but you should always consider the audience and the goals of the piece. Consider the technology and how it may advance your goals.

APPENDIX A

Editing Websites

The World Wide Web is a very fluid and organic information location. These alphabetically listed websites are current at the printing of this book and offer a wealth of data about both motion picture editing and other aspects of the business. As always with the web, take what you read with the understanding that the Internet is an unregulated source of tips, advice and facts. Take the time to mount your own searches, using various search engines and using keywords such as *editing, film, television, careers, technology* and *digital*. And when you see links on this select list of sites, follow them and see where they lead.

Academy of Motion Picture
Arts and Sciences
www.ampas.org

Academy of Television Arts
and Sciences
www.emmys.org

Adobe
www.adobe.com

Advanced Television Systems
Committee
www.atsc.org

Alwaysi
www.alwaysindependentfilms.com

American Cinema Editors
www.ace-filmeditors.org

Andy Pratt's Negative Cutting
Service
www.negativecutting.com

Apple
www.apple.com

Apple: Final Cut Pro
www.apple.com/finalcutpro

Apple: Quick Time
www.quicktime.com

Applied Magic
www.applied-magic.com

Art and Culture
www.artandculture.com

The Association of Imaging
Technology and Sound
www.itsnet.org

The Association of Independent
Video and Filmmakers
www.aivf.org

AtomFilms
www.atomfilms.com

Audio & Video Editing
www.fedele.com/website/tech/
editing.htm

Avid
www.avid.com

Big Film Shorts
www.bigfilmshorts.com

Blossom Software
www.Blossom.com

Blossom Technologies
www.blossomvideo.com

Canopus Corporation
www.canopuscorp.com

The Cinema Audio Society
www.ideabuzz.com/cas

Click2learn
www.click2learn.com

Compaq
www.compaq.com

Core MicroSystem
www.coremicro.com

Creative Planet Community
www.creativeplanet.com

Cyber Film School
www.cyberfilmschool.com

Digital Post Production
www.digitalpostproduction.com

Digital Studio SA
www.DigitalStudio.com

Directors Guild of America
www.dga.org

Discreet Logic
www.discreet.com

Draco Systems
www.draco.com

DPS
www.dps.com

DV.com
www.dv.com

DV Guys
www.dvguys.com

Dvgear
www.dvgear.com

DVline
www.dvline.com

Fast
www.fastmultimedia.com

The Federal Communications
Commission
www.fcc.gov

Headhunter.Net
www.careers.com

Hollywood Reporter Magazine
www.hollywoodreporter.com

IMST
www.imsisoft.com

Inside Magazine
www.inside.com

The Institute of Electrical and
Electronics Engineers
www.ieee.org

In-sync
www.in-sync.com

MacroSystem US
www.draco.com

Mandy's Film and TV Production
Directory
www.mandy.com

Matrox Digital Video Solutions
www.matrox.com/video

Media 100
www.media100.com

Media 100 Ice
www.iced.com

Motion Picture Editors Guide
www.editorsguild.com

Motion Picture Sound Editors
www.mpse.org

Movieworks
www.movieworks.com

Music 2 Hues: Royalty-Free Music
& Sound EffectsProduction Library
www.music2hues.com

The National Association of
Broadcasters
www.nab.org

Newtek
www.newtek.com

Ocean System
www.oceansystems.com

Panasonic
www.panasonic.com

Pinnacle Systems
www.pinnaclesys.com

Pro Max Systems
www.promax.com

Production Hub
www.productionhub.com

Release Print Magazine
www.filmarts.org/releasepr

Res Magazine
www.resmag.com

Softimage
www.softimage.com

Society of Motion Picture and
Television Editors
www.smpte.org

Strata
www.3d.com

Tektronix
www.Tektronix.com

Ulead
www.ulead.com

Variety Magazine
www.variety.com

Video Movie Magic
www.videomoviemagic.com/con
tact.html

Video Systems Magazine
www.videosystems.com

Video University: The
Information Source for
Hobbyists & Pros
www.videouniversity.com

Videography Magazine
www.videography.com

Vitec Multimedia
www.vitecmm.com

Windows Media. Com
www.windowsmedia.com

2-pop
www.2-pop.com

3Cube
www.Videocube.com

APPENDIX B

Postproduction Forms

Footage Dailies Log Sheet

Title _____ Date _____ Page No. _____

Editor _____ Phone/Email _____

Asst. Editor _____ Phone/Email _____

Scene Number	Take Number	Roll/Video-tape Number	Begin Number	End Number	Description	Remarks

Film Processing Form

Date _____ Special instructions _____

Title _____ _____

Production no. _____ _____

P.O. no. _____ _____

Number of rolls _____ _____

Roll nos. _____ Person to contact _____

Email _____ Phone _____

Process: Type of film _____

____ Normal   ____ Force 1 stop   ____ Force 2 stops

____ Return original   ____ Hold original

Video Transfer:

____ Prep for video transfer   ____ Prep for keycode transfer

Video transfer at _____ Time of transfer _____

Workprint:

____ Normal light   ____ Print all takes

____ Best light   ____ Print circled takes only

____ Timed   ____ Return on core/reel

Return materials via _____

Bill to   Ship to

_____   _____

_____   _____

_____   _____

APPENDIX C

Suggested Readings

Bobker, Lee. 1999. *Making Movies from Script to Screen.* New York: Harcourt Brace.

Dancyger, Ken. 1993. *The Technique of Film and Video Editing.* Boston: Focal Press.

Hollyn, Norman. 1999. *The Film Editing Room Handbook: How to Manage the Near Chaos of the Cutting Room.* Los Angeles: Lone Eagle Press.

Johnson, Nels, Fred Gault, Mark Florence, and Keith Weiskamp. 1994. *How to Digitize Video.* New York: John Wiley and Sons.

LoBrutto, Vincent. 1994. *Selected Takes: Film Editors on Film Editing.* New York: Praeger Publishers.

Murch, Walter. 1995. *In the Blink of an Eye: A Perspective on Film Editing.* Los Angeles: Silman-James Press.

Oldham, Gabriella. 1995. *First Cut: Conversations with Film Editors.* Los Angeles: University of California Press.

Reisz, Karel, and Gavin Millar. 1968. *The Technique of Film Editing.* Boston: Focal Press.

Rosenblum, Ralph, and Robert Karen. 1979. *When the Shooting Stops . . . The Cutting Begins.* New York: Viking Press.

Schneider, Arthur. 1989. *Electronic Post-Production Terms and Concepts.* Boston: Focal Press.

Watkinson, John. 1995. *Compression in Video and Audio.* Boston: Focal Press.

Watkinson, John. 1994. *An Introduction to Digital Video.* Boston: Focal Press

Magazines

Cinemaeditor
The Independent
Mac User
Post
Res Magazine
Videomaker
Videographer

GLOSSARY

180-degree rule   States that when on location or in the studio, you mentally place an imaginary line between two people talking or based on the direction of the action. The camera is placed on one side of this imaginary line, and it can move anywhere within 180 degrees of the line. If it stays on that one side, the screen direction of movement and the direction in which your actors or subjects are facing on the screen will not change. However, if you move the camera across the line, the direction of the action or position of the actors or subjects will appear to flip suddenly. This is considered a jump cut and is disturbing and disorienting to the viewer.

3:2 pulldown   The process of transferring or recording the film to video fields during the Telecine transfer. Also known as 2:3 pulldown. See Chapter 11, Figure 11.4 for a visual explanation.

30-degree rule   States that if you are planning on editing together two shots of the same person or thing, the camera should be placed 30 degrees away in the second shot from its placement in the first shot to avoid a jump cut.

4:2:2   Term for a component digital video format. It refers to the sampling rate based on the color subcarrier frequency. The luminance channel is sampled at four times the rate of the color difference channels.

A/B roll model   An editing process that uses two video sources played simultaneously, to be mixed or cut between.

AES/EBU   Digital audio standard established between Audio Engineering Society and European Broadcasting Union organizations.

alternating current   Electrical current that switches in polarity from positive to negative sixty times a second; is found in most standard wall outlets in the United States.

analog   Adjective used to describe signal that is sent out in a continuous stream instead of the bits of information sent out in 0s and 1s in digital. It is usually considered an inferior technology to digital video information.

animation   A series of still images that, when played in rapid succession, creates the illusion of movement. Animation is often now a visual effect that is created on a sophisticated computer system.

answer print   Complete print of a film after it has been edited with picture and sound. It is examined by the filmmaker to see whether any changes must be made before making a release print.

artifacts   Distortions that appear in digitized video images.

aspect ratio   The ratio pertaining to height and width of image on a screen.

assemble edit   Copying footage from one videotape to another. In this type of analog video editing, all signals from the source tape (visual, both audio tracks and control track) are copied onto the edit tape.

A to D (analog to digital) converter   A circuit that uses digital sampling to convert an analog signal to a digital signal.

audio/visual (A/V) drive   A hard drive designed to eliminate image flickers, bounces, pauses, jumps and audio distortion during playback.

batch digitizing   A feature available on most non-linear editing systems that reads through footage and automatically digitizes selected clips on the basis of defined timecode in and out points. Saves time and hard drive space.

Betamax   Also referred to as "Beta." A half-inch videotape format developed by Sony for the consumer market to compete with VHS.

bin   A place to store your various clips, allowing convenient access to footage. Catalogued on the screen by name, keyword, thumbnail image of the first frame of the shot and so on.

bit   Computer term. A binary representation of 0 or 1.

bit stream   Refers to the transmission of digital video down a multiconductor cable.

butt splice   The joining together of two ends of film and securing them with a piece of splicing tape.

byte   Computer term. Bytes consisting of eight to ten bits per sample are typical of digital video systems.

capture card   Computer hardware that captures digital video and audio signal to a hard drive.

chroma key Process of inserting or combining source images so that they appear to exist on the same plane. A special key color is selected, which is then replaced with video information. This technique is most commonly used in TV weather reporting.

clip Comparable to a take or shot in film or analog video editing. Based on control track or time-code breaks.

CODEC A compression/decompression device, such as JPEG or MPEG.

code numbers Numbers printed onto film every foot in sequential order after film and sound have been synced by the editor. Printed numbers help in keeping the film in sync once the editor starts editing individual scenes.

color bars Standard test signal for adjusting video color monitoring equipment containing reference colors that are produced by a color bar generator. Is usually placed at the beginning of a project.

component video In analog, a signal transmission system that separates luminance (1) and chrominance (2) signals to avoid quality loss from NTSC or PAL encoding. In digital, a digital representation of this same component analog signal. See *composite video.*

composite video In analog, a signal transmission system that combines luminance and chrominance signals with horizontal and vertical synchronizing pulses. In digital, a digitally encoded video signal representation of composite analog signal. See *component video.*

compositing Superimposing multiple layers of video.

compression The video signal is compressed so that the data stream is reduced to a manageable level and doesn't take up as much space, making nonlinear editing possible.

continuity The successful and unnoticeable continuation of a scene in terms of placement of objects, weather conditions, camera placement and so on.

control track Equivalent of sprocket holes in film; it is a way that the video "talks" to the VCR and allows it to move through at the appropriate speed. There is a control track pulse on each frame of video, which can be used to gauge approximately where you are on the videotape if you reset the counter to zero at the beginning of the tape.

cut Instant change from one shot to another.

cutaway shot A shot of something within or around the environment where the action or conversation is occurring. Used to avoid jump cuts or to compress time.

cuts-only editing An analog editing process that does not included transitions such as wipes and dissolves and simply shifts from one scene to another.

D1 A component digital video recording format. Successive formats include D2, D3 and so on, up to D9.

dailies The first work print from the original camera negative with no color or lighting correction. Viewed by the director, cameraperson, director of photography and other people concerned with the film.

desktop video (DTV) The synthesis of video components and personal computers for videomaking capabilities.

digital Refers to a numerical representation of information and the ability of this information to be processed electronically by a computer.

digital audio Audio converted to digital information.

digital video effects (DVE) Digitally altering the video signal. Strobing, flipping and solarizing the image are typical manipulations.

digitizing Converting analog video/audio data into digital data for computer storage.

digitizer A device that captures and imports analog data into a computer by converting to a digital signal.

disk mirroring A feature available on a RAID 1 type drive that allows information to be duplicated as a copy elsewhere on the array as a safety device.

dissolve A transition effect in which one picture gradually disappears as another appears.

double system In filmmaking, references the fact that picture and sound are recorded on separate units; picture is recorded by film or video cameras, and sound is recorded on a separate audio recording device.

drop frame timecode Type of timecode that "drops" or gets rid of the extra 108 frames in every hour of video. Whenever the timecode on a videotape must indicate actual running time, the timecode must be adjusted using drop frame timecode.

dropout   Problems that occur when videotape becomes too dirty or has "bare spots." Will show up as white specks or streaks on video monitor.

dubbing   Rerecording a sound or dialog to replace original sound or dialogue because of poor quality in the original recording. Can also refer to simple copying of video or audiotapes.

dupe negative   Film negative printed from the master positive (reversal) or original negative film stock.

edit   Process of reviewing and selecting video/audio sources that results in an assembled project of consecutive cuts. The goal is to create some kind of a story or communication. Motion picture editing involves artistic motivation.

edit decision list (EDL)   A written list of all of the shots in your edit, with each shot's corresponding timecode or film edge number. The EDL describes the shots and lists them in the order in which they will occur in the edit. The EDL is the primary method of transferring information about your edit from one editing system to another and between the off-line and on-line edit stages.

editing bin   A boxlike container lined with a canvas bag in which a film editor hangs film trims to keep them in order and to keep the trims from gathering debris from unclean surfaces.

effects track   Sound track separate from dialogue or music tracks to be used solely to contain any extra sound segments.

encoder   Used to convert or translate video signal into a different format. Also can be used to prepare video for Internet streaming.

equalization   Manipulation of audio or video frequencies with the purpose of eliminating unwanted signal. Used primarily to enhance audio quality.

establishing shot   Often an exterior shot of the location in which the action will be occurring. It is incorporated to help the audience get their bearings and to understand "where" they are.

extreme close-up   A very close shot filling all or most of the frame with the subject.

fade   Editing term indicating that video/audio needs to be dissolved into or out of black in the case of video and silence in the case of audio.

film edge numbers   Small numbers running along the edge of positive film workprints near the sprocket holes. (Key numbers are the corresponding numbers on the film negative.) These numbers ascend at each successive foot of film and are used as a footage count to identify where shots occur on the roll of film.

fine cut   The final stage of editing in which cuts and transitions are fine-tuned.

Firewire   A direct digital output/input transmission protocol. Allows you to go directly from a digital signal to a digital editing system for editing and other image manipulation and back out to digital with virtually no loss in picture or sound quality. Also known as IEEE 1394.

frame grabber   High-speed digitizer capable of capturing frames at a rate that will allow real-time motion.

frame rate   The number of frames per second. Video runs at thirty frames per second for full motion.

freeze-frame   An editing effect in which a single frame is copied many times over to give the appearance that time is standing still. A still photographic image.

full motion video   Video playback on a computer similar to the playback quality of a television or VCR.

fx   Standard abbreviation for "effects."

generation loss   The degradation in picture and sound quality as a result of duplication.

hard disk   Important for video use, hard disks need access time of less than 10 milliseconds, sustained throughput of 3 megabytes per second and a maximum time for housekeeping of 33 milliseconds.

high-definition television (HDTV)   Television designed to enhance resolution for sharper pictures. 16:9 aspect ratio.

individual shot   Close shot of a character as he or she goes through their action or dialogue.

inputting   Transferring a digital signal from source, such as a CD, digital video or audiotape, or MP3 file, into a computer.

insert edit   An analog video edit in which video material from one tape is copied to another tape. The visual and audio elements from the first tape are copied on top of the second tape's previously existing control track.

interlock   The stage of film postproduction in which picture and sound have been edited together and are viewed and listened to together.

internegative   A film negative printed from a color reversal original.

jog/shuttle   The control on a VCR that transports tape forward or reverse frame by frame (jog) or for fast scanning (shuttle).

JPEG   Stands for "Joint Photographic Experts Group." A common compression scheme referred to as *spatial* or *intraframe* compression. JPEG is considered a fairly mild compression factor that promotes few artifacts (visual sparkles, video noise, color streaks, blocky edges around the edge of an image; compression artifacts are the result of the system's inability to correctly reconstruct the original image) and allows for maximum editing freedom. It is the compression scheme used by most nonlinear systems.

jump cut   A cut in which an image or character, because of the edit, appears to jump to a different location on the screen, causing an unnatural effect.

keycode numbers   Numbers placed on the film by the manufacturer to be used as reference by editor and conformer. Not to be confused with code numbers.

L-cut   An editing technique that manipulates aural space by letting the audio of one shot continue under the visuals of another shot. Also called the *split edit.*

linear editing   An editing process by which the final product is assembled one image and sound at a time. Requires shuttling back and forth on videotapes to access the needed footage and once something has been edited, there is no moving it around on the edit master tape.

logging   The process of creating some type of written version of your raw footage so that you can easily locate the shots you need as you proceed through the edit session.

longitudinal timecode (LTC)   A type of timecode that can be laid down instead of VITC if the camera does not incorporate VITC timecode. LTC is striped onto your videotapes after production and takes the place of one of the two audio tracks (thus getting the name *longitudinal*).

lossless   Refers to a compressed data file that is reconstructed exactly from the original data. All of the original information is there, just compressed.

lossy   A compression scheme in which specific parts of the data (meaning video image content) are permanently removed. Lossy compression is acceptable when dealing with video, because the images will be viewed subjectively, and our eyes easily fill in the small amount of information that is missing.

master positive   A special print that is made as an intermediate stop in producing a picture duplicate negative.

master scene shot   A wide-angle shot of all the action in the shot, allowing the viewer to see each of the characters and their proximity to each other.

match cut   Puts the audience in a privileged position of seeing part of an action from one angle and then seeing it complete from a different angle. The action would match so that none of the movement is repeated in the second shot but it matches perfectly with where the first shot left off.

medium shot   A shot that is perceived from a medium distance, in between a long shot and a close-up. If the shot were of a person, it would normally show the body from the waist to the head.

monitor   In video, a television set that is wired to a camera or VCR for display of live or taped signals. In audio, the monitor is referred to as a *speaker.*

montage   Shots assembled in rapid succession to communicate a particular image or mood.

MOS   Film slang term inferring that the scene only has visuals with no accompanying audio. *MOS* stands for "mit out sound." "Mit" is the German word for "with," so officially, *MOS* means "without sound."

Moviola   A brand name of film editing equipment that includes viewscopes, flatbed editing machines and upright editing machines.

MPEG   Stands for "Motion Picture Experts Group." A form of interframe compression (as opposed to JPEG's intraframe compression), meaning that some frames of the image contain all of the information, an entire image, and others record only what differs from the previous frame or succeeding frame.

negative conforming   The process of matching the camera original negative footage to the edited workprint and keeping it synchronized with the final mixed sound track so that projection prints may be produced. The conformed negative is usually assembled in AB rolls for 16mm and single rolls for wider gauge film stocks. 16mm requires A/B rolls in order to keep the splices invisible in the projection print. 35mm and wider-gauge stocks do not have this problem. However sometimes in the wider-gauge stocks for special effects completed in the film laboratory, A/B rolls may be required.

noise Excess signal information in the visual portion of the video. Video noise is usually perceived as speckles or muted edges of surfaces.

non–drop frame timecode A type of timecode that is used when actual running time is not critical.

nonlinear editing An editing system in which the editor has the ability to assemble bits of source material in any order, place shots or audio or titles in between previously placed material without covering anything up and move elements of the edit around easily. Film editing is nonlinear, as is computer-based digital editing.

off-line edit An early version or rough cut of the material. In this stage, one uses dubs of the original footage as sources to keep the original footage in pristine shape. During the off-line edit, basic structural editing decisions are made, often called an EDL (edit decision list). The term *off-line* is also used to refer to footage that has not yet been digitized.

on-line edit The process of creating a final edited master tape or film. Created from the original source footage and guided by the edit decision list. The term *on-line* also refers to footage that has already been digitized.

open editing system A system on which you can accomplish things other than nonlinear editing or a system that incorporates well-established industry hardware, CODECs, applications, platforms and standards and interfaces with these to support your nonlinear editing needs.

optical soundtrack Sound that has been recorded onto photographic film in waveform and is read by an optical sound head.

outtake Footage that is not used in the final product.

pixel The smallest distinguishable area in a video image; can also be thought of as one point on the screen.

postproduction Production that follows the original recording, includes editing.

post-striping Using an external timecode generator to lay down timecode onto your videotapes

after production. Takes the place of one of the two audio tracks.

preview window On a desktop editing system, the location on the screen where you review footage and mark in and out edit points.

program window On a desktop editing system, the location on the screen where you assemble the film; often called the timeline.

proprietary editing system A system consisting of editing equipment (both software and hardware) dedicated as an editing bay and not used for other tasks, such as word processing, video games and so on.

RAID Stands for "redundant array of inexpensive disks." An interconnected stack of inexpensive hard drives.

RAM Stands for "random access memory." Usually measured in megabytes (MB) or gigabytes (GB).

reaction shot A shot that shows the reaction of one person to another person or situation.

release print The composite print of picture and sound that is processed for projection and general distribution.

rendering time The time it takes a computer to compute a transition or effect from video sources.

reversal print A film print made by processing the original camera reversal film stock.

rewritable consumer timecode (RCTC) Type of timecode laid down by Sony and some other Hi-8 cameras, but these are considered consumer-oriented versions and not industry standard.

rough cut State of edited motion picture before the fine cut; cuts and transitions are not smooth, nor is the film ready for general viewing. The rough cut often includes a scratch sound track and might not include graphics.

rubberbanding Manipulating audio levels within a desktop editing system.

SCSI Stands for "small computer systems interface." A transmission protocol designed to move large amounts of data from the computer to the storage device.

sequence A series of shots characterized by inherent unity of theme and purpose.

single system In filmmaking, refers to camera system that records both picture and sound onto the same material at the same time. Videotape cameras are considered single system, as the visual and audio elements are both recorded onto the videotape.

Society of Motion Picture and Television Engineers (SMPTE) The association that governs timecode in the United States.

splicer A mechanism used in film editing to cut film and guide taping of film together.

split reel Reel with removable side that allows film core to be added or removed without need of rewinding.

storyboard Sketches that help to communicate key visual and audio information and to help realize what the final product should look like.

streaming Option for sound and video to play from the Internet as it is downloaded instead of having to be first stored complete in the computer storage system.

superimposition Titles or graphics that appear over video images. These superimpositions can appear translucent or opaque.

sweetening Enhancing the audio track by adding sound effects and music in postproduction.

time base corrector (TBC) If a tape is jittering or breaking up in playback, the piece of equipment realigns the scan lines on a television monitor by digitizing each video frame and storing it in a digital buffer before sending it back out for viewing.

thermal calibration A function of nonaudio/visual hard drives that compensates for internal temperature fluctuations by adjusting the speed of their revolution. Referred to as *TCAL*.

throughput performance The rate at which data travels between disk drives, video capture cards and the video source deck.

timecode A numerical reference for each frame of video. Each frame is given an unchanging and specific "address." The timecode measures hours, minutes, seconds and frames (00:00:00:00). You can quickly and easily locate any shot if you know its timecode address. The primary reason for timecode is to serve as a time reference to facilitate easily locating footage and setting precise edit points. Timecode allows for frame-accurate edits that would be impossible to achieve using simply the control track as a reference device.

timeline editing Editing that is particular to computer-based editing systems in which video and audio clips are shown as proportional bars along a horizontal axis.

timing A lab function in which printer lights can be manipulated to improve the quality of the print made from the original camera negative.

turnkey system An editing system designed for easy setup; in most cases, all of your technical support concerns are handled by just one company.

two-shot A frame that includes two people or subjects.

universal serial bus A stable interface that can pass data at a rate of 400 MB per second.

vectorscope An instrument that measures the parameters of the color within the video signal.

vertical interval timecode (VITC) A type of timecode that is placed on the part of the videotape where the visual signals exist, in between the frames.

virtual reality An artificial environment created with computer technology that allows the user to experience what appears to be a real environment. To enter a virtual reality, the user wears goggles, sensor-equipped gloves and earphones that are connected to the computer system. Three of the five senses are stimulated by the computer technology, and interactions with computer-based scenarios are enhanced.

visual interface The workspace on the computer screen of your nonlinear desktop.

waveform monitor An instrument that measures the luminance or brightness of the video signal.

wide angle A camera lens with a short focal length and deep depth of field capabilities.

wipe A transition from one shot to another in which the new shot is revealed by moving a line or pattern across the screen.

work print The copy of a master videotape or film negative that is to be used to create a rough cut. It is used so that the master tape is not harmed from overuse.

INDEX